PHOTOSHOP ELEMENTS 2
Face Makeovers

DIGITAL MAKEOVERS OF FRIENDS & FAMILY

Gavin Cromhout
Josh Fallon
Nathan Flood
Katy Freer
Jim Hannah
Francine Spiegel
Pete Walsh
James Widegren

APress Media, LLC

Photoshop Elements 2 Face Makeovers
DIGITAL MAKEOVERS OF FRIENDS & FAMILY
© 2002 Apress
Originally published by Friends of ED in 2002

First Printed January 2002

Trademark Acknowledgements

Additional material to this book can be downloaded from http://extras.springer.com

ISBN 978-1-59059-162-8   ISBN 978-1-4302-5179-8 (eBook)
DOI 10.1007/978-1-4302-5179-8

Credits

Authors
Gavin Cromhout
Josh Fallon
Nathan Flood
Katy Freer
Jim Hannah
Francine Spiegel
Pete Walsh
James Widegren

Technical Reviewers
Victoria Blackburn
Nyree Costello
Denis E. Graham
Vicki Loader
Catherine O'Flynn

Commissioning Editor
Jim Hannah

Editor
Alan McCann

Project Manager
Richard Harrison

Graphic Editor
Katy Freer

Indexer
Simon Collins

Proof Reader
Helena Sharman

Managing Editor
Chris Hindley

Contents

Preface
[Pre-face]

The idea of this book is very simple. We take snaps of faces and manipulate them. Easy, eh? Well, yes – but amazing too. You'll be blown away by how simple it is to create fantastic effects, whether it's careful retouching you're after, or full on stomping ogre creation!

If you stick to a small canvas, the result is an explosion of ideas and creativity. In this book we have face painting, oil painting and screen-printing. We dabble with hyper-reality, surrealism, fantasy, romance, horror, tension and serenity. From a collection of everyday faces, we can generate a cast of digital characters – clowns, tigers, glamour pusses, angels, demons, rock stars, monsters and ogres.

This book presents a series of step-by-step tutorials on how to create these amazing facial effects in Photoshop Elements 2, displaying excellent hints and tips that can be stretched out across all of your digital manipulation.

On the accompanying CD, you will find all of the original source files, plus the finished multi-layered files, enabling you to search through the images, turning on and off effects, to see how to generate each finished image.

Between these packed covers you'll find a wealth of material to get busy with – all you need to do is have fun and learn!

As with all friends of ED titles, this book is backed up with free, fast, and friendly technical support from our editors. If you have a query or problem, mail support@friendsofed.com, and we will get back to you as soon as possible.

If you have any comments about this book, good, bad, or ugly, we're keen to hear from you. Mail feedback@friendsofed.com and have your say!

There's a host of other features at www.friendsofed.com that may interest you – interviews with top designers, samples from our other books, and a message board where you can post your questions, discussions and answers.

Enjoy making faces!

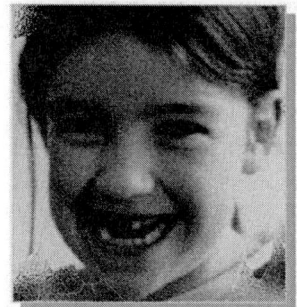
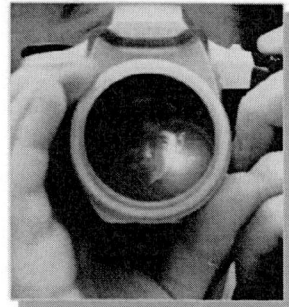
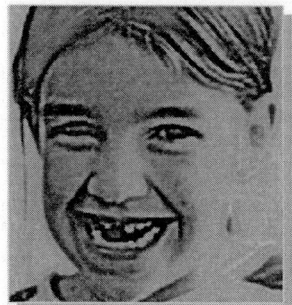

Chapter 1

Inbuilt Features

What you'll learn in this chapter

This chapter is going to take a swift look at some of the things that could be considered *no-brainer effects* in Photoshop Elements 2. They're the things that Elements can do with the least effort on our part. We just have to click a few buttons and it does the hard work for us. That said, we'll have some pretty original uses for these, and you'll see that Elements built-in features can be very useful for many professional-looking effects. Along the way, we'll explore:

- Using Elements vast range of **brushes** and **brush options** to add some neat effects.

- Exploring Elements main ready-made effects solutions – **Recipes** and **Filters.**

- Making **3D objects** out of your faces.

- **Masking** a face to superimpose it into another image.

Most of the rest of this book encourages you to apply a little bit of care in creating your final masterpieces, whereas in this chapter you'll never be more than a few Undo commands away from where you started. So, you'd better enjoy this chapter while it lasts!

> As with all our examples in the book, all our finished PSDs are provided in full on the CD-ROM, named after the model and/or tutorial. Play around with the PSDs to familiarize yourself with the images and techniques, or just use them to check you're following along, it's up to you, but they're all there!

The idea behind this chapter is that you can do anything with any snap. So let's have a look at putting something together using the snappiest of snaps.

The Brush rush

Photoshop Elements 2 has more brushes than you can shake a bristly stick at, and we're going to have a look at what sort of things you can achieve with them. In reality, there are more brushes than you could possibly need.

We're going to be looking quite comprehensively at what brushes can do in one or two later chapters, most especially the **Imitating Artists** chapter, which will examine how to create different *painterly* effects.

However, for these first few tutorials, let's spend a little time getting acquainted with a couple of brushes that can give us an immediate return for our money!

Elizabeth – brush strokes

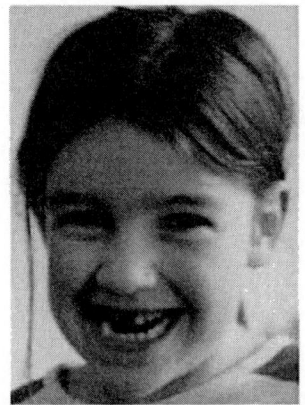

This little brush technique will prepare us for a more advanced technique in the **Fantasy Faces** chapter, where we'll create a fairy (hey, don't skip ahead just yet! Well OK, maybe for a look, but make sure you come back).

I'm sure Elizabeth here would like to be turned into a fairy, so let's make her wish come true!

*As with all the files on the CD-ROM, we've named them after our models, so you'll find this one in the **Inbuilt Features** folder, called* `elizabeth.jpg`. *Open this up in Elements and we'll get started!*

1. First, select the Brush tool, and then in the vast drop-down menu in the Options bar, scroll to the brush that looks like a bunch of five-pointed stars. It's called Flowing Stars.

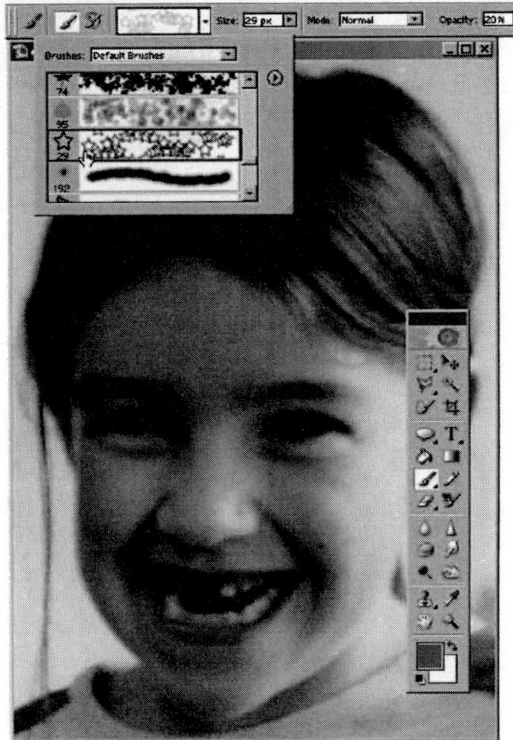

2. Create a new layer with Layers > New > Layer, or CTRL+SHIFT+N. We'll do all of our brushwork on this, so name it flowing stars.

    Then it's a question of getting the settings right. First off, and most obviously, you've got to get the size just perfect. On the hair I've used the largest stars, and on the face I've gone with smaller ones.

    After getting a good layout of stars, we need to apply a **layer effect** called Outer Glow, which will make the whole composition much more ethereal.

3. Open the Layer Styles palette (either docked at the top right of your screen or visible through Window > Layer Styles).

4. Select Outer Glows from the drop-down menu. The glow you should choose here is Simple.

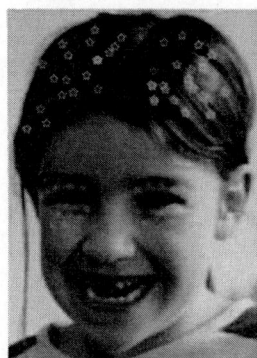

Now, that just scrapes the surface. It seems the makers of Photoshop Elements are way ahead of us. If you look at the specialized menu in the drop-down Brushes palette, you'll see a wide range of other categories. For example, in the Special Effects brushes we have such brushes as Scattered Flowers Mums, Ducks Not in a Row, *and* Butterfly with Chroma. *These are all of course perfect for decoration.*

This picture utilizes the brush from the Pen Pressure selection, called Music Notes - Scatter.

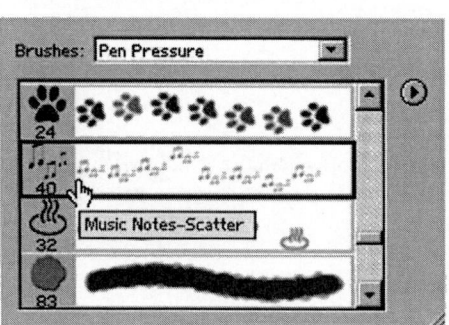

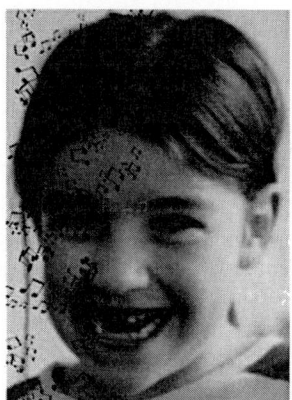

5. To achieve this effect, create a new layer called music notes (we'll put all our brush effects on separate layers, then we can show and hide them at will), and select a good brush size (I've used 250 px). Paint randomly in black over the picture (while on the new layer).

6. When you've got the spread of notes about right (not always as easy as it sounds!) go to the Layers palette and set the **blending mode** to Soft Light – then you'll get that lovely translucent effect!

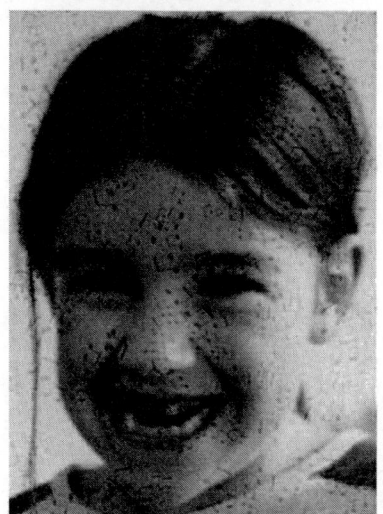
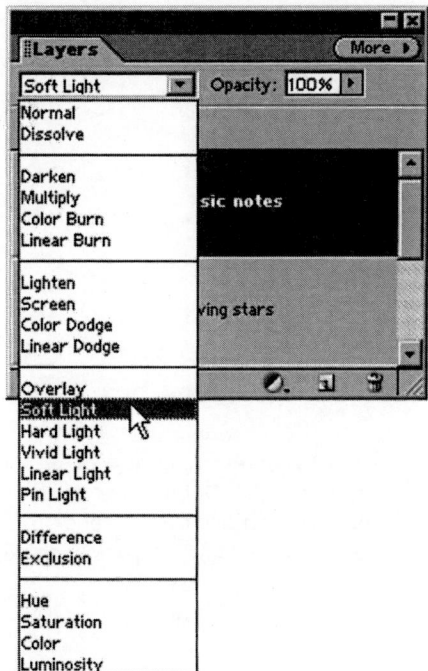

> If you apply a Soft Light blending mode to a layer, it's a bit like using the Dodge or Burn tools across the whole image. The Dodge and Burn tools, as you may be aware, lighten or darken the image. Applying the Soft Light blending mode causes Elements to assess whether to Dodge or Burn the image below. So, if you put a black and white checker board on a layer above someone's face, the black squares will burn the face darker, and the white squares will dodge the face lighter.

7. Let's use another brush from the Pen Pressure selection, and have a look at how the Color Jitter settings on the brushes work. For this effect, use the Confetti brush – it's the third one down – and again, put it on another layer.

7

8. Using a red foreground color and a white background color, with a 40 px brush, paint around the head.

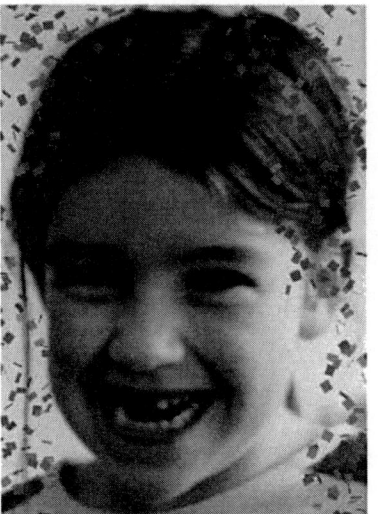

9. Now let's make a change. Click on the last button on the Options bar – the More Options button, and from the pop-up settings palette, increase the Spacing setting as shown:

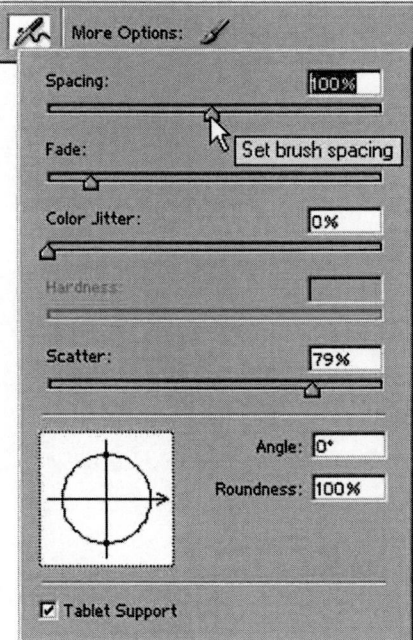

The difference is tangible:

...so now we have a picture at the end of the confetti shower!

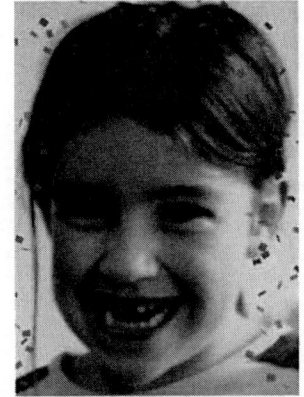

10. If you now set the Fade level to 100#, and apply your confetti you can see how to control the swiftness of the fade at the end of each brush stroke.

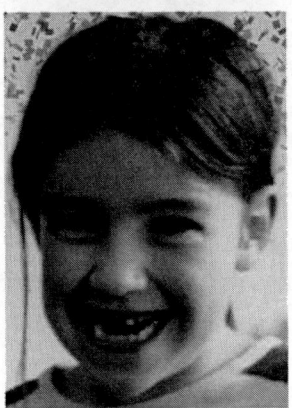

11. Playing around with the Color Jitter will deliver the following effect, this time achieved with an orange foreground and a black background color:

The effect down the left-hand side is done with a 0% Jitter, and the right-hand effect is done with 100% Jitter – so you can control how wild your confetti throwing is getting!

> *You can find our finished PSD for this section on the CD-ROM in the **01 Inbuilt Features** folder, called* elizabethBrushes.psd. *This file has each of our effects conveniently on a separate layer!*

Jolly – the Impressionist Brush

Photoshop Elements 2 also has the facility to create your *own* brushes. Now this may sound pretty scary, but trust me, it's one of the most phenomenally useful things you could ever ask for. We'll have a look at that in the chapter on **Imitating Artists**, so be sure to look out for it!

However, if **Imitating Artists** is going to steal our brush-making, it's only fair we steal an **Imitating Artists** effect! Adobe has seen fit to include an Impressionist Brush, which has one of the best icons around.

Essentially, it acts as a hand-controlled filter. Take a look at the following gallery of easy-to-create Impressionist effects on our model, Jolly:

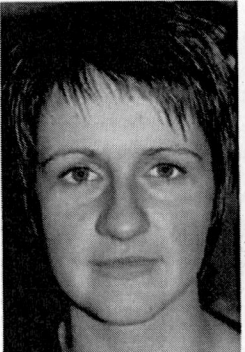
Original

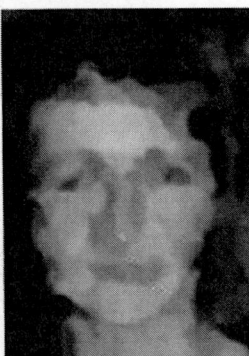
50px brush Tight Short 50px area

10px brush Loose Medium 50px area

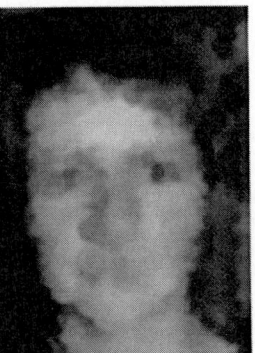
50px brush Dab 50px area

jolly.jpg, *our original image, is available in the Inbuilt Features folder on the CD-Rom.*

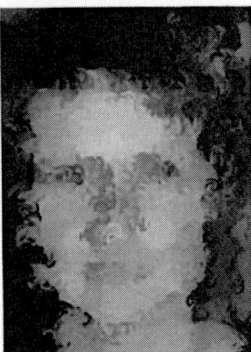
10px brush Tight Curl 50px area

Essentially, the Impressionist Brush is a good way of quickly mussing your friends up to make them look as if they've been painted by a robotic *Cézanne*. However, it does have other benefits, as we will find out in the **Imitating Artists** chapter.

Basically, it's useful for breaking a photograph down into its basic colors, which can be incredibly helpful if you're looking to create a color palette to work from in order to make your picture look as if it's painted. More of that later!

Filter tips

You may have already had a bit of a play with the filters in Photoshop Elements 2, but let's have a quick look over some of the most face-friendly ones.

Recipes

One of the most wanted effects Photoshop Elements offers is the ability to create a sepia-tinted photo, which Elements can handle using its automated **Recipes**.

1. With your picture open, simply click on the How To palette at the top of the screen and select Fun Stuff from the drop-down menu.

2. Click on Create an old-fashioned or tinted photo. Click through the instructions as they appear on the screen.

   Now, this does the job of course, but it's best not to get too complacent. I prefer to have a lovely vignette around my old-fashioned photographs – and fortunately Elements has got that covered too!

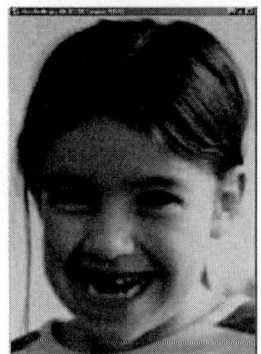

3. Simply make a selection with the appropriate marquee tool, and click the Effects tab from the top right of the interface. From the drop-down menu, select Frames, and then click on the icon Vignette (selection).

This will do the tricky work for you, like so:

Fake sketching

People love to see themselves sketched, and Elizabeth in particular is perfectly suited to a storybook-like pencil sketch.

> *One thing I would urge you to do is apply the right filter to the right picture. Too often you'll see renditions of pictures which have been put through an inappropriate filter. The basic rule of thumb is: we don't want our Photoshop to show! There's nothing better for ruining someone's enthusiasm for a picture than having them realize it took you thirty seconds to make. Applying a filter requires a deftness of touch, so don't get punchy!*

Elements has just pretty nifty built-in filters for the penciling effect, and they can be used beautifully. This one works pretty well, I think, – it's from Filter > Artistic > Colored Pencil:

There are, of course, other choices in the sketch mold, but I feel this one works best. Check out the filters in the Sketch option of the Filters palette drop-down for more Elements wows.

Glass filter

One of the more amazing things Elements can do with a bit of number crunching is create some really effective-looking glass.

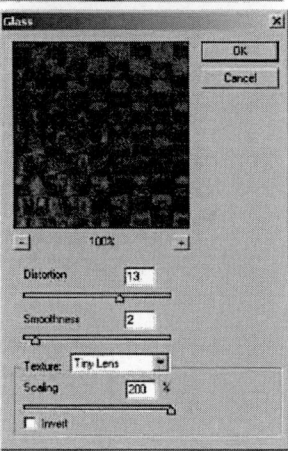

1. Starting with our original `elizabeth.jpg` once again, make a selection with the Rectangular Marquee tool. From the Filter's palette, click on the drop-down menu and select Distort. This will present you with a series of options – and we're interested in Glass.

2. Use the settings shown here:

Why? Well, I guess it's because we had that glass back home when I was a kid. So now our face is looking through a pane of glass!

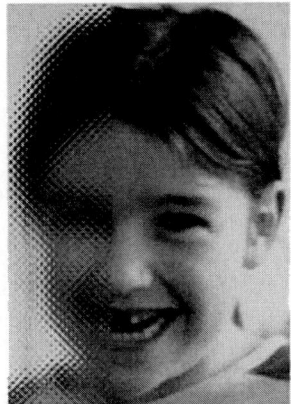

Or, given that children have a tendency to throw baseballs wildly, perhaps we should go for the realistic model:

> *Now, I think what's interesting here is that we've managed to change the context of the whole picture – not by changing the face, but by making simple amendments to the surroundings! By adding in a bit of broken glass we've changed that sweet li'l girl into something rather more menacing. This kind of idea is a great strength when you're fixing up digital images, so use it wisely!*

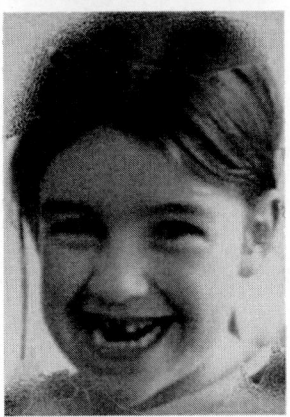

3. The effect can be achieved by using the Polygonal Lasso tool to select a jagged area, and then applying the Glass filter with the Texture set to Frosted. Next, with the selection marquee still flashing, click through Layers > New via Copy.

4. Finally, click through Edit > Stroke to apply a bit of edging around the glass.

5. Optionally, you may want to go around the edges of the glass, adding in extra white lines with a 3 px brush at about 40% opacity. I think that looks pretty realistic!

Gradient Map

One effect you might like to unearth is not really a filter at all. It's the Gradient Map option in the Filters palette:

This basically imagines what your picture would look like in a grayscale format, and then replaces the shades of gray with something a little more exciting. There are a number of different color palettes it uses, so let's take a quick look.

1. Click on the Create new fill or adjustment layer button at the bottom of the Layers palette. Select Gradient Map from the drop-down menu.

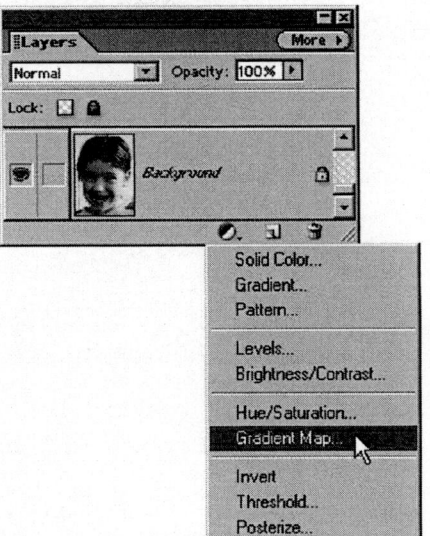

This will bring up a palette showing the existing gradient that it uses when you want it to go grayscale. Not surprisingly, it's black to white.

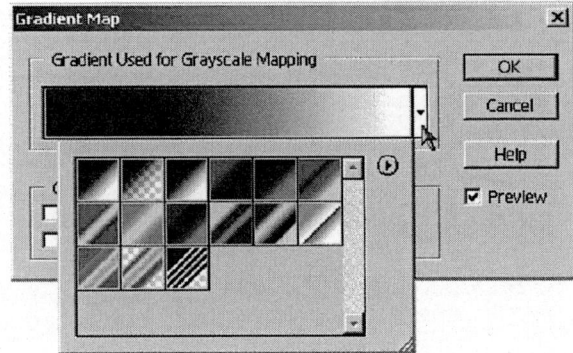

2. Click on the drop-down button beside the gradient to see some variations:

3. A particular favorite of mine is the Copper gradient, which uses a lovely series of browns to create a weird kind of metal (well, copper!) effect.

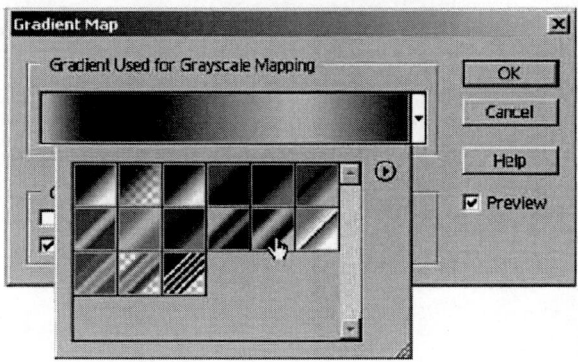
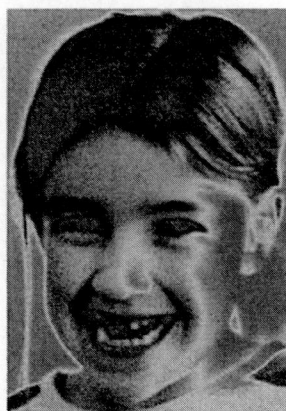

4. If you click on the arrow-in-a-circle button (what do you call those?!) you'll find a whole host of new color palettes available:

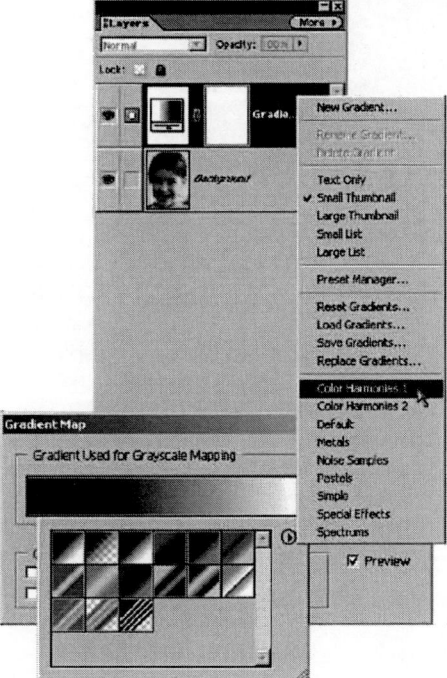

5.   Now take the opportunity to flex your color muscles:

This sort of effect is ideal if you want to incorporate your image into a design that has a strict color palette. If, for example, you wanted to have the face in the colors of your favorite sports team (say, Wolverhampton Wanderers Soccer Team), you can construct your own gradient and swamp the face in these colors.

If you want to do this, you'll have to carry out the following:

6. Select the Gradient tool from the toolbar, or with the shortcut key G, and then press Edit in the Options bar.

7. Rename your gradient (in this case Wolverhampton Wanderers). To select the color of your gradient, click once on the bottom (checkered) arrow. This will allow you to select a color.

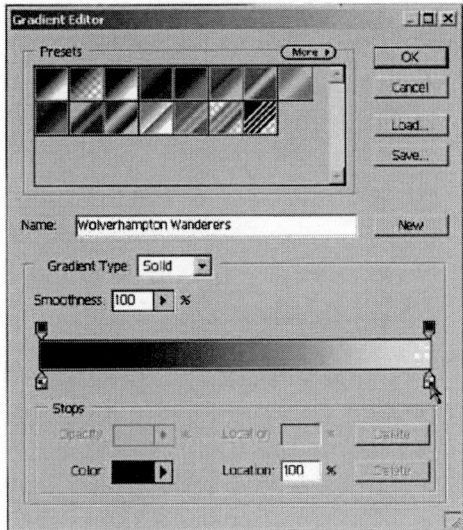

8. Double-click on the colored block, and choose your hue!

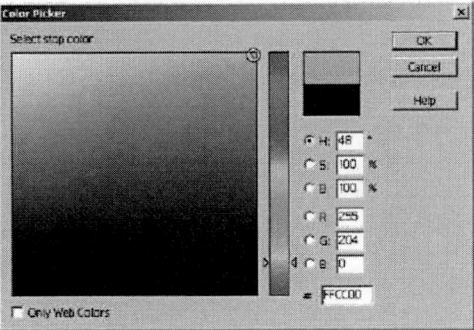

17

9. Then, just press the New button to dedicate your new gradient to the palette, for all posterity.

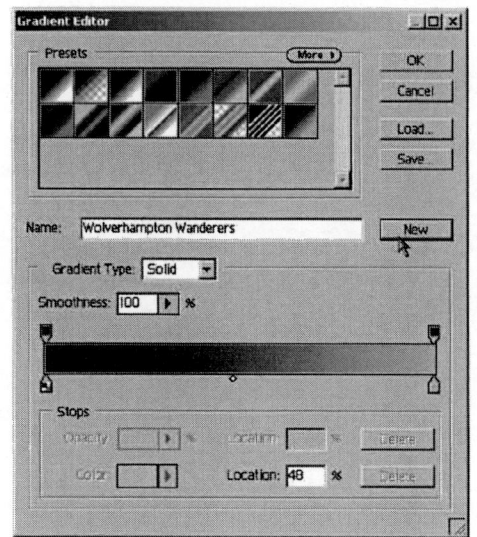

So there we have it, the Wolverhampton Wanderers mascot!

We'll do much more advanced coloring in our dedicated **Imitating Artists** chapter later, where we'll go through a much more detailed example of someone wearing their team's colors!

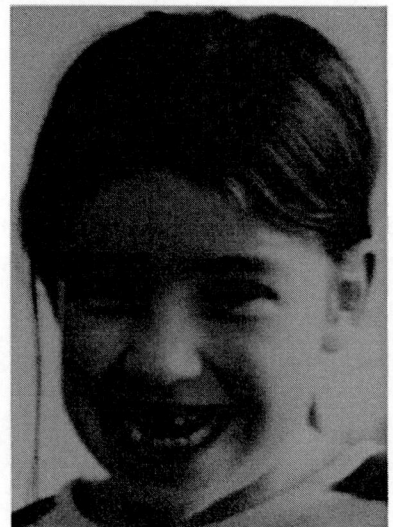

Making 3D objects!

One very lovely aspect of Photoshop Elements is its ability to manipulate images into a 3D format. So, we're going to use that to create an object or two.

1. Go back to our basic elizabeth.jpg image, and duplicate the Background layer so we have a layer to edit. This is easily done by right-clicking on the layer and choosing Duplicate...

2. Fill the Background in with white by clicking Edit > Fill... and then choosing White as shown.

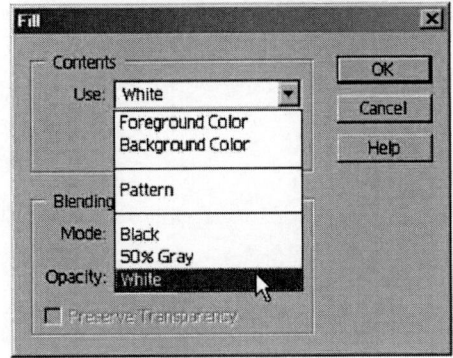

3. We want to have space to throw this picture around a little, so select the Move tool and resize the picture so it sits in the middle of the image.

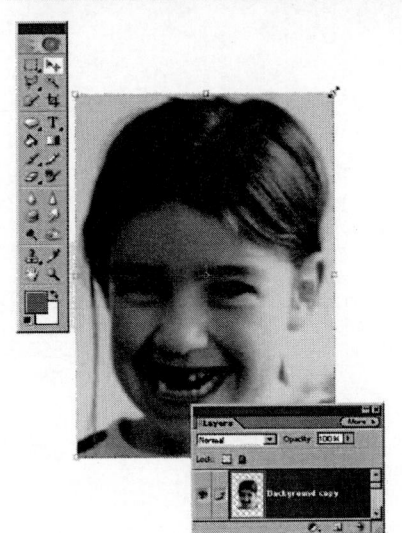

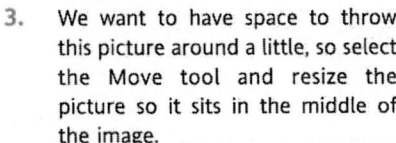

Note: if you hold down the ALT and SHIFT keys while you do this, the picture will stay centered while you shrink it. Press ENTER when you've finished resizing, and Elements will apply the change.

This is the part of the experiment where you can be as creative as you like, before you apply the 3D effect. But for now, let's not be creative *at all*. Let's just deal with the picture as it is, just to demonstrate the 3D effect.

4. While still on your Background copy layer, press Ctrl+A to select the whole image.

5. Click through Filter > Render > 3D Transform to bring up the 3D Transform dialog box.

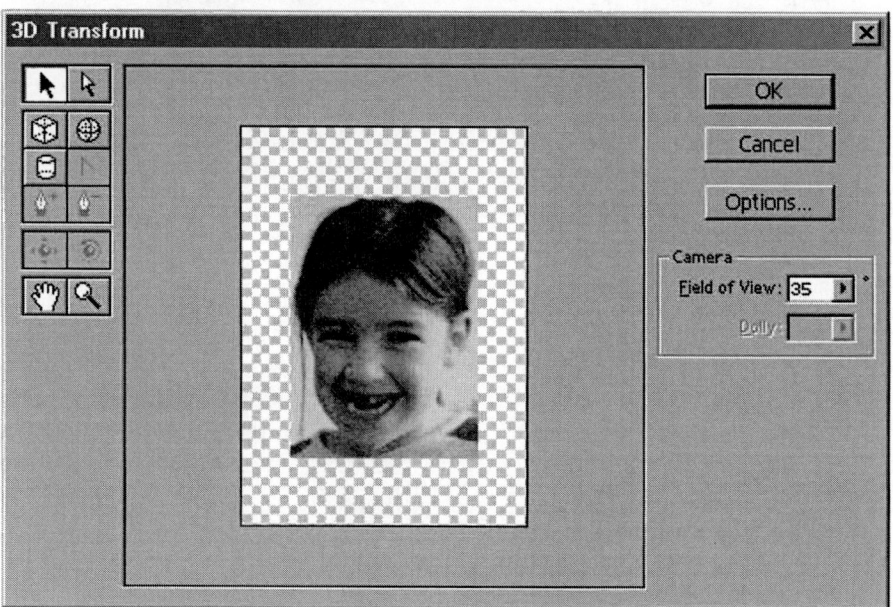

6. Press Options and deselect Display Background. Press OK to that.

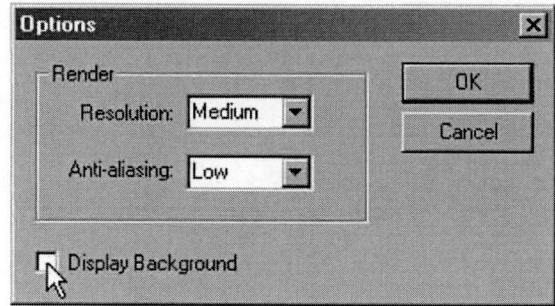

What we're going to do is paste this image on to a tincan. Simple!

7. Select the Cylinder tool from the dialog's specialized tool palette. Now, just as you would with the Rectangular Marquee tool, go to the top left of the picture, and drag out a cylinder, down to the bottom right corner:

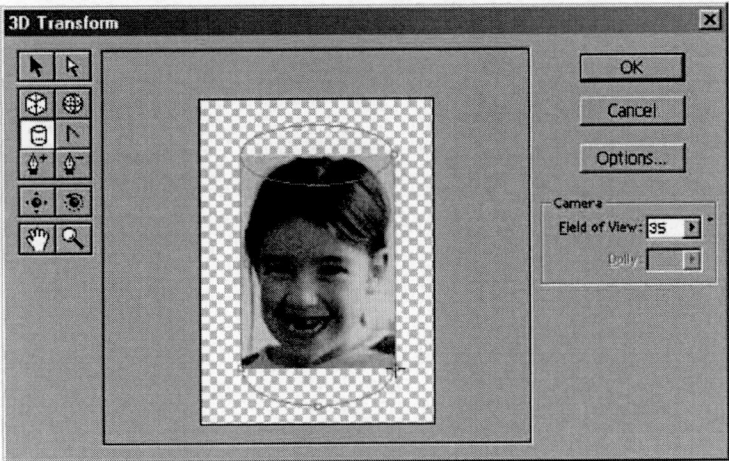

What we have to do now is *pretend* the image we've got is already 3D. So ask yourself – how would we make the picture of the girl flat, if she really were pasted onto a can? Answer – we'd have to look at the can *directly on*, so we couldn't see the top or the bottom. You got me? What we have to do is change the can shape so we can't see the top or bottom.

8. Select the white arrow (the Direct Selection tool). Move it to the little square at the bottom of the can shape.

9. Drag the can shape upwards, and you'll see the can shift until it is full on to us.

So you see? If we assume the picture is 3D already, the can would look like that. What? You don't believe me? Well OK, we'd better shift the can around as if it were 3D. That'll persuade you!

10. Select the Trackball tool, and drag the can in whichever direction you like.

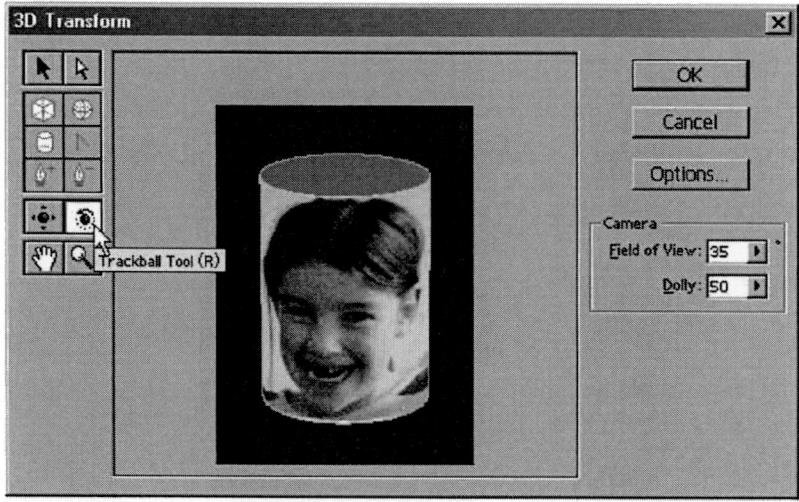

See what I mean? There we have a tin can with our picture on!

11. Just press OK, and see it rendered in full color on our main picture.

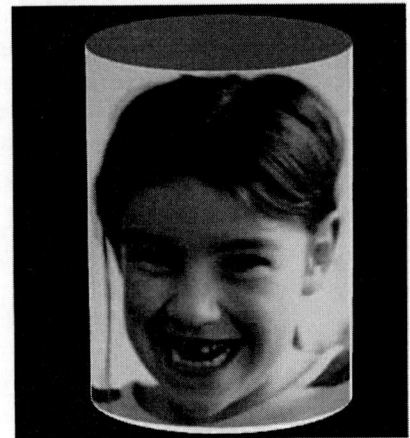

12. Cool huh? Well, now's the time you get to go back to that stage where I said you could be as creative as you liked. At that stage, on our flat picture, I just added a gradient to the picture, and put some appropriately nauseating words on the can. I flattened the image before transforming it into 3D. I also had rather more fun with the angle of 3D – and I expect you'll want to also!

OK, let's have one more go at a 3D object. This time we'll go for a balloon.

Now, balloons aren't quite spherical, and we only have a spherical 3D tool. So the first thing we're going to have to do is make the image completely square so, we can stretch it out later on.

13. Hit CTRL+D to deselect the whole image and instead click on the picture of Elizabeth on its own, or highlight the Background copy layer.

14. Select Windows > Info to show the Info palette. With the Move tool highlighted, drag the bottom handle of the picture so that the Info palette shows we have a completely square picture. In this case, it's 33.66 cm in width and height.

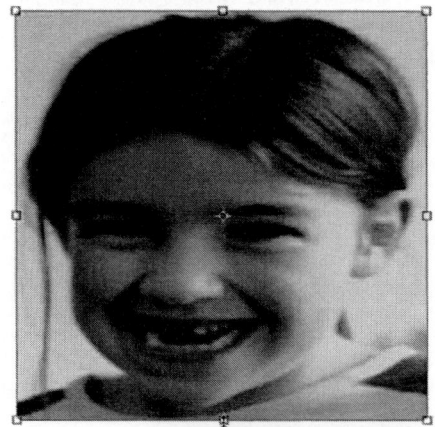

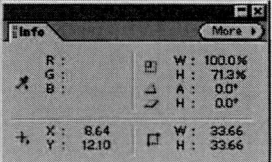

15. Press ENTER, and then CTRL+D to deselect everything.

16. Starting from roughly the center of the picture, and pressing ALT and SHIFT, draw an elliptical marquee. You can reposition it with the cursor keys to make sure it's more or less in the center.

> *Don't forget you can also hold the spacebar while drawing (if you have enough fingers) to reposition the marquee as you draw it!*

Next, we need to create a circle that's an appropriate color for our balloon.

17. Use the Eyedropper tool to select a color from the background of the image (a light gray), and fill in the circle using the Paint Bucket tool. Personally, I also chose to calm the square edges of the picture down with a 30% opacity paintbrush too.

18. I also wanted to add a lighting effect to make this appear more *balloony*, so click through Filter > Render > Lighting Effects and use the following settings:

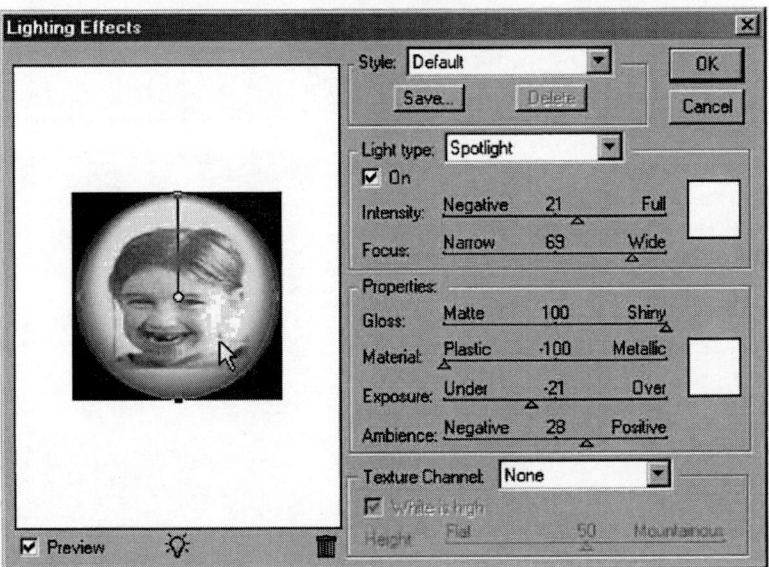

It's already looking quite good:

19. OK, back into the 3D Transform dialog. This time, use the Sphere 3D shape and drag a circle to about the same size as the image. Use the Selection tool (black cursor arrow) to move your circle, if it's not positioned precisely.

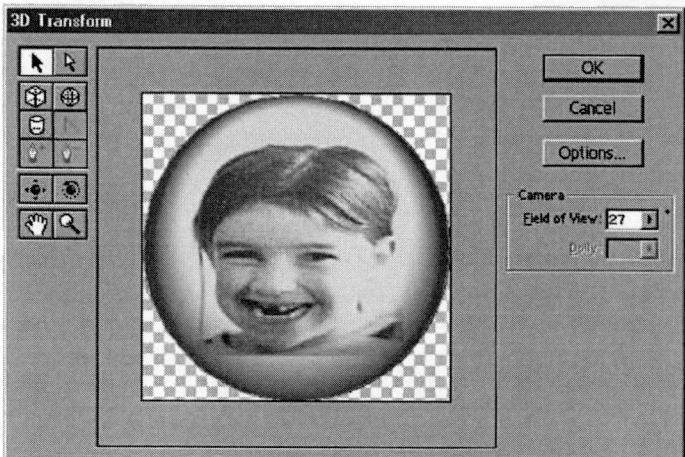

20. And, once again with the Trackball tool, position the image in exactly the way you want it! Now we have the face wrapped around a ball! Press OK to render it to your main image.

That's a nice bouncy ball, but I said I wanted a balloon, darn it! Well, that's easy.

21. Simply select the image with the Rectangular Marquee tool and use the Move tool to drag the bottom down a bit.

    As you see, that brings the squashed face back into proportion a bit.

    If you've got your thinking cap on straight, you'll realize that unsightly pattern on the right of the balloon is caused by the fact that it's trying to go *behind* the image ... which is a bit of a problem, because a 2D image (which is what it was) doesn't have a *behind*. So, it just comes up with any old tat.

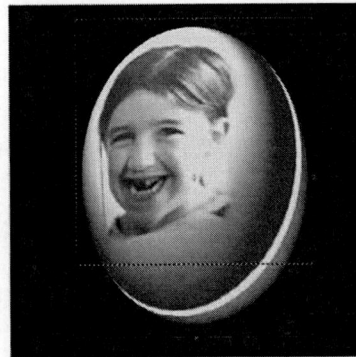

23. Fortunately, it's a fairly sober sort of tat, so I suggest you select it with the Magic Wand tool (Tolerance set to 50%) and then, with the SHIFT key pressed, select the white stripe as well.

24. Then, select a color from the edge of the 'proper' balloon, and click through Edit > Fill > Use Foreground Color. Deselect, and patch the inevitable white line up with the paintbrush.

25. All you have to do now is select it and revolve it how you like. Then, add a little valve at the bottom. I constructed mine out of a couple of ellipses and an adjoining polygon, shaded with the paintbrush. The string is just a shaky white line, made also with the paintbrush.

    You might want to create a bunch of them to stick on a party invitation or some such. The application's up to you!

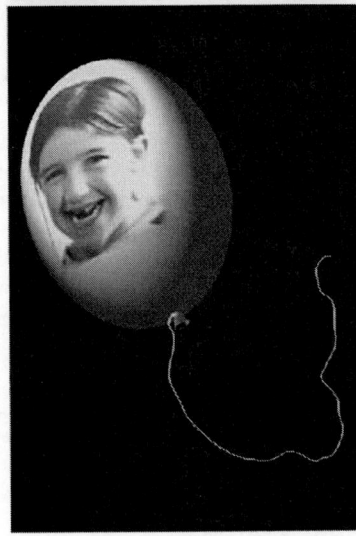

You asking? I'm masking!

One thing we're going to see quite a lot of in this book is **masking**, so I guess we'd better get to grips with Photoshop Elements 2's masking capabilities right away!

Here's a handy picture of a photographer that should suit our purposes well. What we want to achieve with this picture is a neat little effect where we see what the photographer is taking reflected in his camera lens. Here's the face I want to use as the reflection:

Yes, it's her again. Elizabeth's mischief knows no bounds...

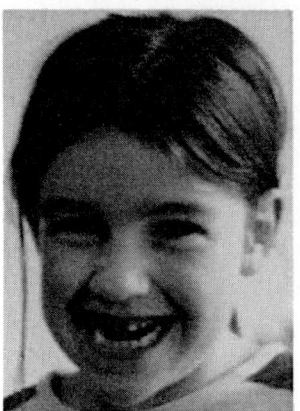

The process will involve letting the second image (the face) show through the first image (the photographer). Wherever we paint our mask, that's where the second image will show through.

1. First things first. Open up `photographer.jpg` from the CD-ROM. This will be our base image.

2. Now select the Layers palette in the menu bar, and drag it out onto the screen, so it sits there permanently.

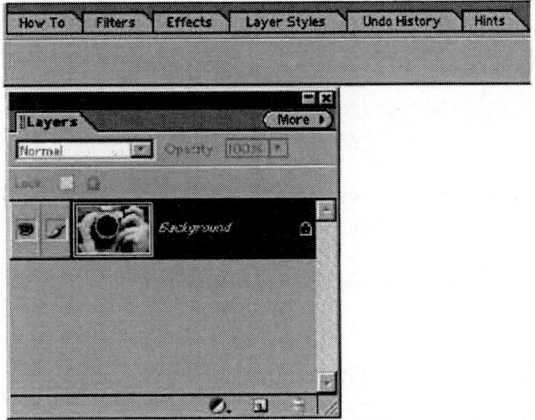

3. Next, using the Move tool, drag the face image from its window into that of the photographer. The picture of Elizabeth is much larger than the photographer, so resize it so you can see her:

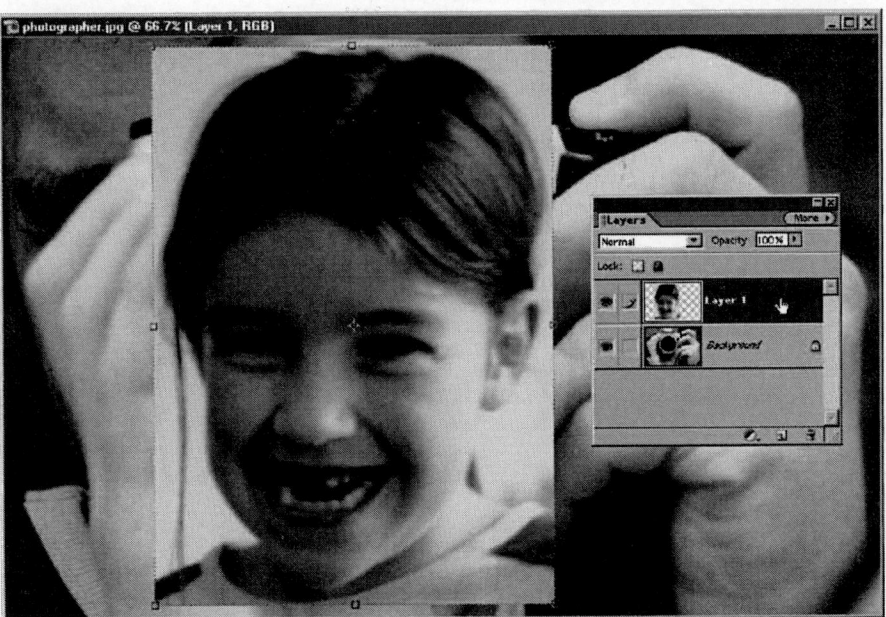

4. Rename the new layer face. So, here are our options. We could:

- Cut away the background of the face image using the Lasso tool. This would be a very permanent way of doing things, and not actually *masking* as such.

- Use the Selection Brush – I guess this would be the best way of approaching things using Photoshop Elements, because the Selection Brush is there and ready for use.

- Create our own editable masking layer. This would be a way more conducive to professional image manipulation.

We'll have a look at the latter two options.

The Selection Brush

1. Choose the Selection Brush. In the Options bar at the top, make sure the Mode is set to Mask rather than Selection.

What we're going to do is paint over every bit of the face we want to keep. Why would we want to do this? Well, it's more accurate than a Lasso tool, because you have scope for error, and the priceless use of the Undo command!

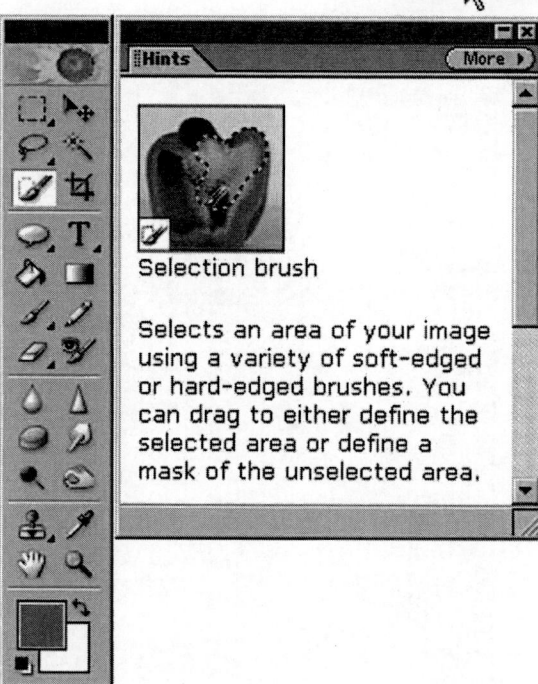

Selection brush

Selects an area of your image using a variety of soft-edged or hard-edged brushes. You can drag to either define the selected area or define a mask of the unselected area.

2. So, with an appropriately sized brush for such a delicate operation, get to painting! You don't have to get it 100% right at this point – we're just flexing our Elements muscles here.

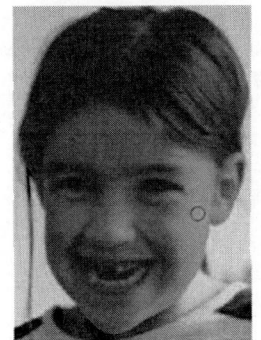

When you've finished this, switch out of the Selection Brush by clicking on another tool and see what happens. Everything you *haven't* painted over is given a selection. It's at that point that you press delete, and the whole background disappears.

But hold on there – isn't that just like selecting and deleting? Yup, it sure is. And that's cheating!

True masking

Here's a neat little workaround which will give us a proper mask. What we're going to do is use a dedicated layer to create our mask. That way, we can alter the shape of our mask at will.

1. First off, let's return to the state where we have the complete face picture sitting on top of the complete photographer picture, as it was before we took out the Selection Brush.

2. Now, create a new layer and call it mask.

    On this layer, we are going to paint with the regular Brush tool, in exactly the same way as we did with the Selection Brush.

3. So, select the Brush, and a bright red paint to go with it.

4. Make sure you're on the mask layer, and begin to paint over the face in exactly the way as you did with the masking brush. Note – you can reduce the layer opacity in the Layers palette if you want to see what you're painting over.

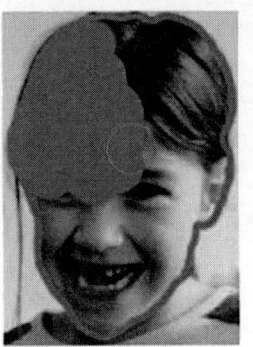

> *It's at this point that really annoying people usually come in and tell you you're not a very subtle painter. Oh, how they laugh. Well, we'll show them.*

5. Once you've finished painting over the face (are you ready for this?) go to the Layers palette, and drag the mask layer down below the face layer.

6. Now, click in the Link box on that layer, and a chain icon will appear.

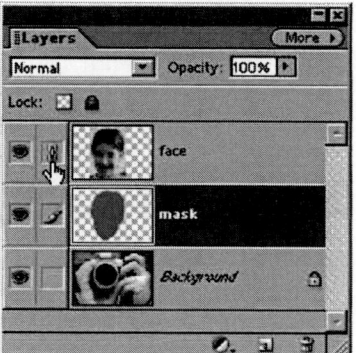

7. Finally, press CTRL+G (or click through Layer > Group Linked)

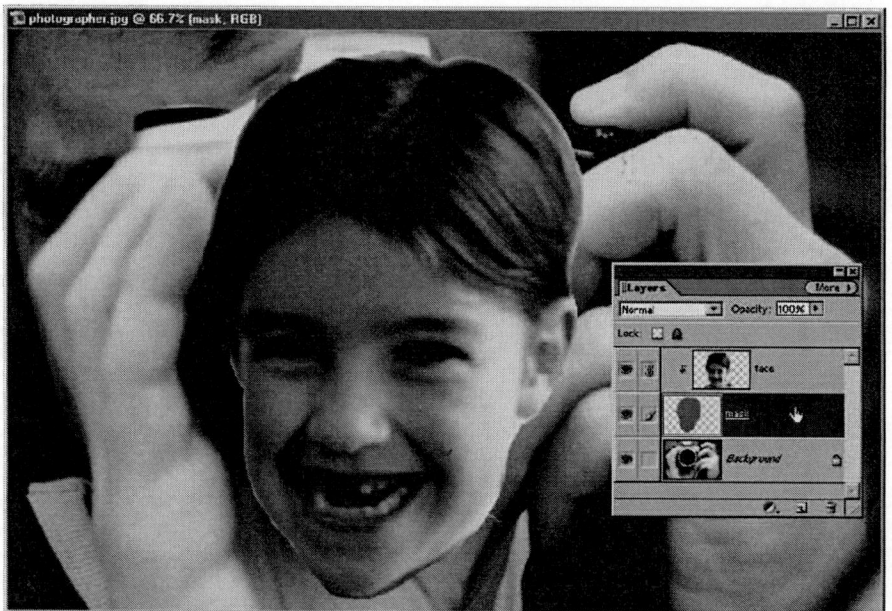

There we have it! A mask layer, completely controlling the layer above it! That, if I say so myself, is pretty amazing. Best of all, it gives us the possibility to amend the mask if we want to!

Say if I decided I wished I'd kept that long strand of hair running down the left of the picture, I would just ungroup the layers (Layer > Ungroup), drag the mask layer back over the top of the face layer, and paint in that extra bit of hair to the mask. No problem!

Also, if you decide you want to resize the face, the mask will resize itself automatically – because the layers are linked! It just works on so many levels! Literally!

Finishing off the effect

Well, you'll have to excuse me – I got so excited about the masking that I forgot we're trying to finish off an effect here. Photoshop Elements can do that to you!

1. Right, we'd better resize that face so it fits in the camera lens. Do this by dragging it around with the Move tool.

Remember to keep the SHIFT button down if you want to keep the face in the correct proportions. You might also want to slightly crop the overall image if you want to focus in on the tiny face. I've cropped a little off each side.

2. OK, so that still looks a little slapdash, so let's fix those rough edges. Making sure you have the mask layer selected, change the layer blending mode properties.

Pin Light works pretty well, I think, giving the face that feel of genuinely being reflected.

3. For that final touch, let's slap on a lens flare ... seeing as this is a lens! Now, where do you put the filter? On the face layer? On the mask layer? On the background?

   The answer is none of these. What we have to do is copy everything we've already done and flatten it on to a new layer.

4. Select All (CTRL+A) and click through Edit > Copy Merged. This takes a snapshot of everything visible, in exactly the format it appears in. Then, simply paste this snapshot on top of everything else (CTRL+V).

5. It's this layer we use to put the lens flare on. So, click through Filter > Render > Lens Flare and choose your Brightness (I went for 100%).

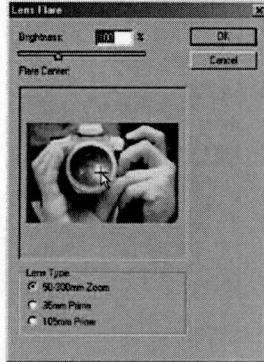

And there we have it! Job done!

> *You can find our PSD on the CD-ROM, called* elizabethPhotographer.psd.

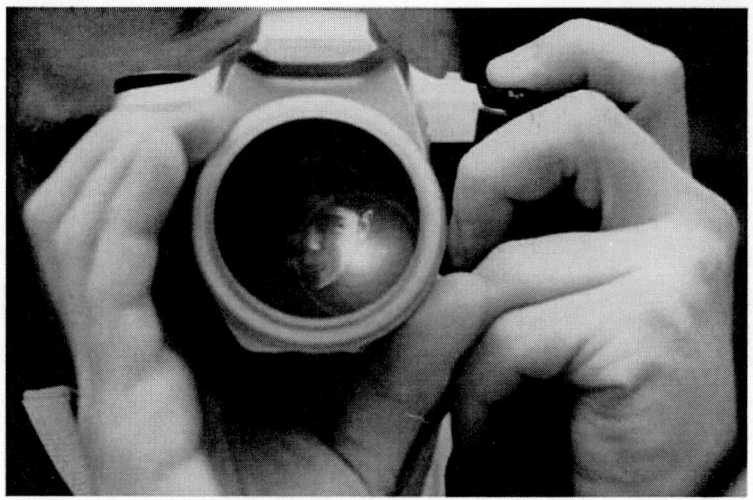

Summary

What we've done here is try to get as many quick results as possible. It's been a case of gain without pain, and Photoshop Elements is excellent for this kind of instant gratification.

Throughout of the rest of this book, we're going to be dealing with some much more involved and careful techniques, which sometimes take a bit of hard work to realize – but don't ever lose sight of the fact that you're just a few clicks away from some great effects!

The tools and techniques we've covered in this chapter will serve you well as we turn our attention to some more original and frankly astounding effects, but you'll be amazed at just how easy even the most complex of facial transformations can be when you have Elements and this book at your side!

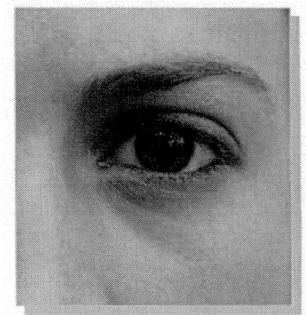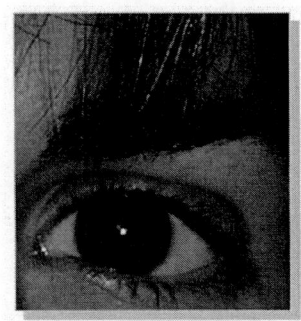

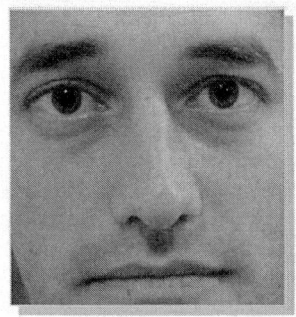

Chapter 2
Retouching Photos

Retouching photos is one of the most common things you'll need to do with Photoshop Elements 2, but there are a wide range of different techniques required to achieve that perfect photo. We'll cover all the bases in this chapter:

- Introducing the **Clone Stamp** tool – sampling skin to clear up a complexion.

- Using the **Red Eye** tool, and some other techniques, to eliminate scarlet peepers.

- Using **adjustment layers** to correct bad lighting and recolor our pictures.

- Finishing off with a full makeover.

In this chapter, we'll look at some of the ways faces can be retouched, enhanced and transformed. Along the way, you'll discover a lot about the way faces are constructed, how imperfections affect them, and how faces are lit.

We'll look at a number of different projects to illustrate the different techniques you can use within Elements to get the best effects and the best results.

Retouching

Before you can even consider adding special effects to your images, you might have to fix some problems with the image. For example, a noticeable pimple on your heavenly model's cheeks, something as simple as a discoloration of the skin, or a small scar caused by a childhood trip or fall.

In any event, Elements has a number of tools created for the specific task of removing small, unwanted areas from your image, and these are especially useful when we come to dealing with faces – no face is perfect. You'll often find you need to spend some time touching up your images before progressing onto anything more creative.

Let's have a look at an example.

Caroline – Clearing the complexion

This image has been very well taken, but there are still a number of small niggling problems that Elements can easily help us remove or cover up. Open the image from the CD-ROM, it's called `caroline.jpg`.

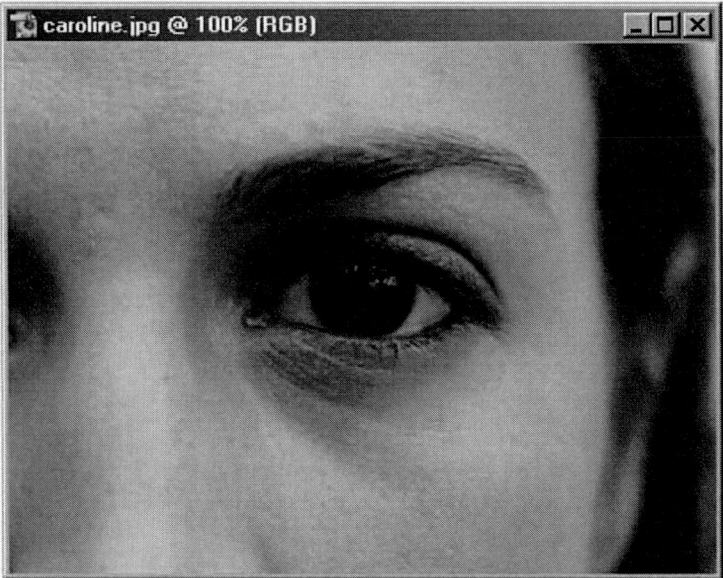

Firstly, what we need to do is make a list of the problems and decide on an order to tackle them:

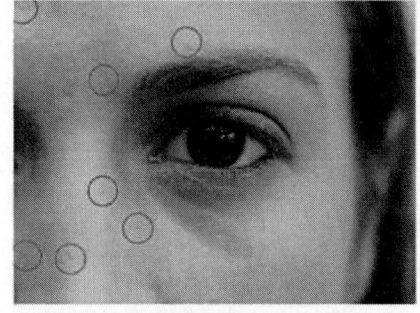

- There is a tiny scar on the bridge of the nose.

- There is a slight yellowing just to the left of the iris.

- There are a few tiny spots around the nose.

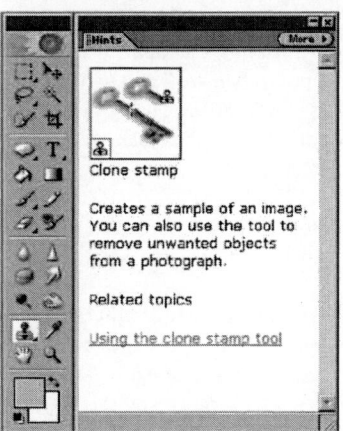

- There are some burst blood vessels in the cheeks.

Nothing particularly major here, but let's see what we can do about them. We'll tackle these in order of complexity – starting with the easiest.

Blemish removal

Elements includes a really ingenious tool called the Clone Stamp tool, which you can activate from the main toolbar, or by using the handy keyboard shortcut S.

We use ALT+CLICK to define a 'source' area for the stamp, and then wherever our brush goes from there, Elements copies the image relative to our source point. So if we draw to the right, we'll get the pixels to the right of our source point, and so on. Basically, instead of using paint, we are using another part of the image.

The Clone Stamp tool is great for removing unwanted objects (by 'cloning' an empty area), duplicating existing objects, and covering up imperfections, as we are about to do now. We'll use the Clone Stamp to stamp out Caroline's very subtle imperfections.

> *Before we begin, zoom in on your first target; I've chosen one close to the nose. You can never be too close to your subject when retouching faces.*

1. Click on the Clone Stamp from the toolbar, or use the shortcut S. We now need to pick a brush size and define a source area.

2. Choosing a suitable brush is actually half the trick. Pick a soft brush, small enough to give you precision – as a general guide, I've picked a brush that's about half the size of those red circles we drew round the spots earlier.

   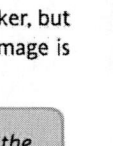

   I've chosen Soft Round 45 pixels from the picker, but these choices will depend on how big your image is to begin with.

   > The soft edge on our brush means that the edges of our 'paste' won't be too noticeable.

   Even with the soft round edge, our brush is actually still way too rough to give us a believable effect. This is a human face after all, and no two parts of a face are identical so you don't want the copying to be too obvious.

3. With this in mind, let's change the opacity of our brush using the Opacity slider on the Clone Stamp Options bar. We'll dab gently over the damaged area as opposed to using 100% opacity brush and completing the task with one obvious-looking stroke.

   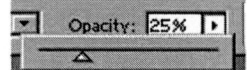

   Now we've got our brush set up and have thought about what we're going to do, it's time to select a source area for our sneaky piece of cloning.

4. We need an area of skin close to the blemish that is untarnished. Start by looking at the spot immediately below and to the left of the eye, on the bridge of the nose. Notice that this area has a gradient of light to dark from left to right, running vertically almost all the way down the nose – caused by the way the light catches it.

5. Select an area to paste (using ALT-click) from the area immediately above the blemish.

6. Now start dabbing on the blemish below – the skin tone and light gradient will be preserved. Keep dabbing until the blemish gradually fades away.

No amount of painting over this area with a single color brush could accomplish anything like this level of realism.

Remember, as with most effects in this book, keep in mind the uniqueness of your subject – the human face. No two areas are the same so if people start seeing repeated parts of skin, they're going to get suspicious and it might even turn out that your 'modifications' are even more noticeable blemishes than the spots themselves.

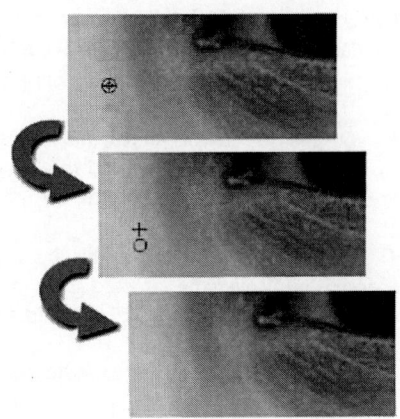

Right, that takes care of the spots, but what about the scar?

The scar

This is a slightly larger area than any one spot. Cloning from any one area will surely create an obvious and recognizable pattern.

Don't worry though, because another great thing about using the Clone Stamp tool is that we're not restricted to using the original unblemished area; we can resample new areas as often as we like.

Using Elements to completely remove the scar will take a few stages, but let's get started and we can deal with hurdles as and when they appear.

1. To fix the top of the scar, sample an untarnished area from immediately above it (which would be most similar color, lighting, and texture wise). Use the same dabbing technique from the previous exercise to lightly paint out the upper part of the scar.

2. Select a new area to sample from for the bottom part – for instance, the area just below the scar. Repeat the same dabbing to paint away our troubles.

3. Once you have begun to see some results, try sampling from all around the scar, filling in the gaps from the first two steps and gradually building up the new area out of healthy adjacent areas. We can use the same process on the burst blood vessels on the cheek too.

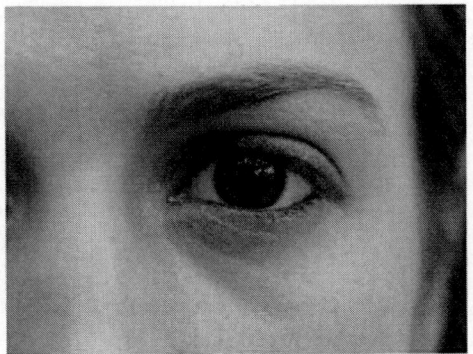

Remember, we're trying to be realistic here, so don't remove every single tiny mark, or you run the risk of losing believability.

Especially with faces, it is really important that the texture of the face is preserved when you're using the Clone Stamp tool. It's pointless if you've got the color, hue and tone of the area right, but suddenly the pores of the skin end in a suspiciously smooth area.

As you can see in the above image, just such a problem has occurred in this image: there is a suspiciously smooth area around the bridge of the nose, where we removed the scar. Wouldn't it be great if we could use some of the texture from the forehead to paste over this area?

There's just one problem with this, if we used our Clone Stamp tool to select this forehead area and then pasted it over the effected spot, the tonality (arrangement of colors) would be all wrong – the forehead is far lighter, and so, changed area would stand out and seem unnatural.

Let's try and solve this using an **adjustment layer**. What we're going to do in a moment is make a new layer, use our Clone Stamp tool, and then add a layer that will adjust the color of our cloned layer, so that it blends in better with everything else. This way we will ensure that the new piece we're cloning doesn't stand out!

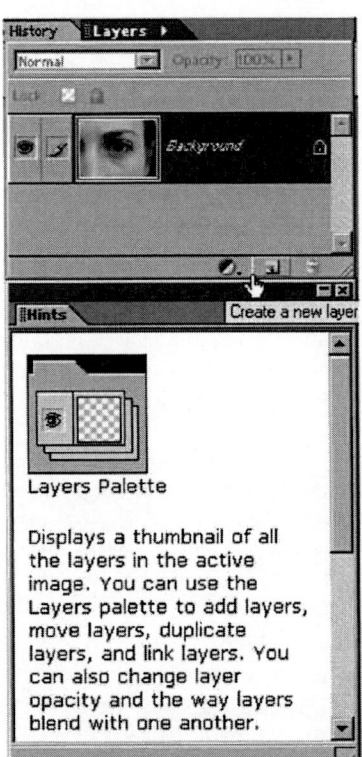

1.   First things first, let's create a new layer. At the bottom of the Layers palette, click on the icon to create a new layer immediately above the Background one – call it scar:

     We're going to clone from our existing layer onto our new layer.

2.   In the Options bar, turn on Use All Layers. This means that the Clone Stamp tool will sample from all layers underneath it when you use ALT+CLICK, and not just the layer that you're on.

Remember that we're going to be stealing texture (skin) from one layer – our background layer – and pasting it over the scar onto another new layer (which we have just created).

Layers Palette

Displays a thumbnail of all the layers in the active image. You can use the Layers palette to add layers, move layers, duplicate layers, and link layers. You can also change layer opacity and the way layers blend with one another.

3.   Go ahead and clone from the forehead. Don't worry about getting it too perfect for now.

As you can see, this cloned area does not match its new surroundings, because its origin (the forehead) was much lighter than the destination area (the bridge of the nose).

We're going to add a layer that modifies the way our cloned layer looks – like looking at the layer through colored cellophane.

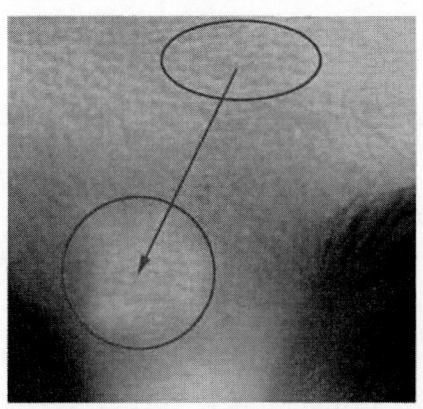

4.   From the menus, select Layer > New Adjustment Layer > Hue/Saturation.

5.   Group this layer (by checking this option) so that the effect applies only to our cloned layer, and not to all our layers. Leave the other options as default.

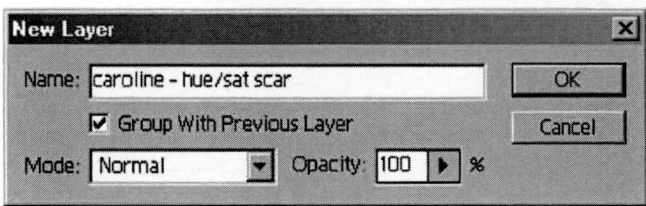

Checking this option means that this adjustment layer will not actually *change* the layer beneath; it will just make it look different. We *could* just adjust the hue/saturation *on* our layer. But what if we wanted to change this later? With the adjustment layer, the hue/saturation effect is applied to the layer – but not permanently – we can turn it on and off as we go. We're going to use the adjustment layer to adjust the color and brightness of our cloned area:

Why these particular settings? Well, as we make the area darker (by adjusting the Lightness slider) it shifts the colors towards black. This obviously has the effect of shifting the colors towards gray (in other words **desaturating** them), so we need to pump up the saturation a bit to compensate for this. Adjusting the Hue slider changes the color range of the image.

With this done, our cloned layer blends in perfectly with the surrounding skin.

The difference is subtle, but if you're going for realism, very effective. You'll probably only find it necessary to go to these lengths when dealing with the larger imperfections such as scratches and scars.

Our final task on this project is getting rid of the yellow area of the eye.

The yellowing eye

Here we have a different problem: The tone and texture of the area are correct; it's just the hue that's gone awry.

This is a slightly longer procedure than spot removal. Obviously, there are lots of different ways to achieve this task. I chose the one we're about to run through for two reasons; firstly it preserves the underlying textures of the eye and is therefore more believable, and secondly because it is alterable at any time.

If you're working on multiple aspects of an image, it's useful to be able to come back and change something at a later date without having to redo all the tasks involved. This is one of the things that makes the Photoshop family of tools so great.

1.   Zoom in on Caroline's eye so that we can properly see what we're doing.

2.   Using the same proximity you would with the Clone Stamp tool, use the Eyedropper to choose a color just next to the damaged area – this will be our foreground color.

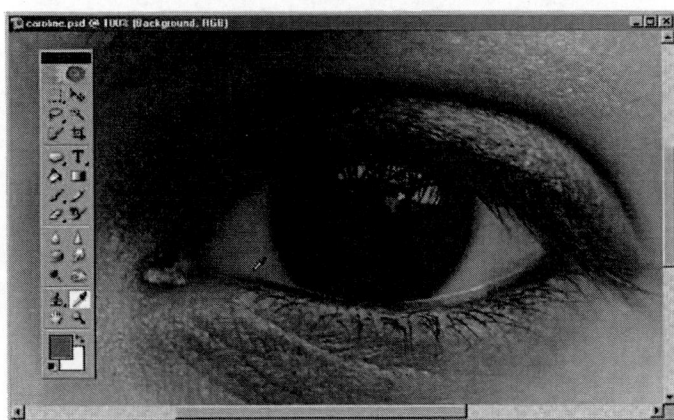

We've done it this way because we need a color that's going to effectively replace the yellow area. To do this, we've picked a color that's near the blemish, but not *tainted* by it. In this case, it's a light reddish gray color.

3. Now let's wrap our lasso round the damaged area. Draw a marquee round the area with the Lasso tool as shown.

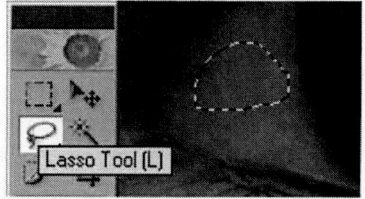

With this done, it's time to add another hue/saturation adjustment layer.

4. Select Layer > New Adjustment Layer > Hue/Saturation.

Note: leave the Group With Previous Layer *option unchecked this time. Because we have an existing marquee, the adjustment layer will only be applied to that area.*

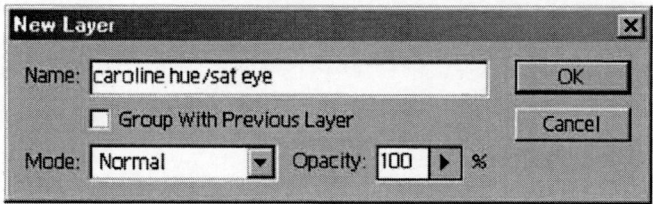

5. Check the Colorize option which will take all the colors in our selected area (within the marquee) and replace the hues using the foreground color, whilst keeping the tonality intact.

This basically means that the damaged area of the eye is recolored using only our foreground color – which we chose from an undamaged part of the eye. So the texture (tonality) remains the same, whilst the color changes:

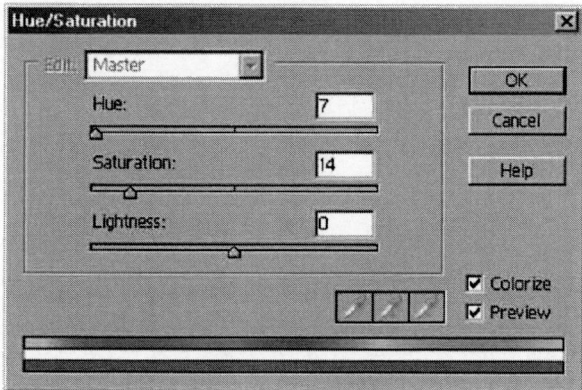

45

Notice, in the Layers palette, you can see that the mask for the adjustment layer is mostly black with one speck of white – the white is the marquee area where the adjustment is being applied.

> *This adjustment layer uses a mask because of the small selection we made when we created it. The tiny white shape defines how much of the underlying layer shows through.*

All that remains to be done is to use the Brush tool to blur the edges of the adjustment layer mask where our marquee (affected area) ends – so that the change from the adjustment colors to the original eye is less abrupt.

Painting (or erasing) on the mask changes the size and shape of the 'adjusted' selection. We don't want to change this shape, we just want to soften its edges.

6. Take out your Brush tool – we want a soft-edged black brush with low opacity, as before.

7. Go around the edges of the affected area with your brush, and you'll gradually remove any rough edges of the effect.

   We have now finished dealing with all the issues we raised earlier, but feel free to continue to tweak the image until you're totally happy.

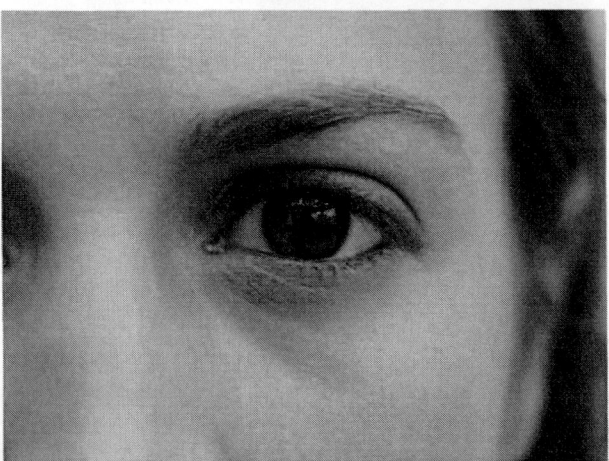

> There are also a few light speckles just to the right of the discolored area, which the Clone Stamp tool can take care of. Finally, I removed the visible blood vessel just above this area:
>
> Feel free to study the PSD of this tutorial which we've supplied on our packed CD-ROM. It's in the **Retouching Photos** folder, called carolineBlem.psd.

Julie – Removing Red Eye

Aside from any imperfections on the face of your subject, not every photograph can be taken perfectly in the first place. Photoshop Elements 2 is the ideal tool for correcting any of the common pitfalls of photography.

A classic problem is red eye. This is far less contagious than pink eye, and a lot easier to clear up. Red eye happens when the flash you're using ricochets off the back of the wall of the eye and reflects back out into the shot.

> *Some more modern cameras have anti-red eye measures – like creating a pre flash to constrict the pupil – which means less light can enter and escape from it.*

It's extremely easy to get red eye creeping into your shots. In fact, I'm particularly good at it. Take a look at Julie – she looks pretty devilish:

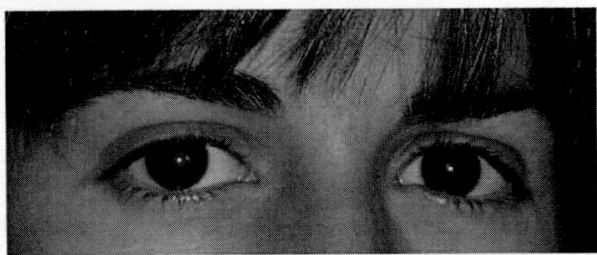

Luckily, getting rid of red eye is about as easy as getting it in the first place. Elements gives us two main ways to achieve this, so let's try one on each eye

First method – the Red Eye Brush

The first method of removing red eye involves using the Red Eye Brush tool. This is a really easy tool to use and will be adequate for many of your photos.

> *The second method I'll show you will give you better results from a little extra ingenuity!*

Let's get started – those red eyes are beginning to burn two holes in the page!

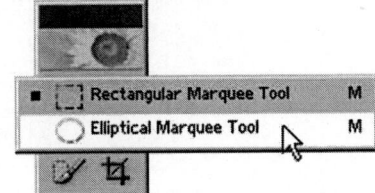

1. To begin, open `julie.jpg` and select the Elliptical Marquee tool.

2. Now zoom in on the eye on the left side of your image, and draw a circular marquee around the red eye area.

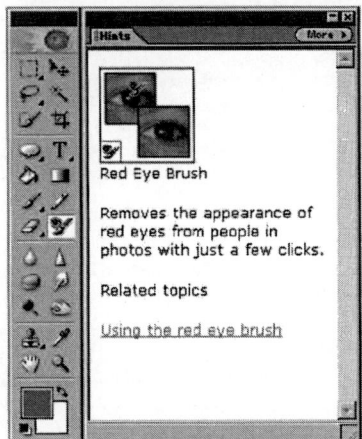

> *Remember that while you're drawing your marquee, if you hold the space bar you can move the shape around. This will help you fit the red area to perfection!*

3. Switch to the Red Eye Brush tool.

Red Eye Brush

Removes the appearance of red eyes from people in photos with just a few clicks.

Related topics

Using the red eye brush

4. Use the Options bar to pick a suitable replacement color (usually black), and set the tolerance to 40% - this way the brush takes into account the various tones of red in the eye, and not just the one specific color.

5. Now all you need to do is dab around inside the marquee using this brush and all the red is replaced with a dark gray.

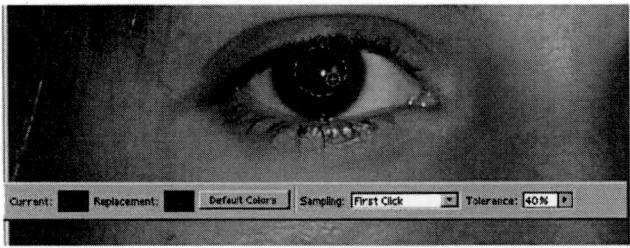

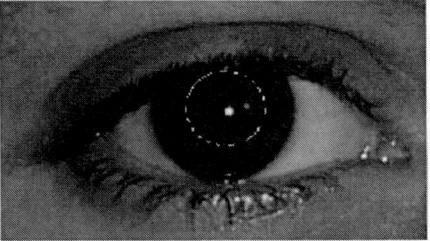

> *This tool basically matches the intensity of the Current (original) color with the Replacement color. So, even though our replacement color is set to black, the resulting color ends up being a dark gray.*

Using the next technique we'll get a superior result, even if it takes us a little longer...

Second way – Layer Blending

1. Let's start on the eye on the right hand side of the picture. Zoom in, if you have to, and select the Elliptical Marquee tool again.

2. Draw once again around the red area. Alternatively, if your last marquee is still there, you can drag it over to the right-hand eye – the red areas of both are of roughly equal size and shape.

3. Now a change from our previous technique. This time, create a new layer using CTRL+SHIFT+N or the Create New Layer button we used earlier.

4. Select the Paint Bucket tool from the toolbar or by using the shortcut K. We want it to paint it black, and a quick way of doing this is to reset the background/foreground colors to black and white, as shown.

5. Fill the selected area with black.

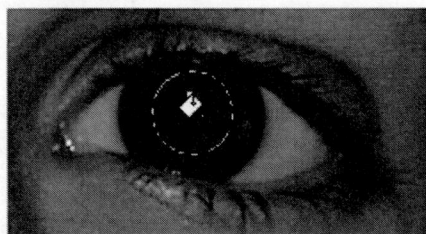

6. Now change the blending mode in the Layers palette to Overlay, and we're almost all the way there already!

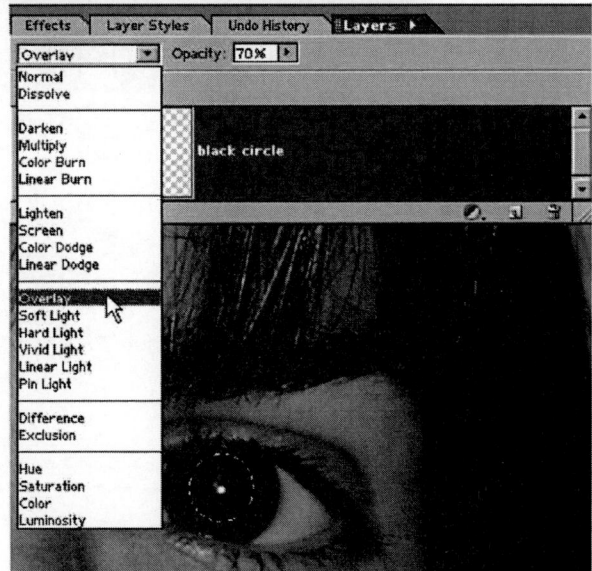

The Overlay blending mode is a great blend to use in this case: it preserves the original (base) colors, especially how light or dark they are, and simply blends in the new colors by mixing them. This is useful when you want to keep your light and dark areas intact – which is one of our goals in this case.

The glint in the eye is still red, however. We want the glint there; we just don't want it *red*.

7. To fix this, once again introduce a hue/saturation adjustment layer. You know the drill by now.

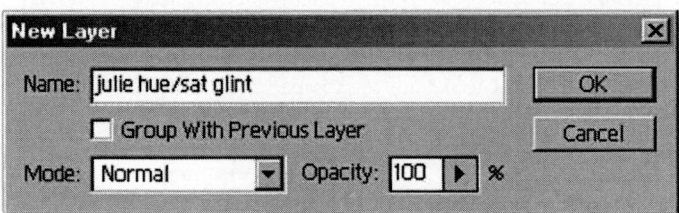

8. All that we need to do is drop the saturation down all the way (-100), draining the color out, and no more red eye.

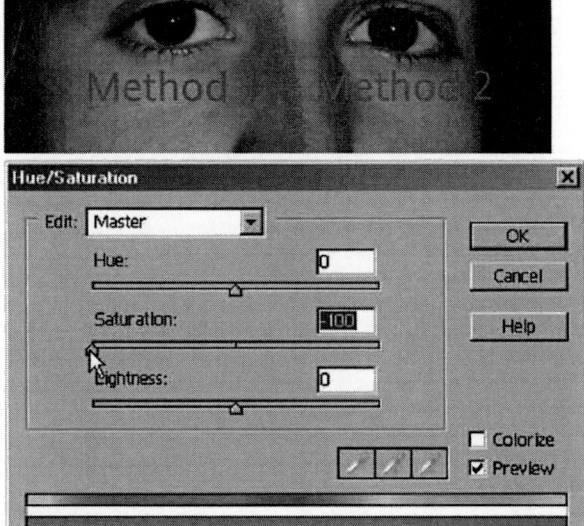

Enhancing

Correcting an image is normally just the first step in working with faces. Often we will want to *enhance* the photograph to improve the overall impact. It's important for us to consider the way in which the face is lit. Even with good lighting on a face, the overall effect can sometimes come out looking quite flat.

Faces have the most amazing number of curves (if you don't believe me, just try modeling one in clay) and it's often nice to accentuate these. Part of the beauty of a face is the play of light along it, and a good place to start when enhancing an image of a face is to reintroduce this tonal flow if it's missing.

David – Adding special lighting effects

One of the most difficult types of faces to work with is the bearded one. This totally breaks up the play of light across the face. Let's see what we can do to fix it.

This picture was taken in fairly harsh light. Because of this, the tone and color of the image has been drastically affected to the detriment of the image.

Remember that if we change the lighting of the image – as we enhance it – this will affect the color of the image, which we are then going to have to tweak. The original color of the image isn't that great to start with, but we're going to make it far worse. If we stopped and analyzed what needed to be done on the image before starting to alter the image, we would probably concentrate on two areas: Fixing the lighting and then fixing the color.

The reason that I've chosen to fix the lighting first, is that doing so will affect the color. If we started by fixing the color and then went on to fix the lighting, this would to some extent mess up the color changes that we had made.

1. Open up david.jpg from the CD-ROM and we'll get started.

2. Start by duplicating the Background layer (call it bg duplicate) and then change the blending mode to Color Burn.

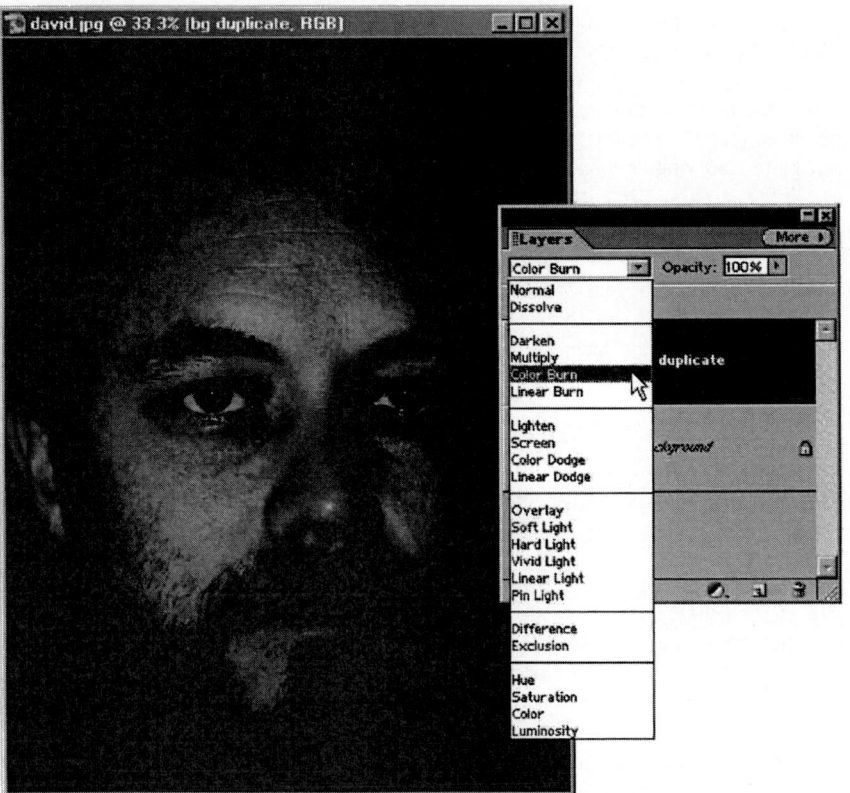

What I'm trying to achieve is to bring out the light – to create some contrast in the lighting on the face. I'm then going to subtly blend this over the original face and in this way enhance the lighting.

I now want to use this Color Burn layer – I want to use the way it has exaggerated the contrast between light and dark areas. However, if I were to use the color burn as is, it would only target very specific areas of the image (this blending mode works a little bit like increasing the contrast of the image, and the areas that would be most affected would be those at the edges of the tone range – extremely light and dark colors) which would then start to look a little artificial. I'm aiming for a kind of rosy glow to the image, so we need to spread this contrast around a little bit.

3. Now create a new layer of the effect of the entire image by using the **Copy Merged** technique. Press CTRL+A (or Select > All) to select everything, and then Edit > Copy Merged (CTRL+SHIFT+C) to copy a merged version to the clipboard.

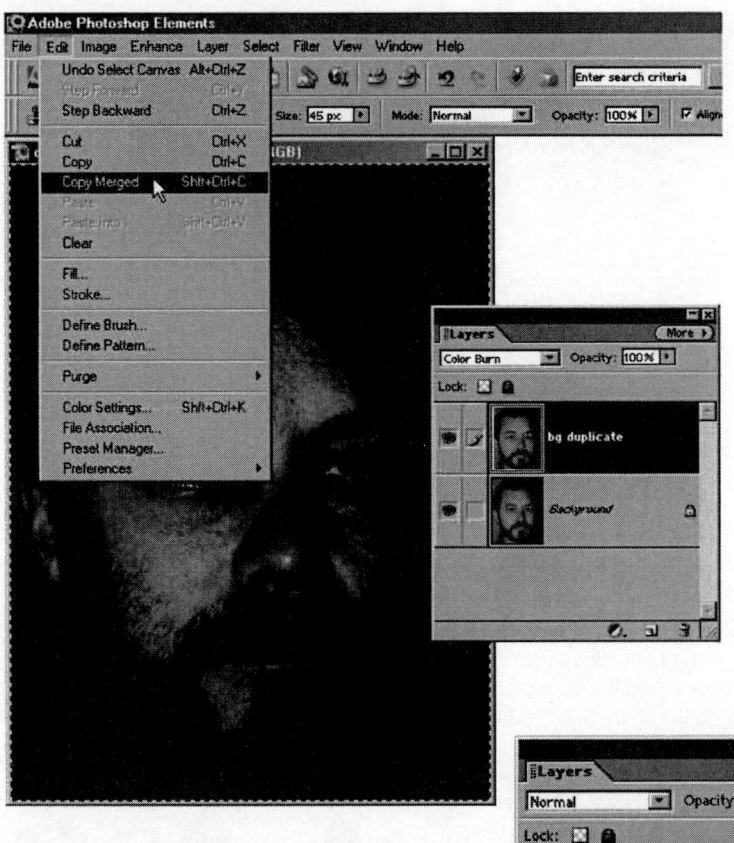

4. Press CTRL+V to paste what we've copied into a new layer, and rename it burn blur. Why 'blur'? Well...

5. Because we're trying to spread the effect, apply a fairly strong Gaussian Blur – Filters > Blur > Gaussian Blur. Set the Radius to 15.

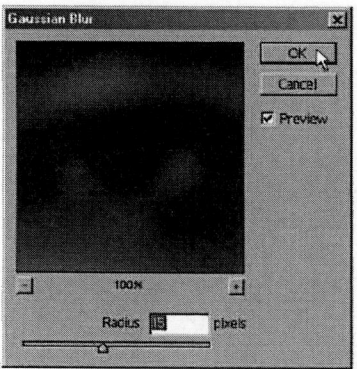

Like with brush sizes, the exact radius of a blur and its relative strength depends on how large your picture is. If our picture was twice the size it is here, the blur would seem only half as strong. Bear this in mind.

6. Now when you change the blending mode of this layer to Screen, a fairly rich glow is added to the image. It proved to be a little too rich for me, so I dropped the Opacity of the layer to 80%. You'll also want to make sure the bg duplicate layer is hidden.

As you can see, the color of the image has been fairly drastically affected. A lot of unwanted red and yellow has crept into the image. This is obviously because some of the color from the Color Burn has come through and is affecting the image.

7. To achieve this, add a solid color adjustment layer using a fairly earthy brown as the fill color and change the blending mode to Hue. On the mask of this layer, I used black to remove the effect from the eyes. Not bad, but I think you'll agree that the image now looks a little plastic.

8. To get around this, add a Hue/Saturation adjustment layer and shift the entire hue range slightly into the red (shifting the Hue slider to –4), enough to reintroduce a realistic looking skin color.

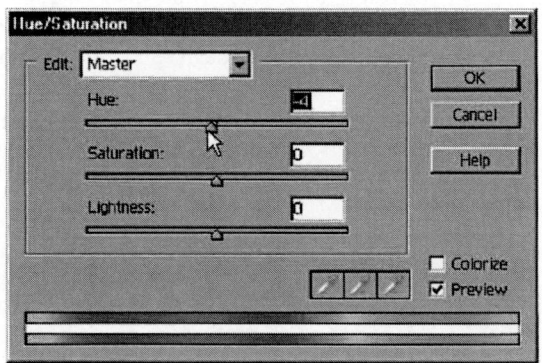

Admittedly, we have lost a fair amount of the color range, which we consciously narrowed by using the Hue blending mode. The Hue/Saturation adjustment layer has not in fact addressed this problem – while we have shifted all the colors, we have not introduced any new ones.

9. To address this, drop the Opacity of the Solid Color adjustment layer to 80%, which lets in a small percentage of the original color.

The end result, therefore (hopefully), has the correct blend between interesting tone and aesthetically pleasing color, without departing too radically from being realistic.

So even though we are dealing with a bearded face, we are still able to introduce an interesting flow of light that enhances the image and increases the visual depth.

You can find the finished Photoshop Elements file on the CD-ROM, called davidEnhance.psd.

Marc – Recoloring an image

Sometimes we need to adjust the color of an image before we start altering the lighting. In the case of the following image, fixing the color is far more important than introducing enhancing lighting elements.

The important thing to watch for when radically changing the color of an image is the way the range of hues is affected – as we saw with the previous image (even when the amount of change was fairly small).

Open up marc.jpg from the **Retouching** folder on the CD-ROM to see for yourself.

Poor lighting (or to be technical, wrong color temperature) in this photograph has severely affected the color, giving it an unnatural yellow sheen. Let's see what we can do to change this.

1. As always, duplicate the Background layer. I'm always paranoid that I'm going to irreparably alter the original and therefore have no point of reference, so I always make a copy, just in case.

    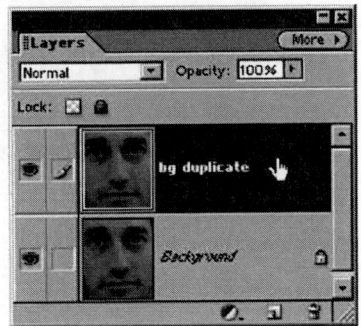

    Also, with this exercise we are going to apply a lot of adjustment layers to the image in order to preserve the original Background layer.

2. Now let's add a Hue/Saturation adjustment layer.

I just wanted to start chipping away at the skewed color in the image, and at least get the range of color more towards pink than yellow. I also figured that the color present in the image was too rich, and so desaturated the image slightly at the same time.

3. Similar to what we did with bearded Dave, adjust the Hue slider to –4, but this time also drop the Saturation slider down to –27.

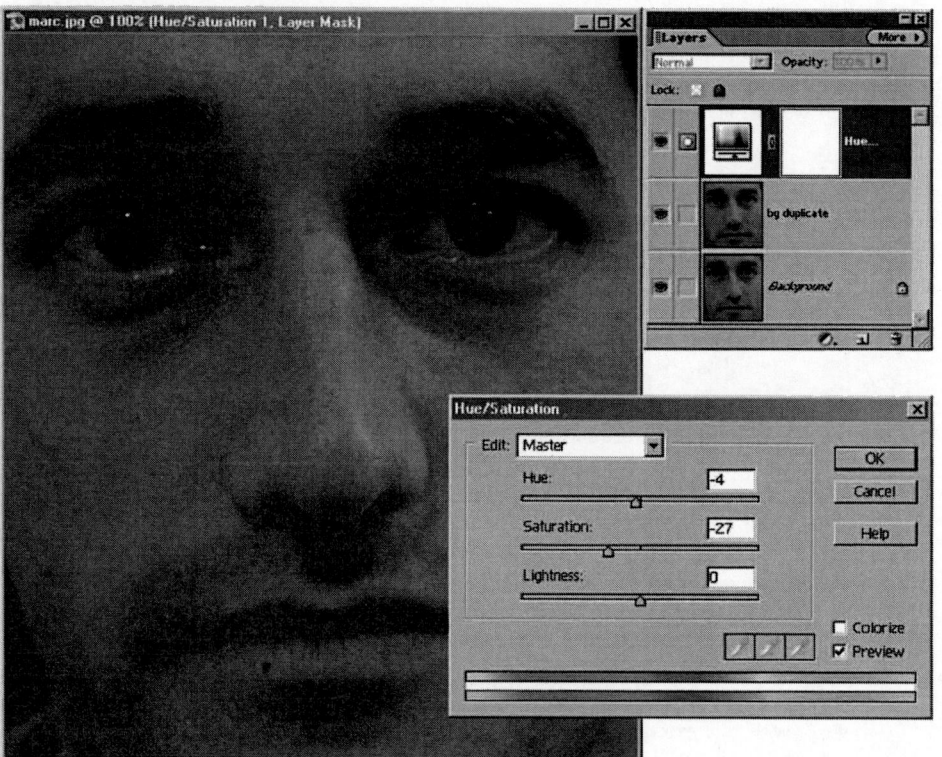

A good start, but the image is way too dark. We need to address this before we can continue altering the color of the image.

4. Create a Brightness/Contrast adjustment layer. In this case, I increased both the brightness and the contrast to simply amplify the entire range of color. But how much? Well, that's really up to you.

I used +35 to Brightness and +23 to Contrast, but the best way to decide on what values to use is to see what looks best for you. At this poin, I could have started messing with levels and suchlike, but I knew I still had a fair amount of color manipulation to go before that, so in the mean time, as mentioned, I just raised the entire hue range.

One important thing that I noticed from this was that even though I had drastically changed the brightness of the entire image, the color of the eyes was still staying fairly dull.

Work would have to be done on the eyes alone. In order to achieve this, we're going to create another Brightness/Contrast adjustment layer, but this time with a twist.

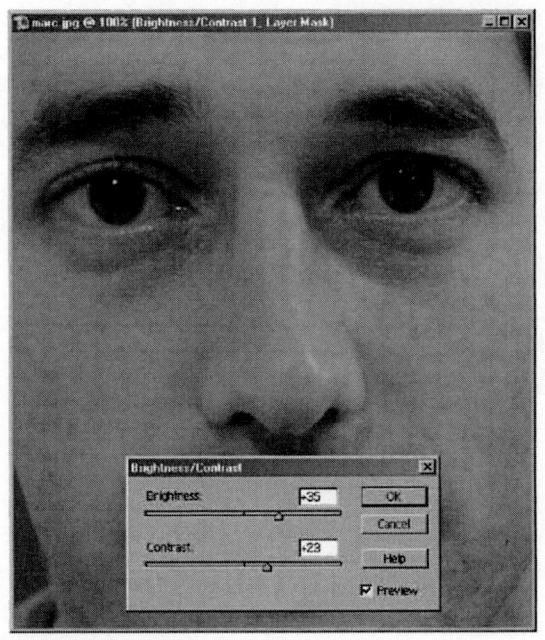

5. Use the Lasso or the Selection Brush to select the whites of the eyes, as shown, then create the new adjustment layer.

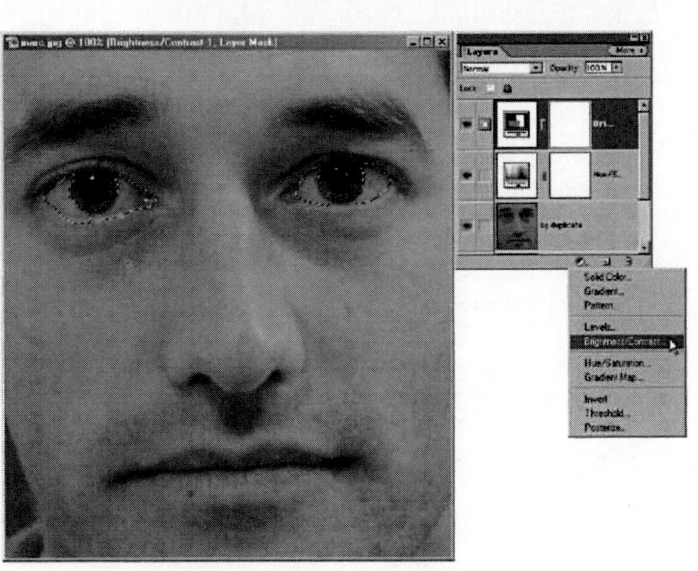

The important thing for me here was not to go overboard. We are still quite a way from completing the transformation – the face is still incorrectly lit and colored, so making the eyes perfectly white would therefore mean that at a later stage they would become over-bright, as we address the rest of the face.

All we're doing now is just subtly making them stand out a bit. If you're working on separate features, it's important to try and keep all the overall effect cohesive. Artificially enhancing a particular feature so that it stands out from the rest is not desirable if you're going for realism.

6. With this in mind, set your Brightness to +68, and your Contrast to +23, and then give the new layer 15% Opacity as a finishing touch.

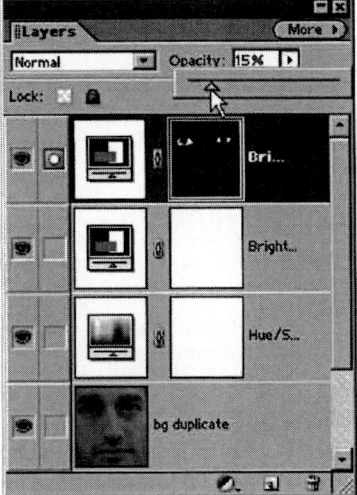

7. Now add another Hue/Saturation layer, this time desaturating a little more and increasing the brightness slightly. This brings the range of color fairly close to normal. Remember what we're going for here is a realistic look – reintroducing realistic color into the image. Obviously, this is open to interpretation. Perhaps I should rather say we're going for believable color.

Here's my settings, but do feel free to play around:

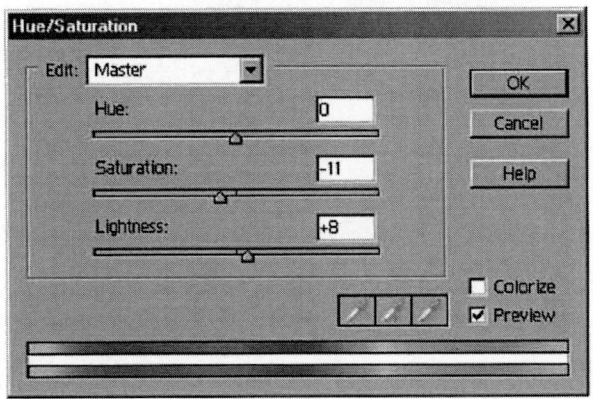

With the addition of this adjustment layer I felt that the range and tone of color in the image was almost there. Most of the yellow had gone, and even though the image was still a little bit on the dark side, things had certainly progressed. I did, however, feel that the Brightness/Contrast layer had desaturated the overall color of the image a little too much, so I dropped the opacity of the layer down to 60%.

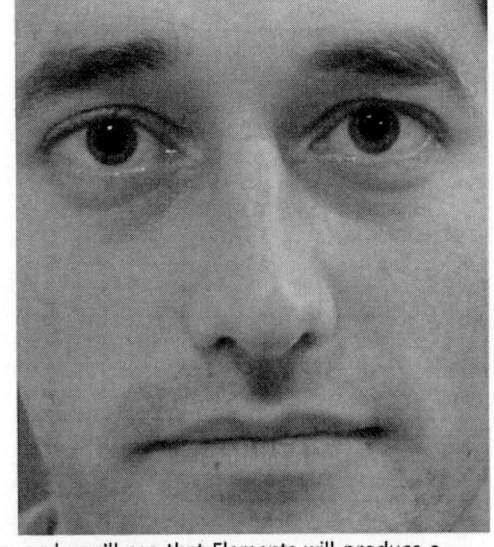

This gave me enough of an alteration in the brightness, without the undesirable desaturation creating problems.

8. Almost there. A final Levels adjustment layer should see us through, so add one to your project.

For the purposes of this image, just choose Auto, and you'll see that Elements will produce a fairly impressive effect. This good result though is only because of our careful earlier preparation.

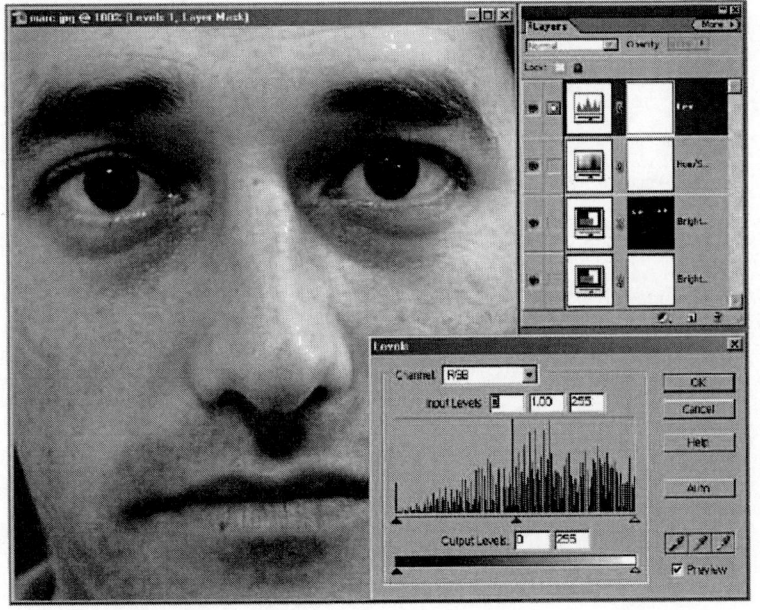

As I stated before, when you're trying to make something realistic, this is an entirely subjective goal. We have, however, managed to effectively increase the color range of the image, and at the same time introduce a healthy amount of contrast.

To complete the above task we had to add a lot of different adjustment layers, each one slightly changing the image.

But how do you know which layers to add when?

While there's no hard and fast rule here, a good point to remember is: when you're trying to alter the color or lighting of an image, realize that it's unlikely that you're going to pull it off in one step. As you change the hue, often this will affect the lighting, and visa versa. Start with whatever seems to be the biggest problem. I usually start with the lighting, because as we've seen before, if you start with altering the color, a lot of the time you'll have to come back and redo it.

Always be careful of decreasing the color depth too drastically: if you add a very strong contrast adjustment this might remove too much of the midtones of the image which might not be recoverable. Using Elements is a lot like using makeup: if you plaster too much on too quickly, people can spot it a mile away. Try to avoid doing this!

> Check out `marcLight.psd` on the CD-ROM to see our finished file.

Transforming

While a nice diffuse lighting effect (or lengthy session with the Clone Stamp tool) can go a long way to removing freckles and even hiding wrinkles, structural elements of the face – the *morphology* – will be relatively unaffected by these alterations.

So how far can we go? Well, with Elements the sky is pretty much the limit. In fact, the only real limit is your imagination, and available time. Let's look at a combination of all the techniques discussed in this chapter and demonstrate their application in a complete makeover project. In this way, we can see the order of techniques and the progression of the image – from stock standard shot, to finished product.

Nadia – Full makeover

Let's have a critical look at the image we are going to be working with; `nadia.jpg`:

There are a number of areas that we can improve on in this image. I like to work on the face before altering the color balance of the image. Let's list the tasks for the face then:

- There are some minor skin **blemishes** to get rid of.

- The **lighting** on her nose is particularly unflattering, making it look bigger than it should. We will need to change either the lighting, or the shape of the nose.

- The **shadow** on her eyes makes them look rather small; it would be better if they were slightly bigger.

That about covers the work we need to do on the face.

Once we have accomplished these tasks, we can address the fairly poor color and lighting in the image.

Obviously, different people will find different tasks to address. Altering the look of a face to make it 'more pleasing' is almost entirely subjective. Certainly there are some aspects of beauty that are universal: regularity of features, good skin tone and color, lack of blemishes etc., but on the whole, you'll have to decide for yourself.

Blemishes

We've already covered how to get rid of minor blemishes. There aren't many to worry about, so you can go ahead and do those yourself.

If you need any guidance, look back at the first model in this chapter, Caroline, or look up our final Nadia PSD, `nadiaMakeover.psd`, on the CD-ROM.

I had no texture to worry about in this image, so the task was relatively easy. But what about the shape of the face?

Morphology

Changing the entire shape of the face was slightly trickier. No matter the shape of the marquee you draw, Elements will apply changes to it using a rectangular bounding box. So, for instance, if you're using a diamond shaped marquee, Elements will draw a square around it and resize it according to that square. So here's the problem: what if you want to push the sides of the diamond closer together, and not the points?

Apply this poser to our face: if I apply a rectangular marquee around the face and then resize it, the face will be squashed out of proportion – the correctly positioned marquee would be tilted slightly clockwise (in accordance with the fact that the face is presented to us slightly diagonally). What we want to achieve is to narrow the face. If we rotate the entire image until the face is parallel with the canvas, and then scale it to narrow the face, we can achieve this task (about 25 degrees clockwise). Once done, the face can simply be rotated back.

You'll notice when doing this (Image > Rotate > Custom) that Elements rotates the entire project, and not just the layer you're on. This makes your canvas a lot larger, as it has to accommodate a diagonally shaped image. When you rotate the image back this is still the case, so you will have to crop away this now unnecessary space.

We could have also used the Image > Transform > Free Transform option to both rotate and distort the image, but this is probably not a good idea for the following reasons:

Firstly, distorting along any plane, other than the vertical (i.e. narrowing the face), produces results that to my mind are too artificial and unnatural.

Secondly, while it's useful to rotate the image in this way to check what angle we need to get the face parallel with the canvas, actually using this option to perform the rotation means that the diagonal corners get cut off – as this command does not resize the canvas – so we lose quite a bit of our image.

I think I might have got slightly carried away on the shape of the face – it's a lot thinner than the original, but it's amazing to see how much we can actually get away with here!

Color

The color in the image up until now is fairly drab and uninteresting. Let's change this. I decided to go for a healthy summer glow. The first thing to address is the slightly washed out pink color of the image. A quick and easy way to change this is to use Enhance > Adjust Color > Color Variations (also accessible from the main toolbar using the icon of three colored circles).

With a couple of clicks we can adjust the color and the contrast of the image:

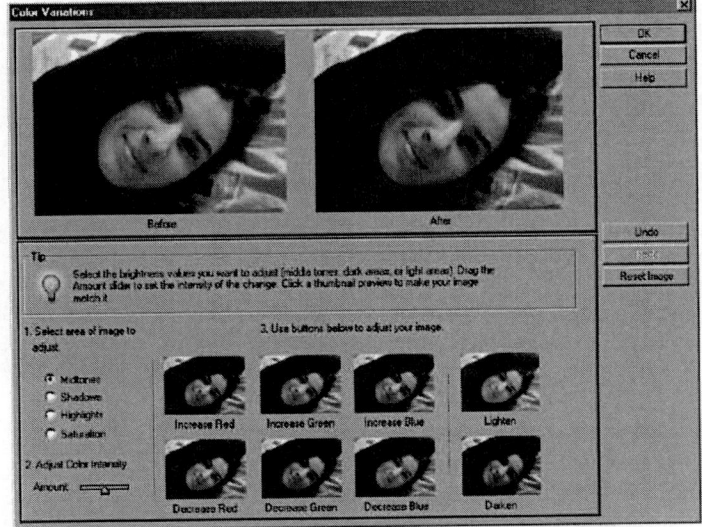

This goes a long way to sorting out the color, but the lighting is still pretty boring. Let's create a glow, similar to the one we completed earlier in the chapter with David.

Once again this involves duplicating our working layer, setting the blending mode of this new layer to Color Burn and then creating a merged copy of this effect (Select > All, Edit > Copy Merged).

With this result pasted onto a new layer, we can Gaussian Blur it (with a Radius of around 7) and then set the blending mode of this new layer to Screen, just as we did before. I also dropped the Opacity of this layer to 70% to make the glow more subtle.

Let's add one further special effect to the image. What we want to do is turn off our Background and copy of background (working) layer and do an Edit > Copy Merged of just the new Color Burn layer that we've got set to Screen.

Turning off these layers leaves our image slightly transparent, as the Screen blending mode is now blending with nothing (the layers below are turned off, remember).

So, when we do our Edit > Copy Merged on this layer and paste the result to a new layer this result will obviously also be semi-transparent – which is what we want – we're creating a wash over effect, and don't need it to be opaque. This new layer we are going to apply Filter > Noise > Median to, will smooth out the effect we're creating. Essentially, this is a similar effect to the one we've just created except we will be tweaking the contrast and increasing the smoothness of the overall image.

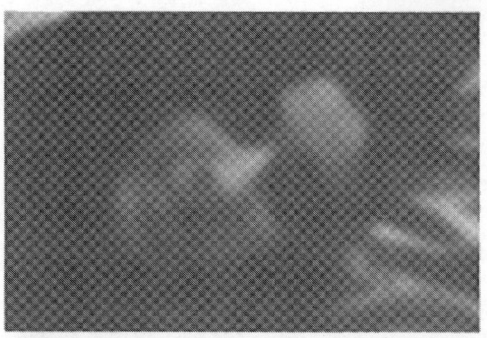

Finally, we need to desaturate this layer (this effect has a tendency to mess with the color which is undesirable in this case) using a new Hue/Saturation adjustment layer.

Drop the opacity of the median layer to around 50% to give it a more subtle effect, and add a Soft Light blending mode.

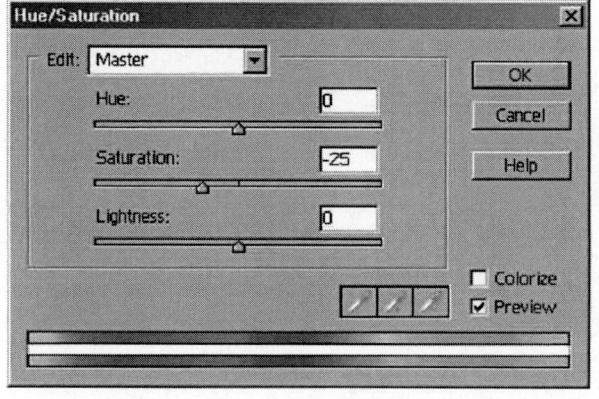

Lips

On final inspection I decided that the lips needed a little bit more color, so I added in another layer, painted some flat color over the top of them (that I got by using the color picker in the middle of the lips to select an appropriate color) and setting the blending mode of this new layer to Color. A final Hue/Saturation adjustment layer to drop the color saturation by about 20 gives the image a more realistic feel:

Summary

So, in conclusion, I'm forced to offer some slightly schizophrenic advice. While it's important to plan ahead, and decide in advance what needs to be altered/improved in an image, nothing is quite as powerful as experimentation. Exploring the use of different blending modes for layers is always really interesting when working with faces.

One of the strangest things for me as a young child was to hold up photographic negatives to the light. Here were shapes that I understood, but in totally unnatural colors. Experimenting with different blending modes is along those lines. If you're just starting out in Elements, using faces is a nice way to get into working out how blending modes work – you already understand how a face *should* look, and it is therefore really easy to see how changing the blending mode affects the overall look.

If we were working on cars, and we decided to completely change the color range this might not look so startling. But change a face to bright blue and you know just what the effect is doing to the original.

In any event, regardless of your skill level with Elements, I'll leave you with one really valuable exercise:

Duplicate an image onto a new layer and apply a blending effect on that new layer. Make a new layer that is a merged copy of the previous two layers. Now experiment with altering the blending mode for this new layer. We used this technique in this chapter to create a warm glow to the image, but there are lots of different permutations of blending modes to be discovered. Give it a try.

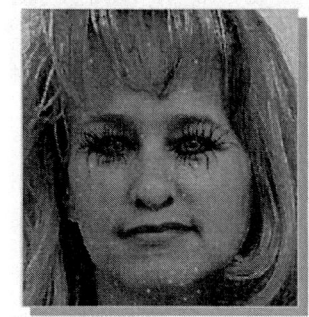

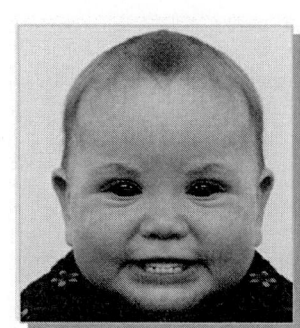

Chapter 3
Freaky Faces

What we'll learn in this chapter

We've done some quick and painless effects, and a little retouching, but it's now time to get a little freaky. Now we're aiming to shock as well as to please with our gallery of the unusual, the weird and the downright crazy! Our journey through Elements' palette of face-meddling tools continues:

- Using **masks** to isolate individual facial features, to play with **eyes**, **lips**, **teeth** and more...

- **Cloning** eyelids and **recoloring** eyes.

- **Blending** features of more than one picture to create a freaky alternative.

- Removing eyes, extending eyelashes, teething a toddler, and more.

Imagine waking up on a typical morning and after customarily hitting the snooze button on your alarm clock seven times, you drag yourself into the bathroom. After running cold water through your clammy hands and splashing your face to remove the sleepy-dust, you raise your head to confront your mirror image. How would you react if you discovered that your eyes were solid black? What if one of your eyeballs was missing or if your eyelashes had grown to four times their normal length? Welcome to my world...

In this chapter, we're going to look at the ways in which you can take a face in Photoshop Elements and make it look really freaky. Sometimes it is enough to just unsettle our viewers. And sometimes you have to blow them away with plain weirdness. No end of people have managed to turn it to their advantage. How do you think hardcore weirdo Marilyn Manson managed to infuriate all the elders and hypnotize the kids? Simple eye techniques, a little bit of foundation dabbed on here, an eyebrow carelessly tossed away there. We can do all this without touching our model's actual skin.

OK, let's get started. Open up Photoshop Elements (unless you've been making an evening of it and are coming straight from the last chapter) and I'll introduce you to our first victim ... sorry, *model*.

Charlie – Taking an eye out

This is Charlie – his portrait was a prime candidate for this effect because a lot of people are drawn to his trademark lazy right eyelid. But let's see what people think when you *really* give them something to gawp at. We're going to take his eyeball out altogether!

Are you sitting uncomfortably? Then let's begin.

Masking Charlie

1. Open up `charlie.jpg` from the **Freaky Faces** folder on the CD-ROM. This is our original image.

2. First off, we're going to have to clear out the area where the eyeball will become just the eye socket. Since we want to work *behind* the shape of the eyelid, the best option here is to mask out the eyeball.

3. Choose the Selection Brush tool.

4. This is a very nifty piece of kit we're going to be seeing more of later (unlike Charlie) in the chapter.

5. Make sure it is set to Mask mode rather than Selection mode in the Options bar. This will allow us to mask out the area of the face we want to see through.

6. Zoom right in on Charlie's eye, and paint over the area we want to omit.

   I've chosen a nice bright red. You might find it easier to reduce the Opacity to 50% just to make sure you're painting in exactly the right areas. The initial brush size should have 100% Hardness and should be small enough to move around the eye comfortably.

   > Note – you change the Hardness *of a brush through the* More Options *button on the Options bar.*

   Don't skimp on changing brush sizes to get the really fiddly bits. If you paint over an edge, press CTRL+Z to retract your brush stroke.

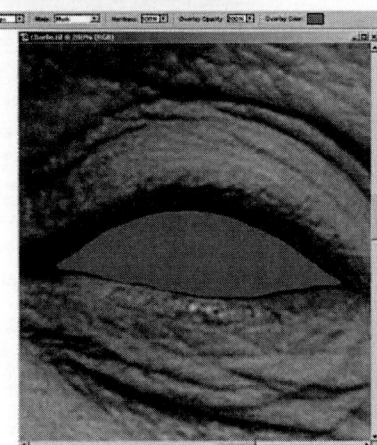

7. If you now click on the Move tool, you'll find a selection marquee appears, selecting everything *except* the area we've painted over.

8. Next, click through Layer > New > Layer via Copy. Double-click on the layer name and call it mask. While you're in the Layers palette, turn off the visibility of the Background layer, so we can see through to the checkered transparency.

What we end up with is this:

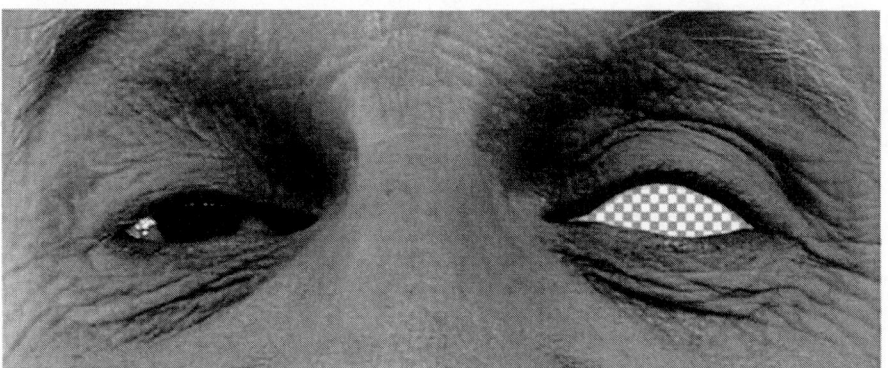

This mask of Charlie will allow us to happily work beneath Charlie's face without ruining any of his beautiful features. What we have is a single masked layer of the image with the eye cleared out, ready to have more layers added beneath it to help compose the socket underneath.

What we want to do with the socket is convey the right amount of depth, and add some type of organic texture inside the socket. The texture should be visible but very subtle, so the viewer has to almost strain to see it. Drag them in!

My Layers palette looks like this at the moment:

What we're going to do is add layers *above* Background, and *below* mask. Really, you could just delete the Background layer, but I like to keep a copy of the original in case everything goes belly-up. Now, however you want to do this is up to you – it depends what you want inside his head – but let's look at what I did.

Filling the void

1.   Create a layer below the mask layer and fill it with a dark red color.

     I sampled a color from a portion of Charlie's skin that was in shadow, using the Eyedropper tool.

2.   Create another layer on top of that (still below the masked layer) and use black paint with a large, soft brush to create the shading.

> *Imagining the way that light would enter the eye socket, I made the shadowing darker toward the top of the socket and gradually lighter toward the bottom.*

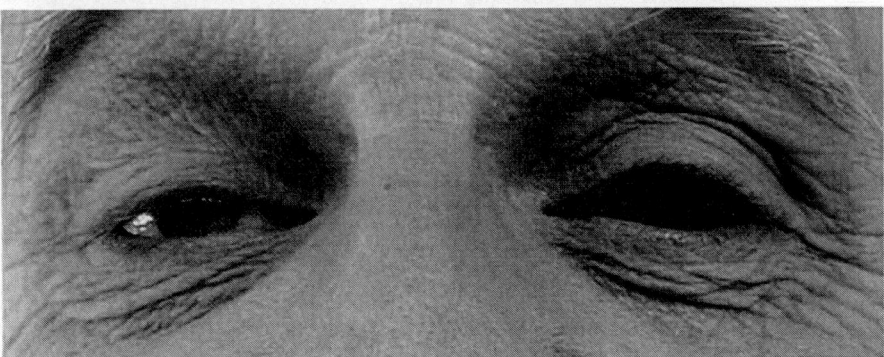

3. Next, to utilize the red tint from the layer below, set this layer's blending mode to Multiply. This has the effect of combining the black shadow with the dark red color to give the socket a fleshy tone.

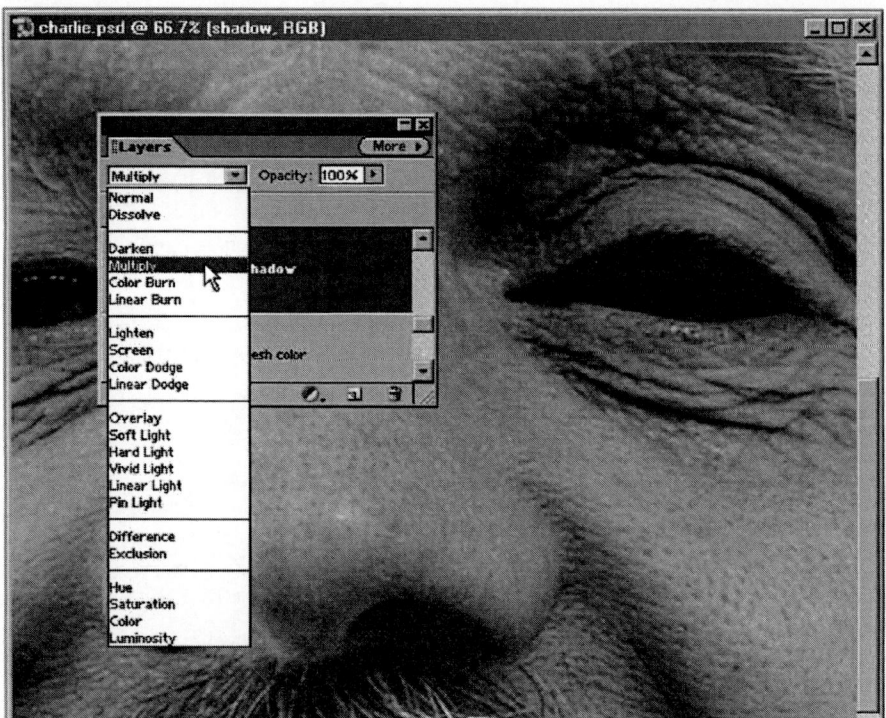

I determined that the shadowing wasn't dark enough, so I duplicated the shadow layer and left it set to Multiply. This was a little too dark, so I reduced the layer opacity down to 60%, which made me happier. Feel free to play around with these basic techniques until you get a result you're pleased to continue with.

Now it's time to figure out how to go about finding the perfect texture for the socket.

> *It's often better to sample from the source than to try to create something from scratch. Charlie's face is an amazing textural landscape, and has plenty of areas that are suitable to sample from. In my opinion, the eyes have it.*

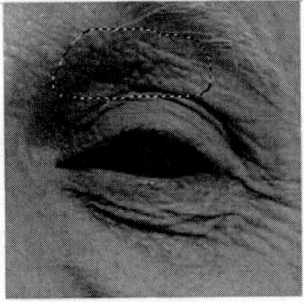

4. With the mask layer active, use the Lasso tool to make a selection considerably bigger than the size of the eye socket area.

5. Then, click through Layer > New > Layer via Copy, name the layer socket skin and drag it over the eye socket. Then, on the Layers palette, drag it below the mask layer.

6. To stop it looking so much like a duplication, select Image > Rotate > Flip Layer Horizontal and then Flip Layer Vertical. You might have to drag it into place to make sure it's covering the whole socket.

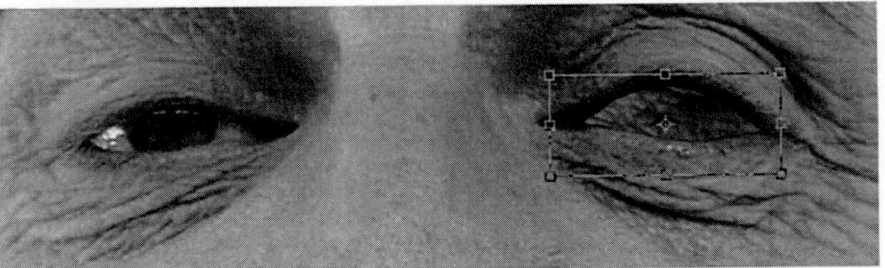

As you can see, the skin texture is not subtle in the least. It's actually covering the other layers that make up the shadowing and skin tone.

7. Blend the texture with the other layers below, by setting the layer blending mode to Overlay, and reducing the Opacity to 80%.

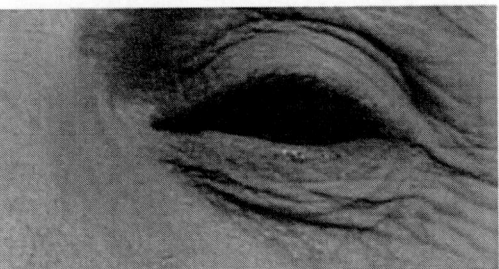

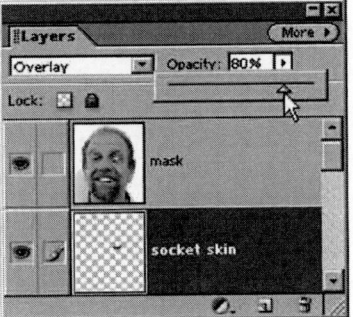

The composition is finally coming together, but there are a few areas that require some extra attention.

8.   The coloring of the eye socket is too strong – the red tint is too unrealistic for my tastes. If you agree, add a Hue/Saturation adjustment layer just above the layer filled with the red and set the Saturation to –75. This helps to make the image look just a little more real.

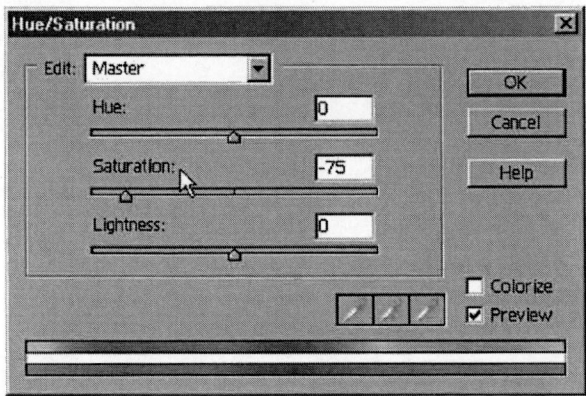

The image is now complete – the socket is believable and the eyelid has been corrected to blend better with the now dark area that it encloses.

The texturing and shading looks OK, but this image has a problem. If an eye socket was truly missing an eyeball, the lid wouldn't have any form to it. It would most likely just be closed, or in the way I imagine it (which means more creepy), the lids would eventually grow together and close off the socket. That's where our next little project lays!

Lifting the Lid

To achieve this effect, we should switch over and use the left eye, because there is more flat, visible eyelid available to clone from.

1. Starting from the original photo, first create a selection around the upper part of the top eyelid with the Lasso tool, and feather it a little. Copy the selection as a new layer and move it down. You might need to rotate it a little in order to match the curvature of the socket.

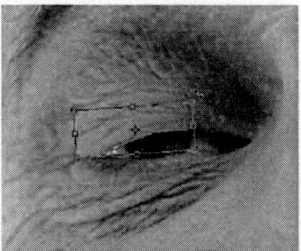

2. In this way, select and drag piece by piece until you've created a total coverage for the eye.

3. Once you have a base covering, link all the pieces of eyelid cover together (by clicking the link box for each skin layer on the Layers palette, then clicking Layer > Merge Linked).

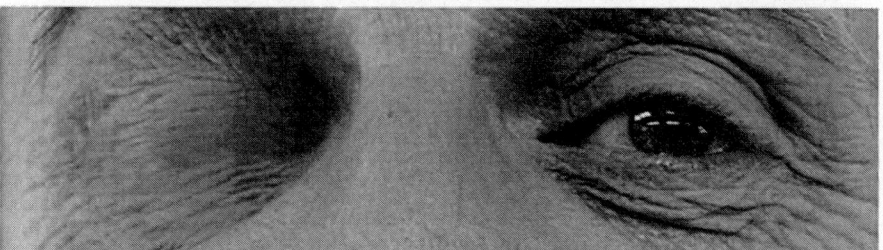

Naturally, the pieces don't mesh very well (ain't no such thing as a free lunch!), so this is where the Clone Stamp tool is once again our best friend.

What we need to do is go through the layer and used the Clone Stamp tool to touch up the areas that look too 'duplicated' (the patterned look you get with repeated layer copying).

4. Grab random areas to blend the wrinkles more seamlessly. A good technique for doing this is using the Clone Stamp tool at 50% opacity to make the blending look smoother.

I think that just about finishes Charlie off! The only other thing I was desperate to do was shove a monocle in there, but that might be pushing the taste boundaries just a little ... I'll leave it up to you!

> *You can find our PSD versions of each 'Charlie' on the CD-ROM, saved as* charlieEye.psd.

Ashley – Not-so-bright eyes?

After all that subtlety, let's go a bit sci-fi. We're going to give Ashley here black eyes, and she won't feel a thing! How do we make this freaky effect look real? Bear in mind, I'm not talking black eyes as you see in the next chapter on **Face Painting**. I mean *actual* black *actual* eyes! I guess these will work well in this picture because dark eyes will contrast well with Ashley's light complexion.

First off, we need to build the base of the dark eyes. There are several approaches we could choose to achieve this, such as drawing a selection around the exposed part of the eyeball and filling it black. However, this option doesn't allow much flexibility, and the key to the realism in the picture is *using as much of what is already there as possible*.

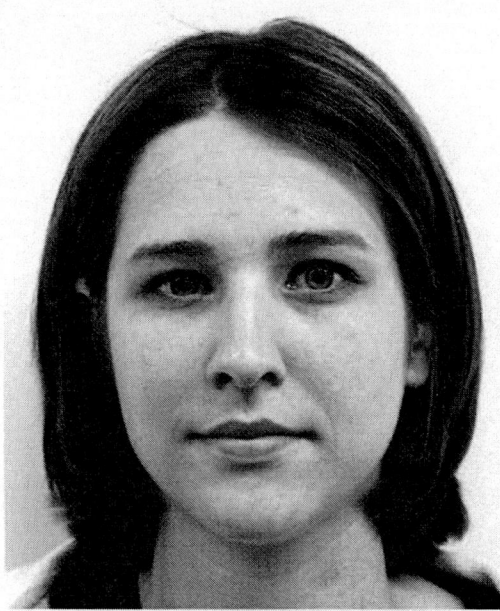

Instead, we'll look at a more freehand way of approaching things. Open ashley.jpg and we'll get going.

1. Working on a new layer, use a medium-sized brush (around 20 pixels) with 50% hardness to paint the bulk of the dark base.

2. Leave the black pupil alone, and brush over the colored iris, making sure to airbrush around the reflections.

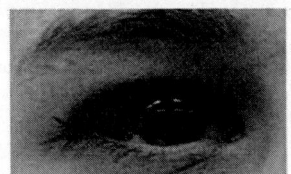

3. Make sure you are totally accurate in brushing the black color right to the edge of the eye. If the black coloring is not close enough to the edges, then white of the eye will show through and the effect will look unrealistic. Go carefully, reduce brush size as you near the edge, and perhaps choose a softer brush at the final boundary.

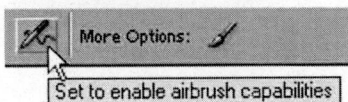

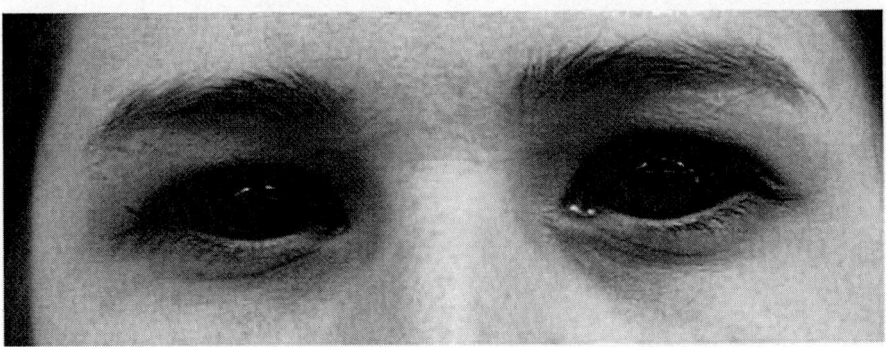

> My own preference is to have the airbrush capabilities checked to allow for greater control of how much "paint" gets laid out.

The composition looks reasonable, but the bottom of the eye looks a bit flat-black to me. To help add a bit more photorealism, we'll airbrush in a very subtle inner glow to help give the impression that a small amount of light is entering the eyes.

4. So, working on a new layer for each eye, and using a medium sized brush with 0% Hardness, softly brush in the highlight with white paint for each eye. You'll probably find the highlights too strong in their initial application, so you should use the Gaussian Blur filter to soften them up a little, then reduce the Opacity way down to around 30%.

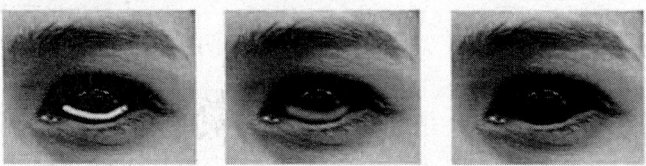

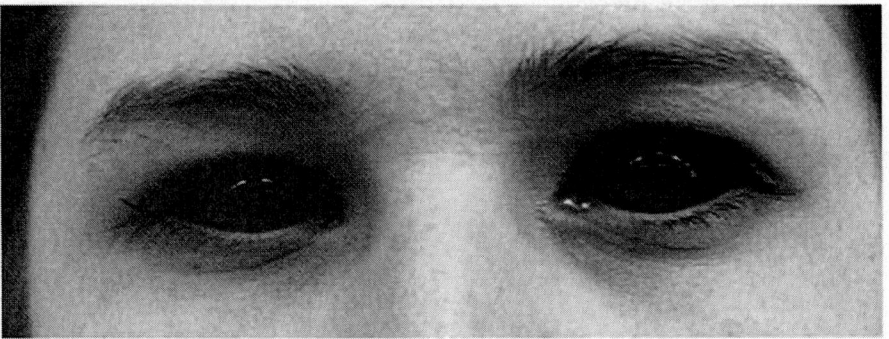

Job done! Ashley looks decidedly unsettling.

Where else can we go with this? Well, I guess we could have a go at doing the Marilyn Manson thing and removing the eyebrows.

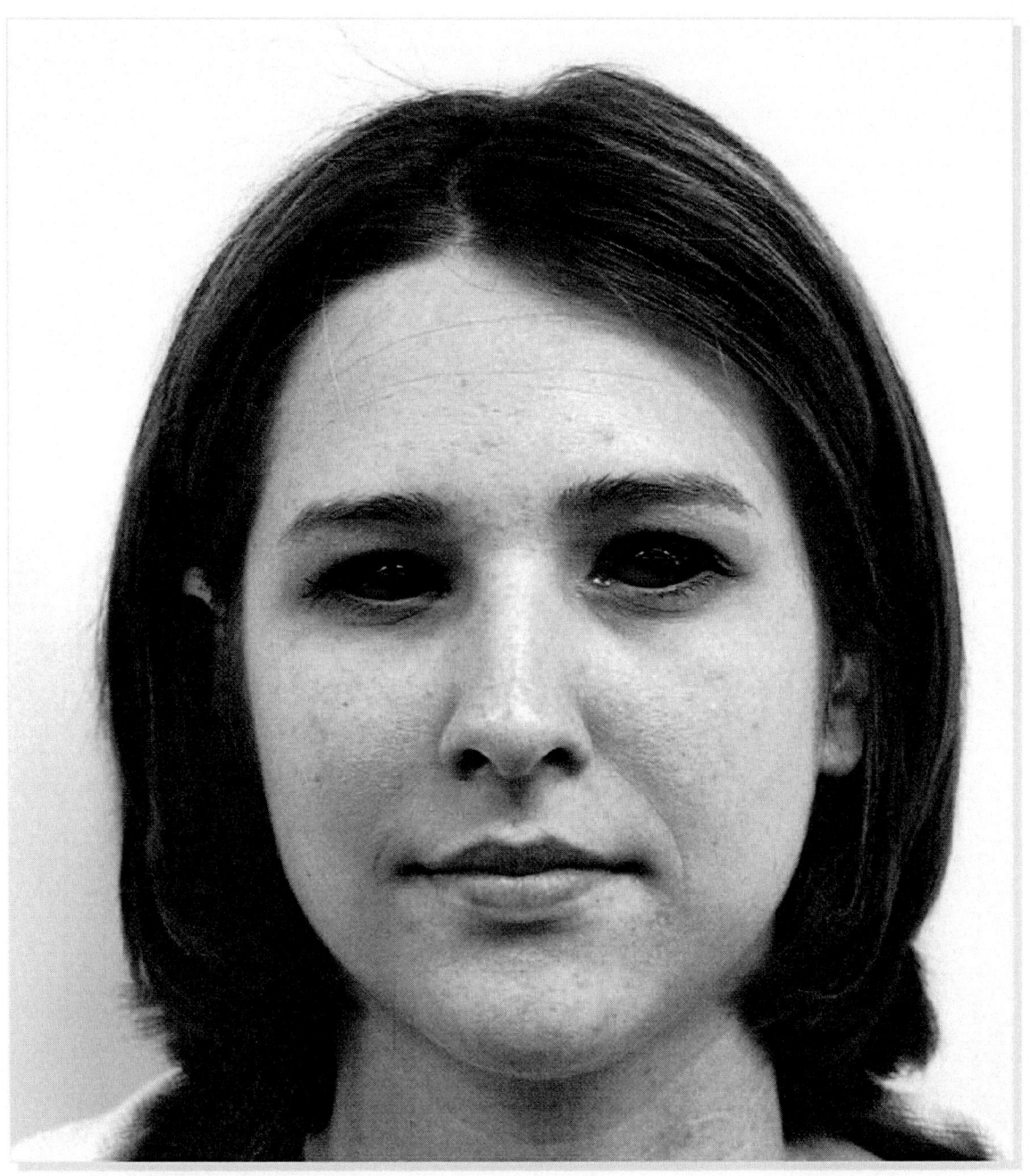

Eyebrow removal

1. Select a big area, encompassing the eyes, eyebrows and surrounding area.

2. Click Layers > New > Layer via Copy and call the new layer Eyebrow mask. Now we're going to get going with some serious concealer!

3. Using the Clone Stamp tool, clone an area directly above and below the left eyebrow. Through a series of long strokes, you will be able to cover the eyebrow completely, leaving a line where the dark underside meets the light brow.

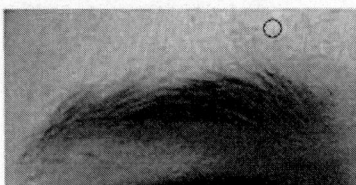
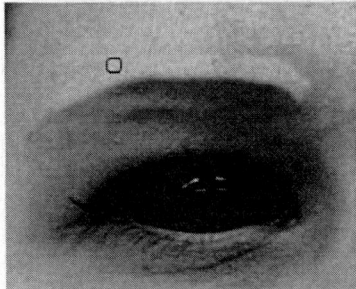
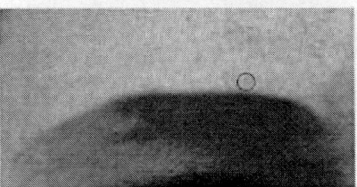

4. Bear in mind, as we're making wholesale structural changes, it's better to use a brush with 100% opacity. Of course, it's tempting to go lower while we find our feet, but that results in a blurred cloning that just never seems to look right. Trust me, I found out the hard way! But if you're doing subtle retouches, a reduced opacity is essential.

   The result is pretty freaky in itself!

   OK, so the eyebrows are a little wonky, but I kinda think that gives a bit of personality.

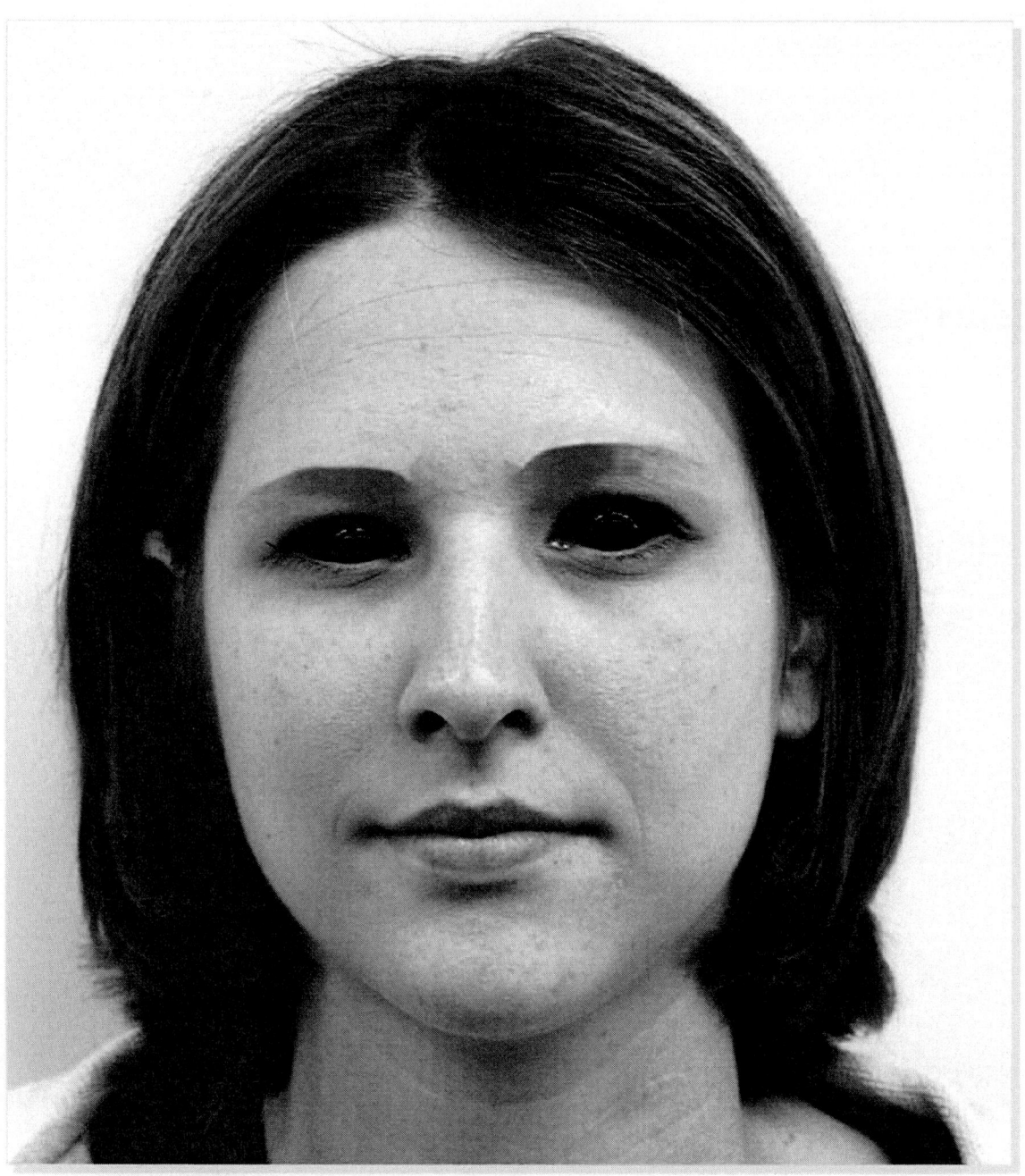

Further possibilities

Where can we go from here? It's up to you which part of Ashley you'd next like to amend – when you're setting out to create increasingly weird effects, the stars really are the limit.

The next area I chose to mess with was the hair. Using the Smudge tool (set to quite a high strength of 75%), I carefully combed all of the hair, in order to create a sort of other-worldly effect, with stylized follicles curling off Ashley's head. I also removed any stray hairs (which I deemed a little unkempt) by using the clone tool, and I accentuated the parting into something akin to a reverse Superman effect!

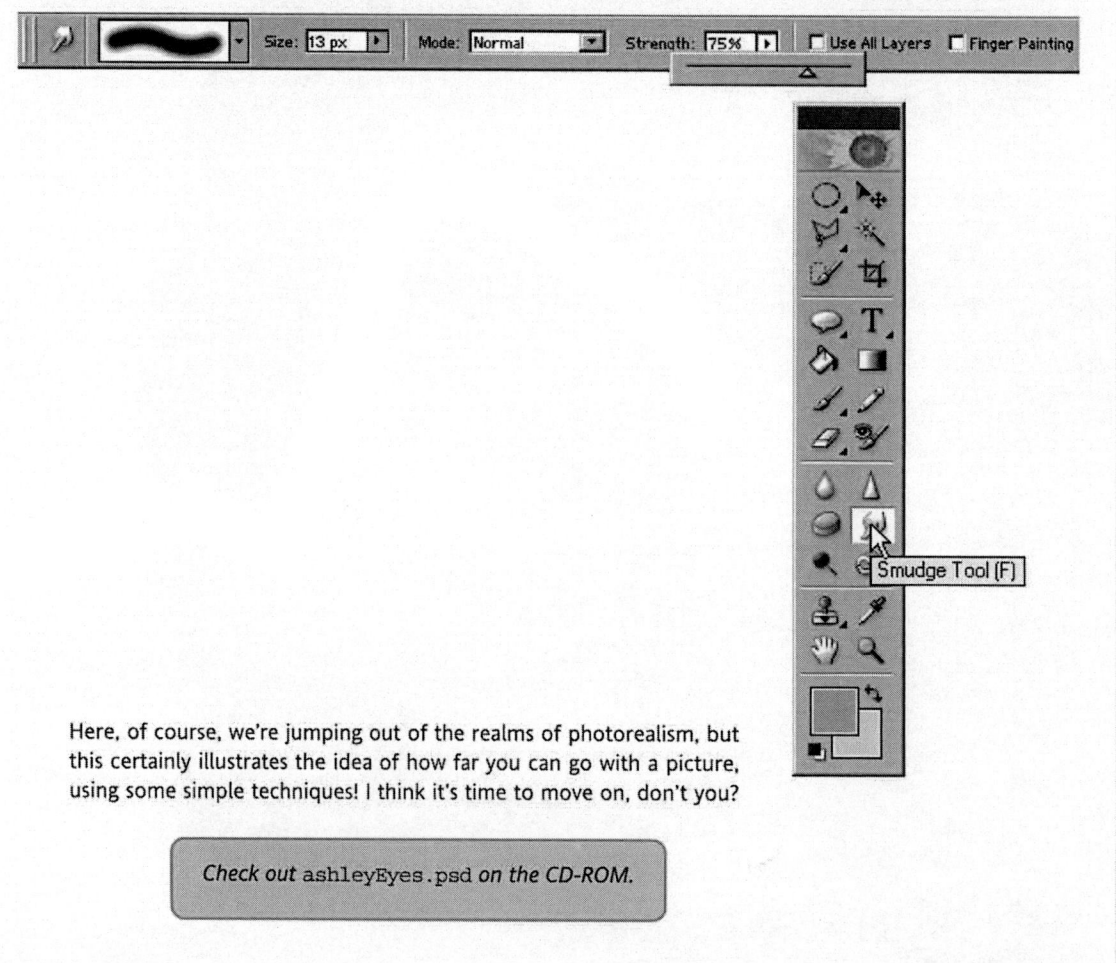

Here, of course, we're jumping out of the realms of photorealism, but this certainly illustrates the idea of how far you can go with a picture, using some simple techniques! I think it's time to move on, don't you?

Check out ashleyEyes.psd on the CD-ROM.

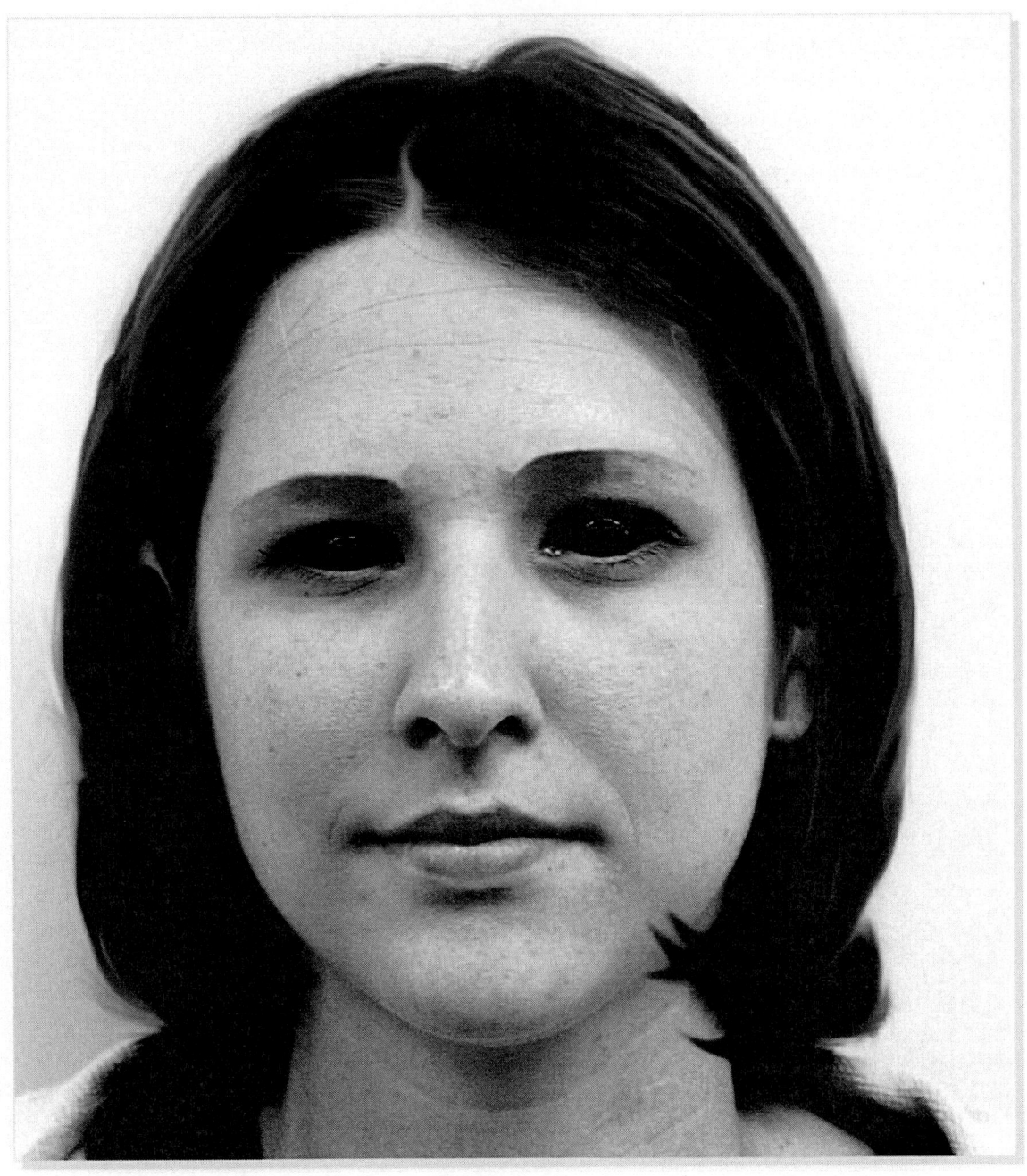

Jake – Teething troubles

Some people might see Jake's portrait and wonder if anything has even been changed. However, the fact that Jake is an eight-month-old child should tip you to the fact that he shouldn't have a full set of teeth yet. The challenge with Jake's portrait was to realistically blend the teeth taken from another portrait, which happen to be the teeth of a 53-year-old man.

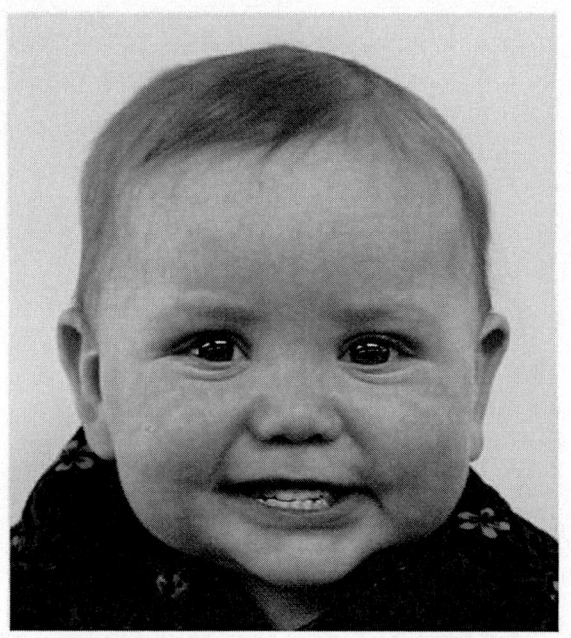

On the surface, it wouldn't appear that there would be much work required to create this image. Simply sample the teeth from one image and drop them on Jake's face – perhaps a little cleanup, and it's all done, right? Well, there were actually a few more crucial steps involved that really pulled the composition together and made the effect blend in perfectly.

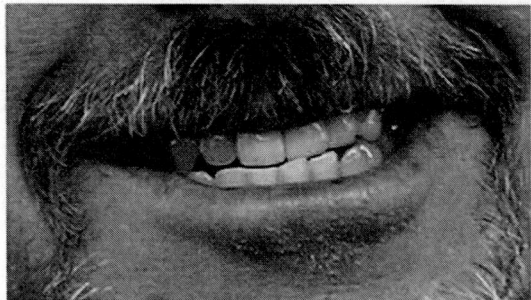
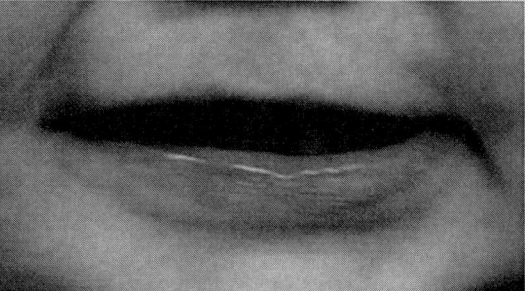

First, let's go back to the beginning – I determined that I wanted to use the teeth from a portrait of a 53-year-old man to replace Jake's one tooth mouth, since they both appear to have a slight underbite. Additionally, I thought it would be even more interesting to feature the drastic age difference between Jake (8 months old) and the teeth he would borrow from Tom (53 years old).

> *Don't worry if you don't have any teeth lying around. We've supplied Tom's on the CD-ROM; called* tomTeeth.jpg, *which is where you can also find* jake.jpg, *our source image.*

1. So, beginning with the picture of Tom's mouth, drag it over wholesale to the portrait of Jake, and name the new layer Tom's teeth.

    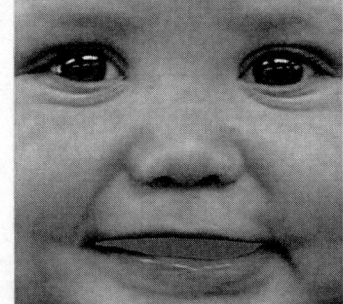

2. Next, while on the Background layer, create a mask (with the Selection Brush tool) of the inside of Jake's gooey mouth.

3. Then, create a new Layer via Copy, and drag it above the Tom's teeth layer. Now *that's* starting to look unusual!

> *The choice here is very much yours. Big teeth look unusual, so you might want to resize the teeth to make them look more natural. A bit of scale and a bit of rotate should see you right, so long as you're on the* Tom's teeth *layer with the Move tool at your disposal.*

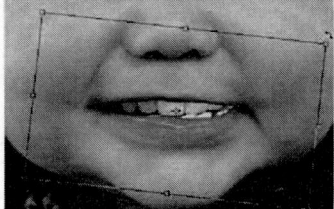

89

Whatever you choose to do, you're going to need to finish the effect off by shading up those teeth a little, to take account of Jake's upper lip.

4. To do this, create a new layer called Teeth shadow above Tom's teeth and select a smallish brush at a low opacity (say, 40%) to fill in those shadows.

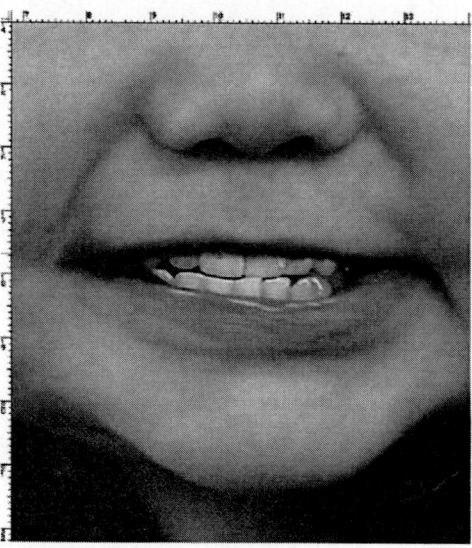

5. To introduce a little more realism to the image, borrow some of the original glare from Jake's bottom lip that has been covered by his new teeth and place it on the portion of the lip that's now visible.

   This was a simple task of creating a selection around the glare on the original layer, feathering the selection and then creating a new layer from the selection. This new layer was then positioned over the bottom lip. I ended up adding a mask to the glare layer so that I could feather it even more, helping it to blend a little better.

This composition demonstrates that even the simplest of effects can always be improved by taking notice of small details, and what can be added or modified to make that simple effect blend more seamlessly. If you're not one for subtlety, don't worry. We'll be seeing more of Jake in a little while...

> *Have a look at* jakeTeeth.psd *on the CD-ROM if you want to see our final Elements file.*

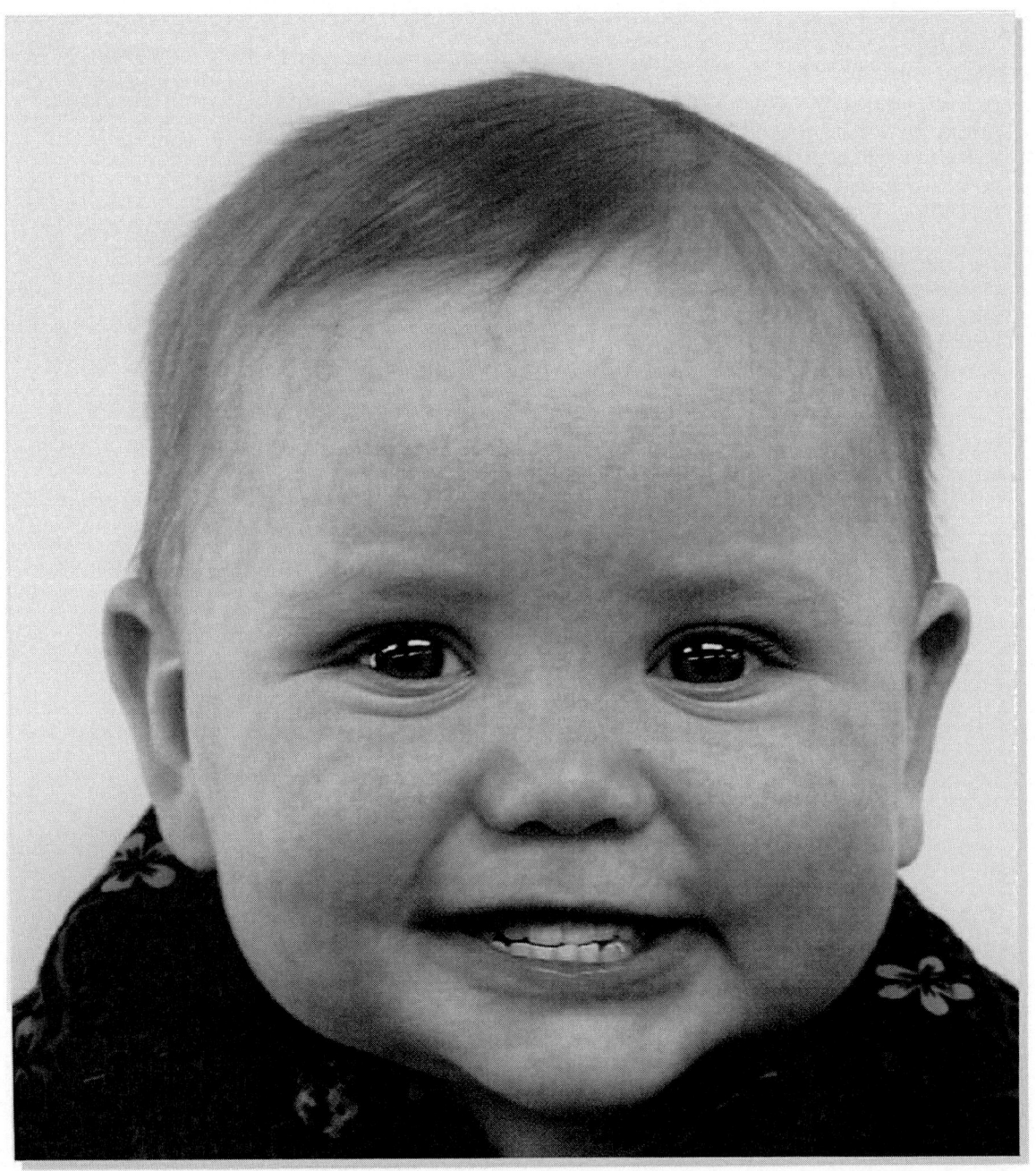

Josh – Focus Pocus

OK, we're going to do a couple of things with this picture. First up, we're going to do some more eyework, because that has a terrific effect on an image. Then, we're going to have a play around with the whole structure of the picture, to look at what special effects we can pull off.

The main task with this composition is to change the iris to the same color as the white of the eye. We want to maintain the same little imperfections and color variations that are present in the visible white part of the eye in the iris that we're going to create.

With such a small area to work with, it would be a nightmare to try and use the Clone Stamp tool accurately. The alternative is this:

1. Use the Lasso tool to draw a selection around the light, lower area of the left part of the white of the eye.

2. Feather the selection by 3 or 4 pixels and create a new layer from the selection. Duplicate and move this new layer several times – enough to cover the iris. Don't worry too much about covering the edges of the iris or pupil at this point.

Once you've covered the iris, click in all the layers' link boxes and **merge linked**. As with Jake's teeth, you find yourself having to create an extra layer to paint in a little shadow on the eyeball.

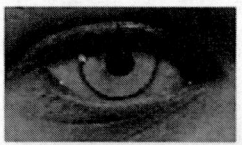

As a result of the iris base covering some of the elements of the original iris, we now have to recreate the highlights and shadowing of the eyeball.

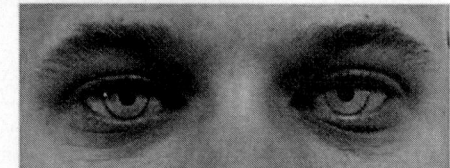

3. Working on a new layer, use the Airbrush with white paint and a small brush to paint in the highlights. Set the iris cover to 50% so that you can use the original highlights as a guide.

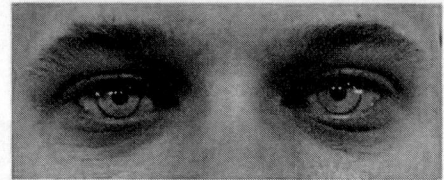

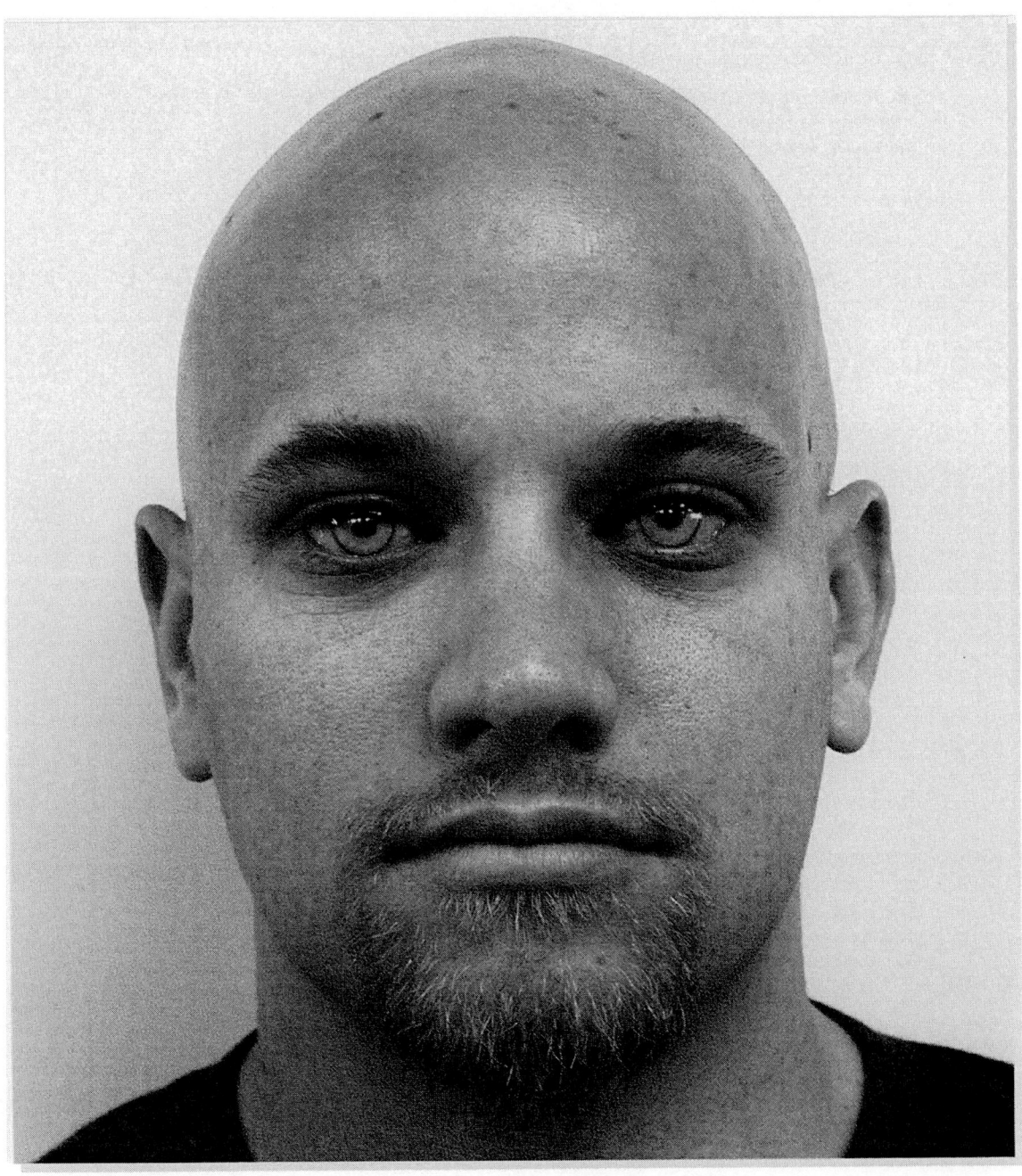

Changing the look

OK, so we've done our initial manipulation – let's have a look at playing around with the whole look of the photograph. What I want to do is throw Josh's face into dramatic relief, so I'm going to toy with the focus on his picture.

I'm going to have a play around with that really useful little Elements initiative – the Selection Brush tool.

4. We're about to select his whole head, so we're going to need a big brush. (No slur on Josh intended!). Basically, the thing to do is paint over his entire head and shoulders, and watch those marquee outlines grow!

This tool is ace – it may be a little sluggish (I don't want to think of how much number crunching is going on on your PC's hard drive) but it's very specific in its selection. Take care around the edges, and don't hesitate to revert to a smaller brush if you fear going over the line.

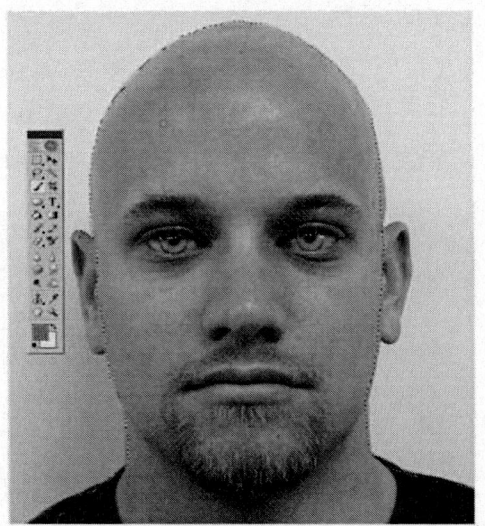

Of course, if you're on your toes, you might be thinking there's an easier way to go about this – you could, of course, select all the white background with the Magic Wand tool – that would work – or you could carefully draw around Josh with the regular Lasso tool. However, the Selection Brush tool will help us out when selecting parts of the face that are not defined by an outline. You'll see what I mean!

5. With this selection blinking at you on the screen, click through Layer > New > Layer via Copy. In the Layers palette, you'll see the action confirmed like this:

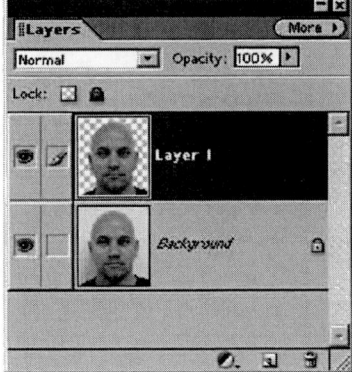

6. The next thing to do is make another selection, this time, a little further 'forward' than the previous one. Make sure Layer 1 is selected, and use the Selection Brush once again. Personally, I selected all of the face forward of his neck.

7. Then create a new layer as before, through Layer > New > Layer via Copy.

8. Continue in this fashion, selecting sections of Josh's face further and further forward until you have this rather fetching collection of layers showing Josh's face disappearing under a checkered ocean. Note that you can pay particular attention to his eyes, as they are set quite far back – your selections should pay attention to this.

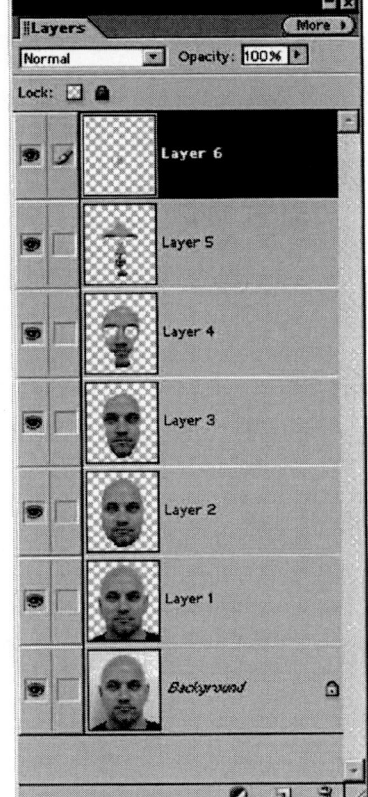

9. With this basic file (which I suggest you save as a Photoshop PSD file, retaining all the layers), you can have a lot of fun.

10. With the picture on the previous page, I've put a Gaussian Blur on each level – the "furthest away" is the most blurred, and the nearest is in perfect clarity. So, that's:

Level	Gaussian Blur setting
Level 6	0
Level 5	2
Level 4	4
Level 3	6
Level 2	8
Level 1	10
Background	12

11. And here's a go at keeping those striking eyes in focus:

...where I have doubled the amount by which I've blurred everything, so:

Level	Gaussian Blur Setting
Level 6	12
Level 5	8
Level 4	4
Level 3	0 (this is where the eyes are)
Level 2	4
Level 1	8
Background	12

I guarantee, you'll see so much of this in advertising, you'll start to get really mad that people are making money out of it! Here are a few more bang-for-your-buck variations, just using that same source file we created:

...if we want a closer look at Josh's lovely ears:

This one was done by clicking CTRL+U on each layer and altering the Hue to values of 100, 75, 50, 25, 20, 15 and 10.

The one on the opposite page actually makes me feel like I'm gonna barf if I look at it too long. The technique's exactly the same as before, only with a Radial Blur (with Zoom).

Feel free to browse through our final file, joshBlur.psd *on the accompanying CD-ROM.*

Linda – Mom's makeover

Here we have an image which is going to take some careful handiwork. This effect is a huge plug for using a pen and tablet, which made it much easier to airbrush the smooth strokes required to create the extended lashes.

If you're into freehand drawing, this image is going to be your favorite to create. Broken down, the effect is really very simple; it's just a matter of keeping a steady hand. Personally, I have very unsteady hands, so to do this I had to constantly back up and start over, but that's just part of the process ... right? Have you ever drawn a detailed image on paper without having to erase? Think of it that way.

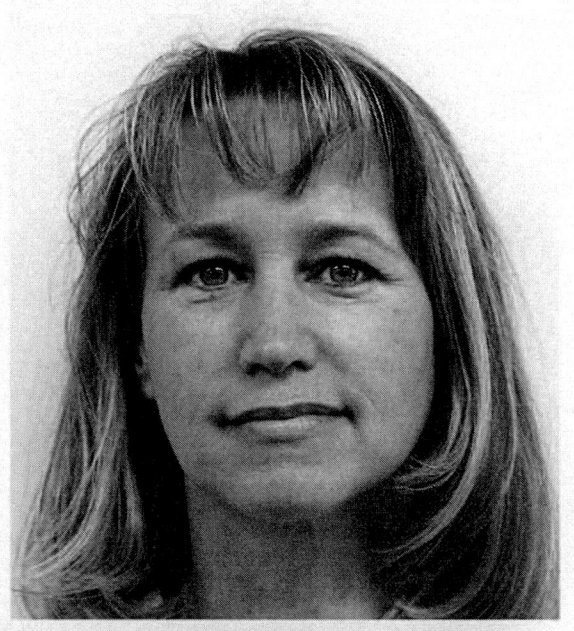

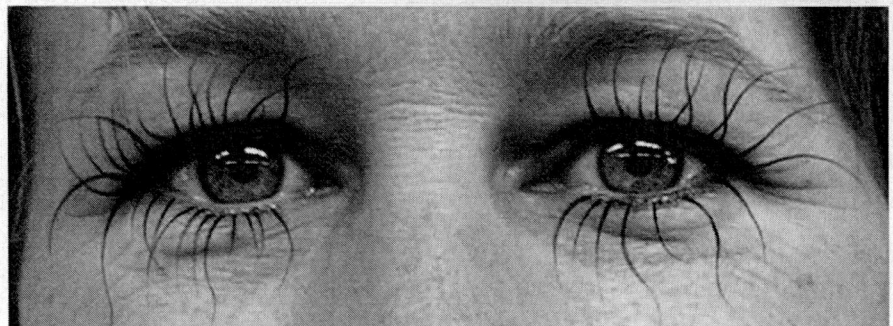

OK, down to business.

1. Start out each set of eyelashes by simply creating a new layer and using a 1-pixel brush to airbrush in the lashes with solid black.

2. Pay special attention to ensure each lash starts out with a thick base and gradually tapers out to a fine point. This is where a pen and tablet play their part – they'll allow you to create natural, sweeping strokes that would be much more delicate with a mouse.

3. With a solid set of lashes brushed in, we're ready to move on to the next step in bringing them to life. If you look at the existing lashes to see how they reflected light and showed other colors, you can see that they have a hint of brown in them – a feature that adds depth as well as color.

4. To replicate this effect, use the Eyedropper tool to sample the brown from the original lashes and, working on a new layer above the original lashes, use the same 1-pixel airbrush as before to paint in the brown color hues. Draw them into random places on the lashes – mostly around the edges and closer to the roots.

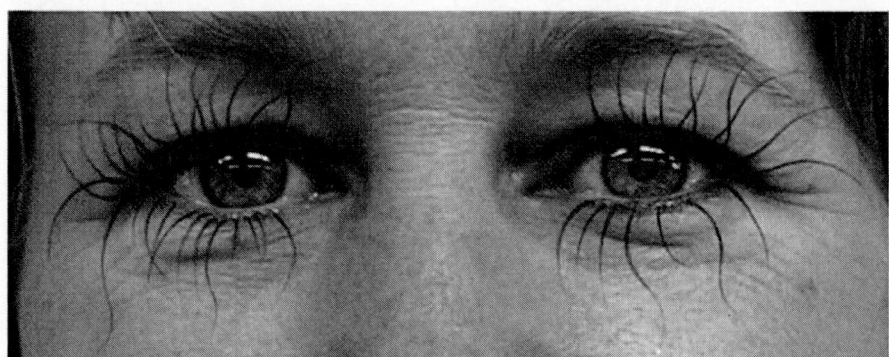

5. Another thing you may notice about the original lashes is that they have individual highlights. So, in much the same manner that we created the brown tints on the lashes, we should go for the 1-pixel brush again on a new layer above everything else, except using white paint to airbrush in the highlights on the lashes. Additionally, instead of drawing on the edges of the lashes, draw the highlights on the middle of the lashes. You should also put the highlights in random sections, which helps to emphasize the fact that lashes are really out of control and reflecting light at all different angles.

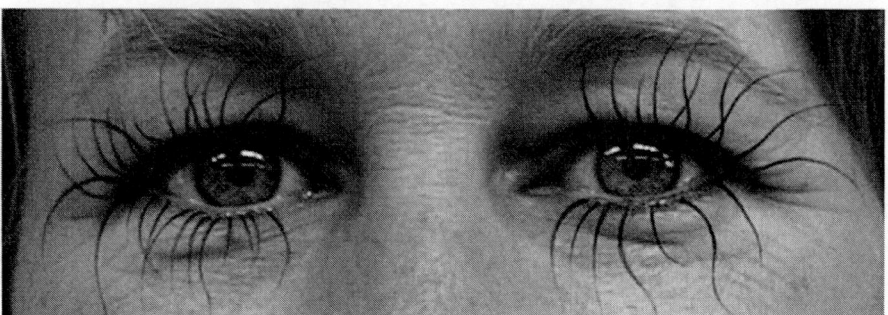

6.   To pull the lashes together with the rest of the image a little better, give them a very subtle shadow. Duplicate the base lashes and move the duplicate layer below the base lashes. Next, apply a Gaussian Blur to soften the strokes and move the layer slightly so the shadow looks offset. Then reduce the Opacity down to 40% to achieve the necessary subtlety.

There we go, the composition is now complete. Although the description makes it sound like a quick process, achieving a realistic effect is a very time-consuming process, as you may have discovered (is it that time *already*!).

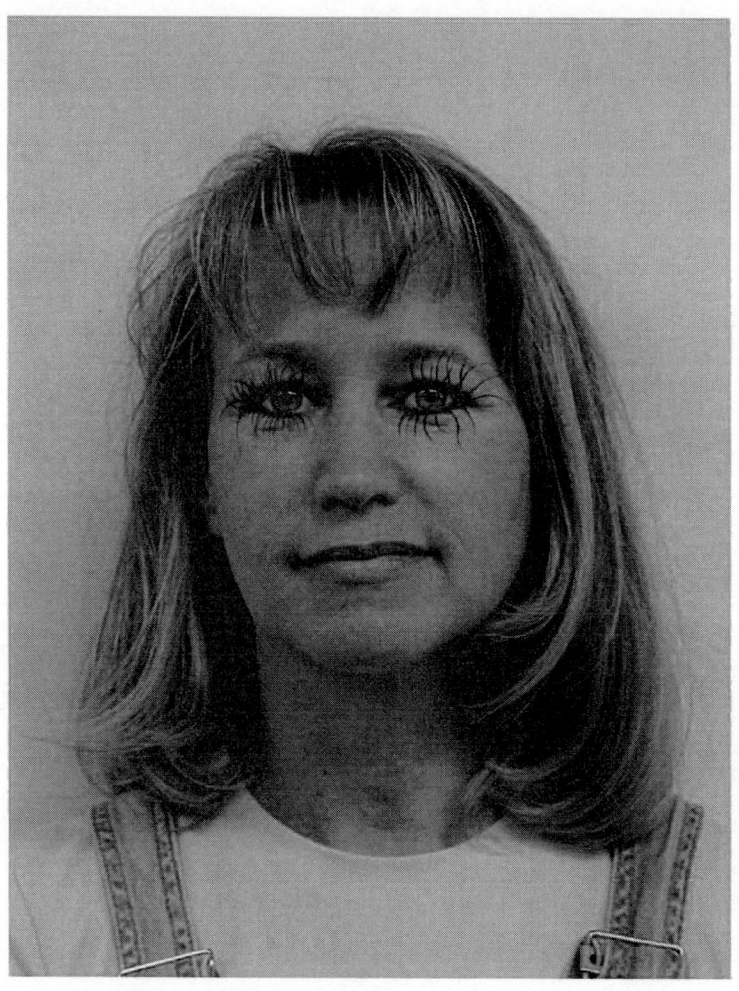

Pushing the boat out

Having done our horrific eyelashes, it would be a crime to leave this image alone now, wouldn't it? So, let's carry out a few extra simple changes.

7. First off, let's flatten everything with Layer > Flatten Image, so we have no layers to worry about.

8. Next, select the eyes (just the colors and black) and open the Hue/Saturation dialog box with CTRL+U. Set the Hue to –120, the Saturation to +85, and leave the Lightness. Now we have some pretty acidic eyes, with a mighty fine shine!

9. Next, select the whites in the same fashion and, through the Hue/Saturation dialog, check the Colorize box and set Hue to 360 and Saturation to 0.

10. OK, now it's time to move on to the Liquify tool. It's pretty tough to describe what goes on in this dark art, but basically choose a nostril sized bloat-tool brush for each nostril, and then a nose-sized bloat-tool brush for the end of the nose.

11. Next, let's give her warped dimensions with a Filter > Distort > Pinch, set to 50%.

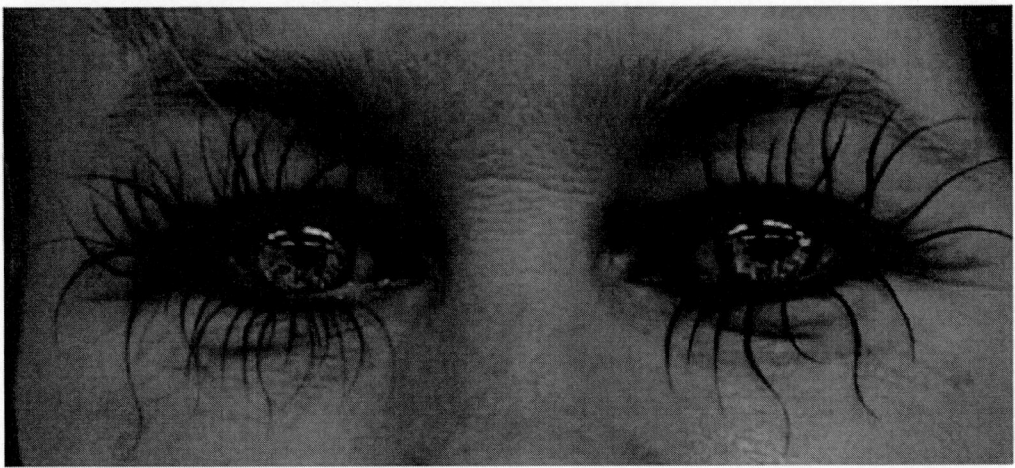

12. Now it's time to color the skin, so carefully select all the flesh tone with the Selection Brush. Through the trusty Hue/Saturation dialog, set the Hue to 50, with everything else at 0. Now we have a green monster! Make sure you keep that selection marquee live.

Now it's time to create a pattern.

13. On a new canvas, create a new layer. On the new layer, use the paintbrush to create yellow dots of varying sizes. Then click through Edit > Define Pattern. Call it Dots.

14. Using Edit > Fill, set the dialog to fill with a pattern, and on the drop-down menu select the pattern Dots. You may now fill the skin area with yellow dots – sickening!

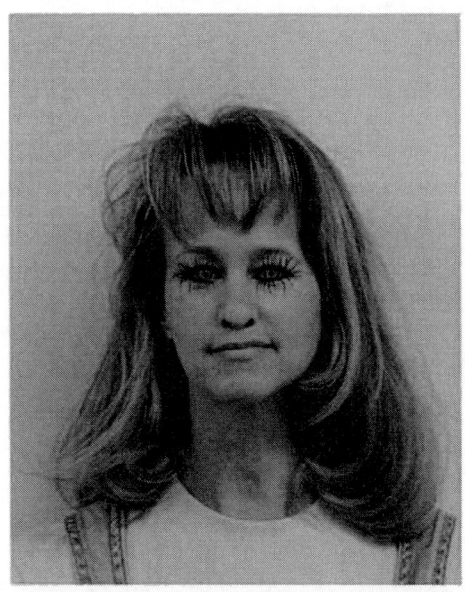

15. Now, simply invert the skin selection and click through Filter > Brush Strokes > Accented Edges. This gives the hair a weird plastic look. Next, change the Hue/Saturation to Hue 270, and Saturation 50.

16. Select the lips and give them an extra boost of Hue +50, Saturation −25 and Lightness −10.

And there it is – through little more than a few color changes, we've a totally freaky mom!

> *Look up* lindaLashes.psd *and* lindaFreaky.psd *on the CD-ROM to browse through our finished files.*

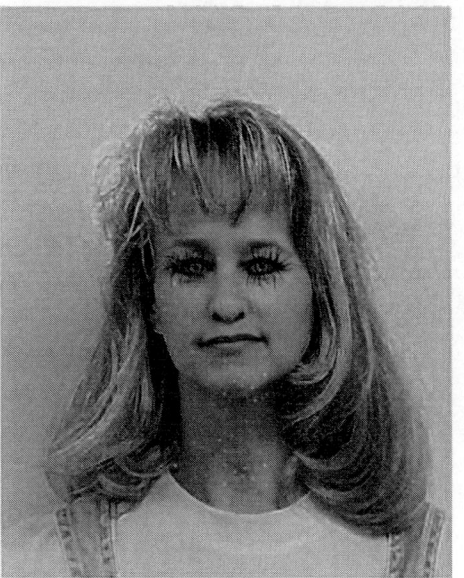

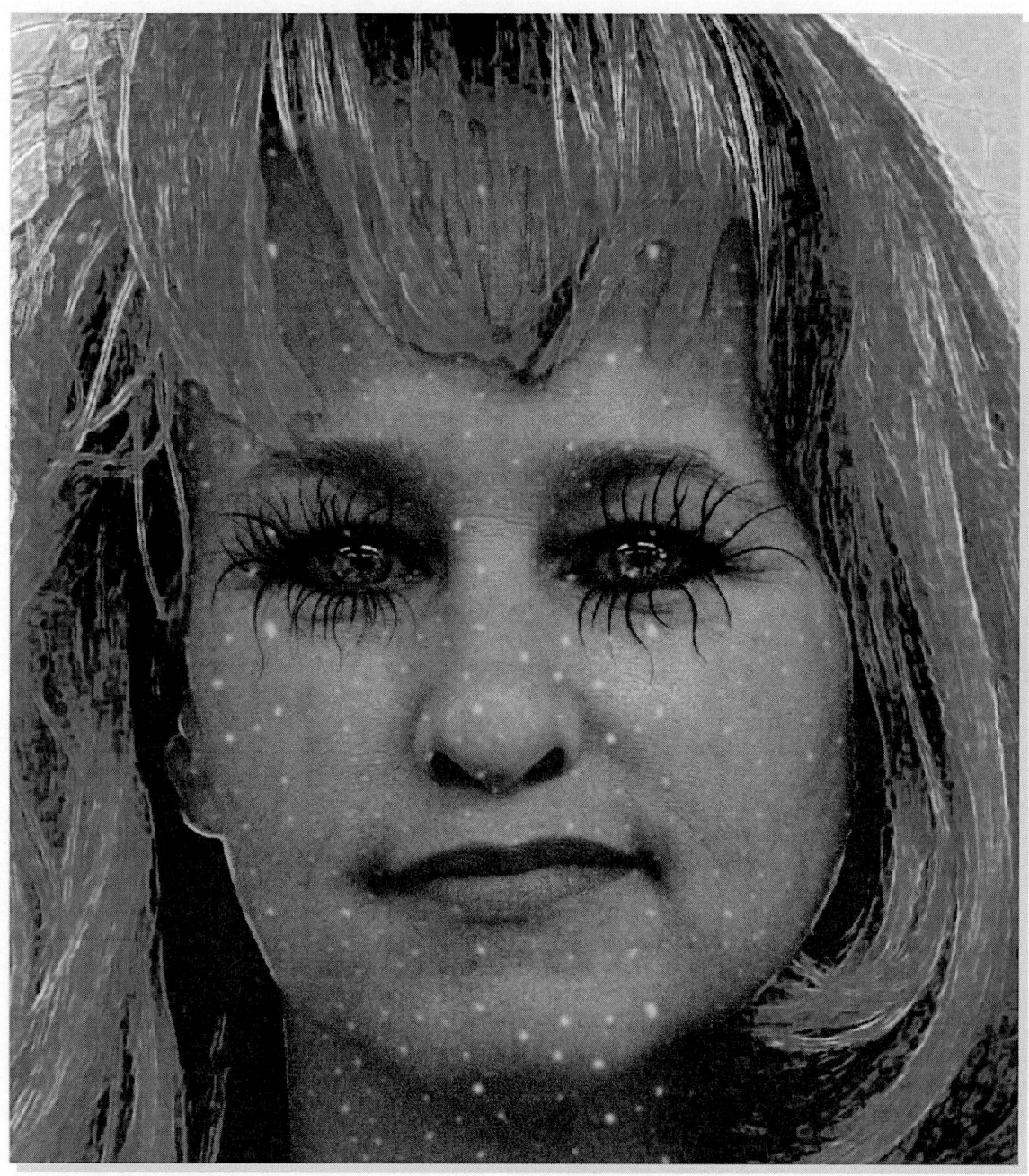

Peter – Two-faced

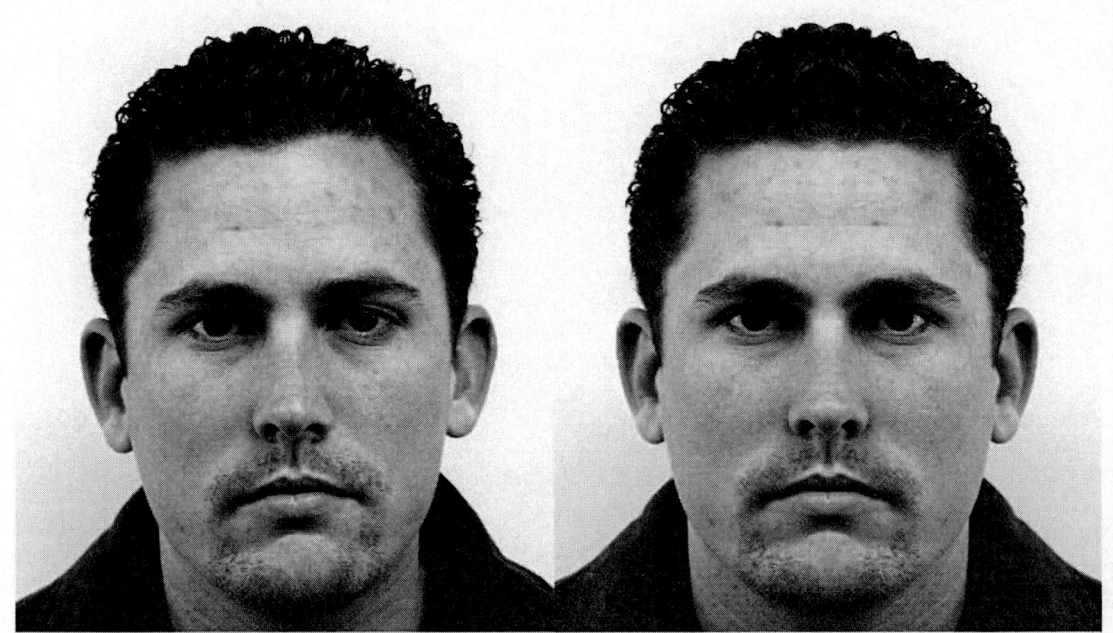

You really have to look hard to find the effect in Peter's portrait. Here's a hint: take a look at the moles and wrinkles on his face. You should be able to see that his face in the finished portrait is perfectly symmetrical, right down to the hair on his head. I initially thought that the challenge with this effect would be to make it look realistic, but it works surprisingly well with Peter's portrait.

1. The first thing we have to do to get Peter's portrait (peter.jpg) ready for the effect is to get his face perfectly straight – as symmetrical as possible, with the eyes level and nose straight up and down. Otherwise, when we reflect one of the halves of his face, nothing will match up right.

The next thing to do is add a mask to the layer and mask the right-hand side of the face. Here is the cool thing about this effect – we're going to learn a new way to mask!

2. Duplicate the background layer and call it face. Create a new blank layer above it and call it mask.

3. Using a bright color (I've chosen red) paint on the mask layer every section you wish to mask. When you have done this, drag the red layer down below the face layer. Click in the link box of the face layer, and press CTRL+G to link them both together. The mask is complete. In order to show it, fill the original Background layer in white, and you'll see half the face disappear! Marvelous, no?

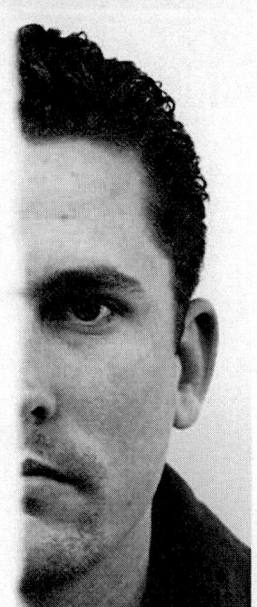

4. With one side of the face ready to go, duplicate the face layer (call it face 2) and then click through Image > Rotate > Flip Layer Horizontal.

5. Create another blank layer above it (call it mask 2) and fill in as before, only on the other side. Drag mask 2 below face 2, link the layers, and hey presto, you have a symmetrical face! All you need to do is line them up and they should fit perfectly!

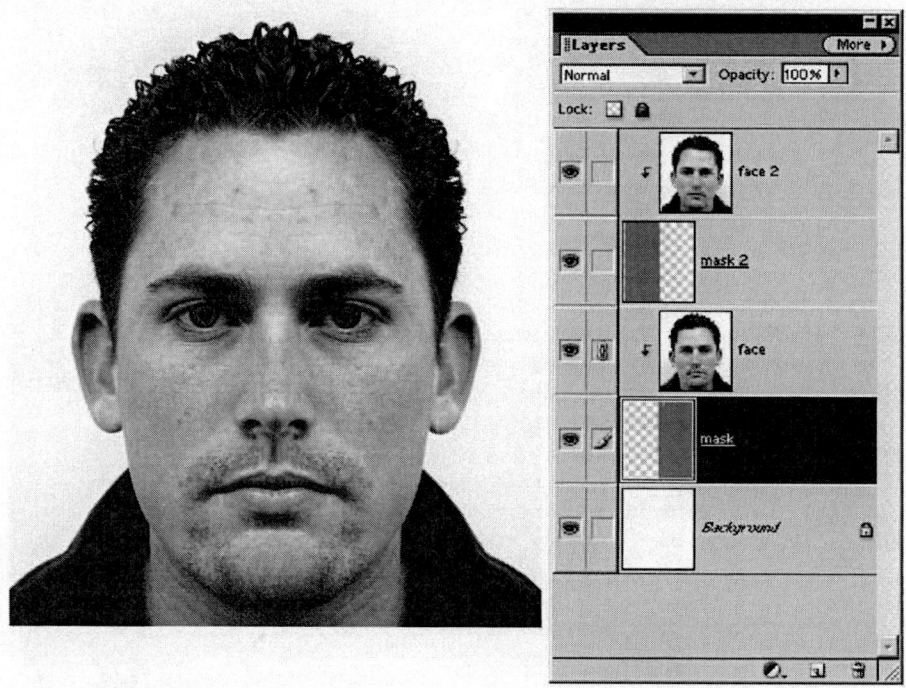

6. And finally, to get the reverse effect, and see the other side of Peter's personality, simply swap the images round on their layers!

Our finished PSD is on the CD-ROM and is called peter2Faced.psd!

Up to this point, I've focused on one specific effect on each portrait. Here is a chance to see a portrait with several effects applied, and create a true freak of nature.

Jake – Problem child

Let's go back to the image of Jake, our favorite toothy toddler.

There's no need to revisit the descriptions of the effects here, but just to be aware that I used the eye effects from Ashley's portrait, the symmetry effects from Peter's image, and borrowed the eyebrows from Charlie, while the chin stubble came from Peter. The end result gives quite a disturbing montage!

Whoa, Jake just aged about 25 years (and also looks like he's from another planet, to boot)!

The entire process of creating these freaky faces was really enjoyable. The concept is so simple, yet it is a great exercise for anyone interested in Photoshop. We get down to the roots of why we use Photoshop Elements – plain and simple – we just love to mess with photos!

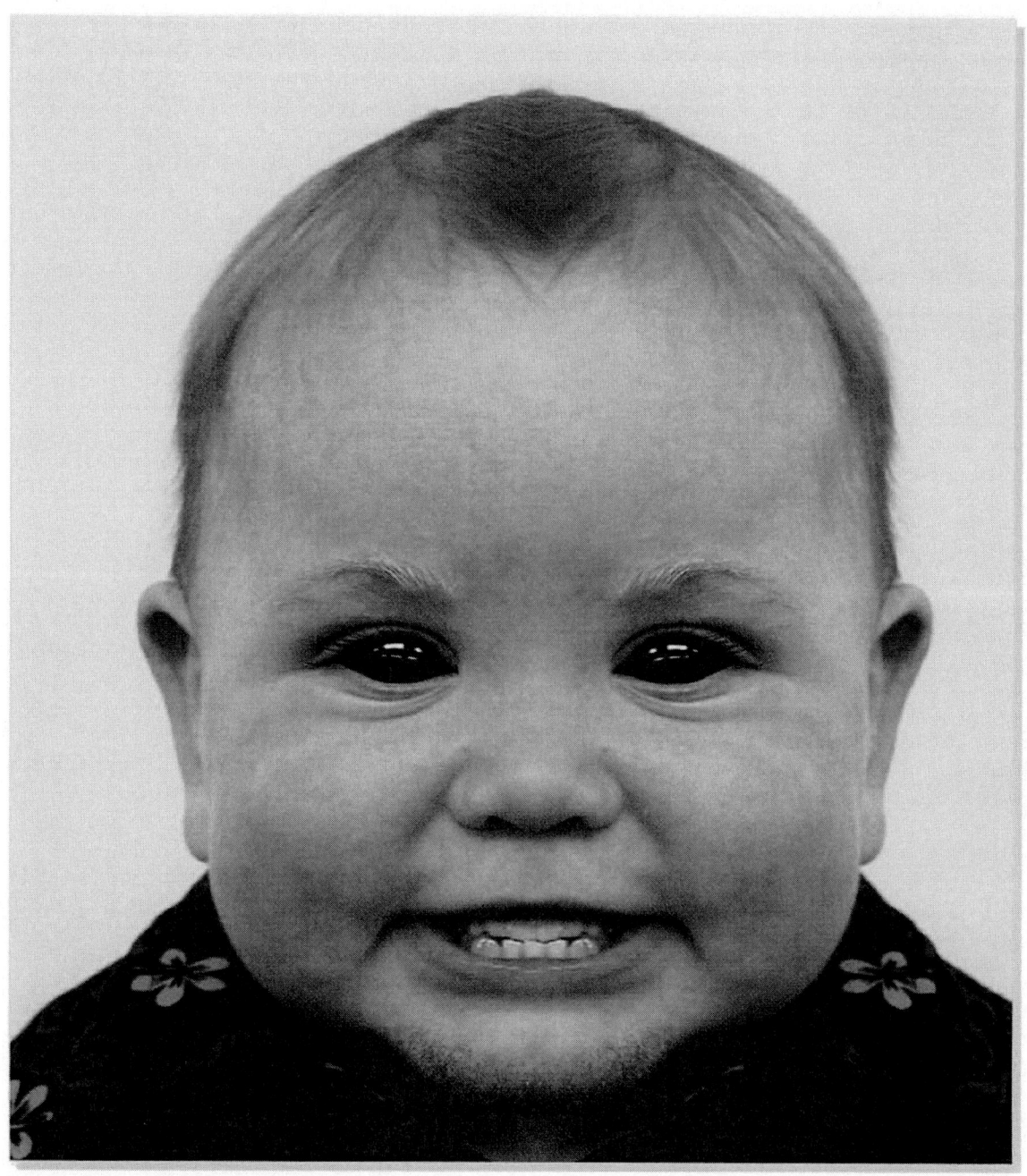

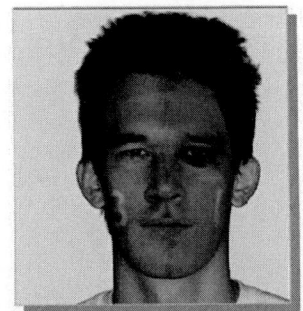

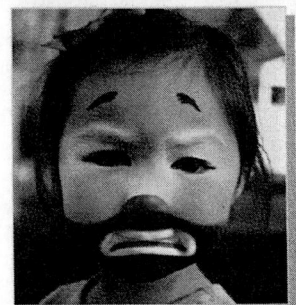

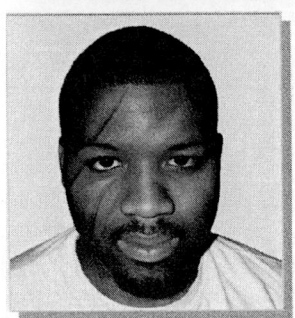

Chapter 4

Face Painting

What you'll learn in this chapter

One of the first things anyone ever wants to do in photo manipulation is paint on a photograph and Photoshop Elements contains some pretty potent tools to help you do this. In this chapter, we'll paint half a dozen faces, exploring along the way:

- Using different **brush styles** to paint faces easily and convincingly.

- Experimenting with a wide range of **blending modes** to add realism and blend paints into the complexion.

- Create a cute little clown, a face-painted sports fan, a chubby-cheeked tigress, and more!

Whether it's black and white photographs you want to bring to life, or a really bad snapshot of yourself you want to improve on, or even if you want to add a black eye to someone without actually socking them, this chapter will tell all.

The main tools we'll be using are the Brush and careful use of those tricky layer blending modes. You'll soon be creating real water-cooler moments with your snaps!

When we've figured out the best ways of using it, we'll concentrate on how we can best optimize the brush control we have at our disposal in order to achieve the makeup effects we want – whether they're subtle or extreme.

Takeshi – sports fan makeover

Now you've got to take your hat off to the dedication of sports fans. They take the time to go out and buy paint, make a design for their face, and then sit uncomfortably with this non-breathable goo all over them for hours in the heat. It is, to look on the positive side, a very theatrical and dramatic expression. This makeover pays homage to those people, and gives you a look into exactly how we should go about totally transforming the color of a face.

You might want to note that this makeover also pays homage to the New York Mets – my favorite baseball team. If you don't like it, choose your own team – but I'm writing this chapter so you'll have to suffer my own allegiances! To that end, this makeover will include the colors blue and orange, along with a number 31 for catcher Mike Piazza.

I guess because of the extreme look of dedication mixed with a degree of messiness, I imagined this kind of fan to be over excited and rowdy. To exaggerate the rough and rowdy element, I decided I would give our portrait a hockey player look, with bruises and a black eye to complement his face paint.

As I wanted to show the paint application as realistically as possible, I studied some photos of painted fans partying at sporting events. Their makeup often looks sloppy and is often smeared. It's best not to cut corners on your research, and these days it's as easy as surfing on the Web to get a couple of reference images. One recurrent theme I noticed was it seemed common to apply paint sloppily around the eye area without a distinct shape. Usually eyebrows were painted but there was often a gap in the paint where skin showed through underneath the eye area. This worked well for me when I was thinking about the black eye as it gave me enough space to focus on realistically incorporating the painful feature.

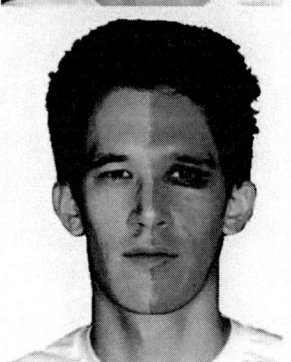

Preparation

1. Open takeshi.jpg in Photoshop Elements, and click through Layer > New Adjustment Layer > Levels to create a new adjustment layer to sort out the Levels of the picture.

2. Play with them a little until the light and color quality are to your satisfaction. You may choose simply to press Auto, which most often does a good job!

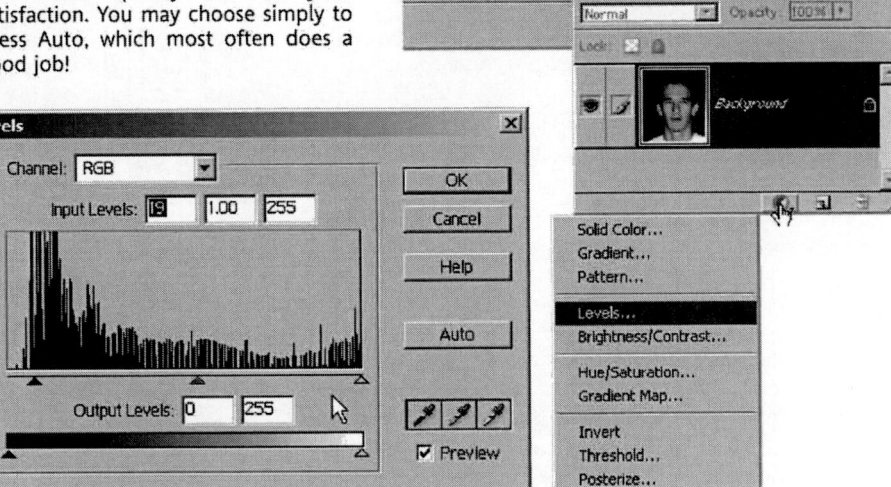

It's always a good idea to start properly by getting the levels right.

Making a face mask!

That horrible dark background doesn't really do us any favors in this picture, so it's time to get rid of it.

3. Use the Selection Brush (set to Mask) to select every part of the face. For subtlety, you're going to have to be very careful around the hair, and I suggest using a very small brush at a low opacity, and eating away. It depends how obsessive you are!

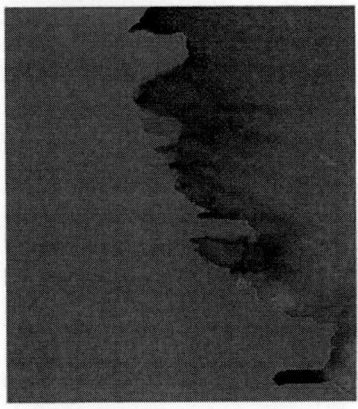

4. Once you've done that, create a new layer. Call it white background. Click through Edit > Fill, and fill the area with white. This will present you with our sportsfan neatly placed on a white background!

> *Why have we done it on a new layer? Well, the fact is sometimes you get dissatisfied with your masking, and if you have a preserved original of the background, you can always go back and sort things out.*

OK, now we should turn our attentions to getting that black eye and facepaint together.

Black eye

To create the black eye you need to start thinking about colors that say "bruise" to you. To my mind that means greeny purple. Layering these colors lightly on top of dark browns will deepen the tone without making it muddy.

5. Create a new layer, and call it blackeye. Select Multiply from the new layer's blending mode drop-down.

> *As this layer is grouped, Multiply mode combines new colors with existing colors in the photo to create a third, darker color. Any dark areas or lines on the skin are enhanced, which works well towards achieving the effect of a black eye.*

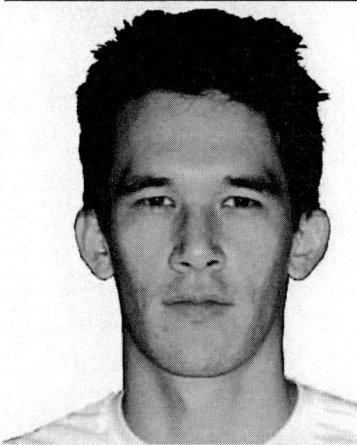

6. So, paint with a reduced opacity – at 20% maximum, with a brush at 0% Hardness, being careful not to over saturate the dark colors. Making slight marks helps add realistic light and energy to the surface, so work lightly from the ground up.

Oof!

The next step is to apply the greasepaint!

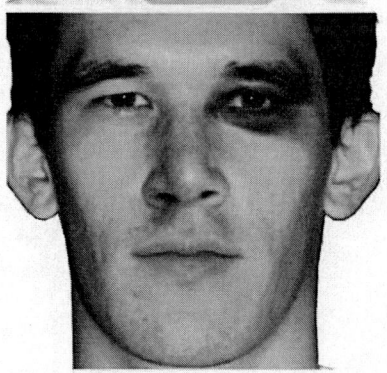

Team Colors

To help achieve our face painting effect, we need to make a mask of the face.

7. Let's copy everything we've done so far. Press CTRL+A to Select All, and then press CTRL+SHIFT+C to Copy Merged (that is, to take a snapshot of everything we've done up to now). Press CTRL+V to paste it on top of the layer stack. Call the new layer facemask.

8. Once again, using the Selection Brush (set to Mask) paint over the face, but this time in just the areas you wish to have the 'paint' appear.

    When you're satisfied with your selection, click out of the Selection Brush and press DELETE. Now we have an independent face to play with!

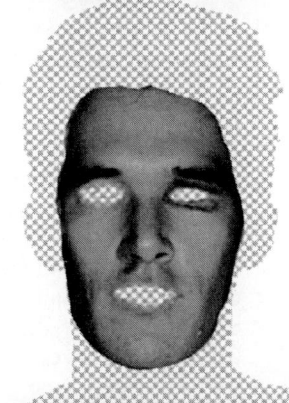

9. What we're going to do now is think ahead a little. The place where we want to put the paint is going to be a little smeared around the eyes, so it's time to take a soft-edged Eraser with about 10% Opacity and muss up the edges of the eyes a little – that is delete them from the facemask layer so the paint only fills those areas. It will help you to make the Background layer invisible while performing this task.

10. Next, create a new layer called paint. This will provide the basis for the color on the face. The blending mode that best imitates light and dark is Overlay, so use the Layers palette to apply the mode to the paint layer.

    > When Overlay mode is painted on top of existing colors, it enhances contrast and helps boost color's saturation. I've found that this doesn't work so well with lighter skin because the color tends to over saturate. In this case, orange turns fluorescent and yellow, blue turns iridescent purple.

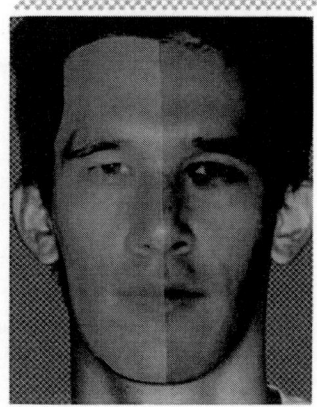

11. With the Polygonal Lasso tool, draw a box, with a line down the center of the nose, encompassing the whole left hand side of the face. Fill it with a vibrant orange. Create another box for the right side of the face and fill it with blue.

12. So now we have a rectangular paint job, which looks purple and orange on the face. Now, click in the link box of the facemask layer and click through Layers > Group Linked. This associates the two layers and rather usefully deletes any of the paint that we don't want!

13. What is almost infinitely useful at this point is the fact that we can edit both the **paint** and facemask layers together. So, the thing to do now is go on to the facemask layer and use the eraser to soften up those hard edges at the side of the face. The paint needs to look like it's been blended in. After you've done that, work over the facemask layer with a low opacity Eraser (say, 10%) and randomly delete areas of the mask in order to make it look like the paint has worn away in areas. What we're doing – just to keep you ahead of the game – is deleting the face mask, and revealing the unpainted face layer right at the bottom of the layer stack!

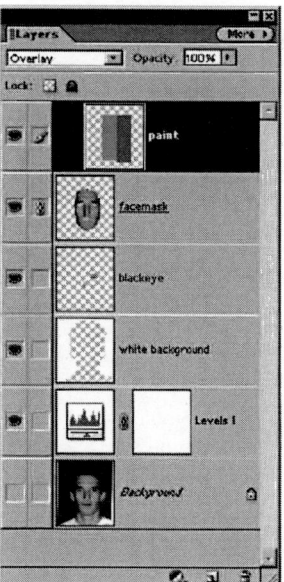

Man, you've just gotta love it when Photoshop Elements comes together like this!

14. OK, now we still have that *real straight* line down the center of his nose, so we'd better sort that out. It's going to involve mixing the colors – so let's head back to the paint layer. Use the Smudge tool and make a gestured smear across the hard line of color in between the eyebrows. We want the smudge placed here in relation to the black eye to help accentuate battle scar evidence. After that, have fun messing up that straight line by scribbling over it with the Smudge tool!

15. To finish off, we need to line up the layers so that the blue is genuinely blue and the orange is genuinely orange. The way to do this is to select the facemask layer and press CTRL+U to bring up the Hue/Saturation dialog. Set the Saturation to 0, and you have yourself one blue and orange picture!

> Check out takeshiSports.psd *if you want to look at our final Elements file.*

The finished image looks pretty wild compared to our original. The next makeover also possesses a wild element – attempting to combine the features of a tiger and a female.

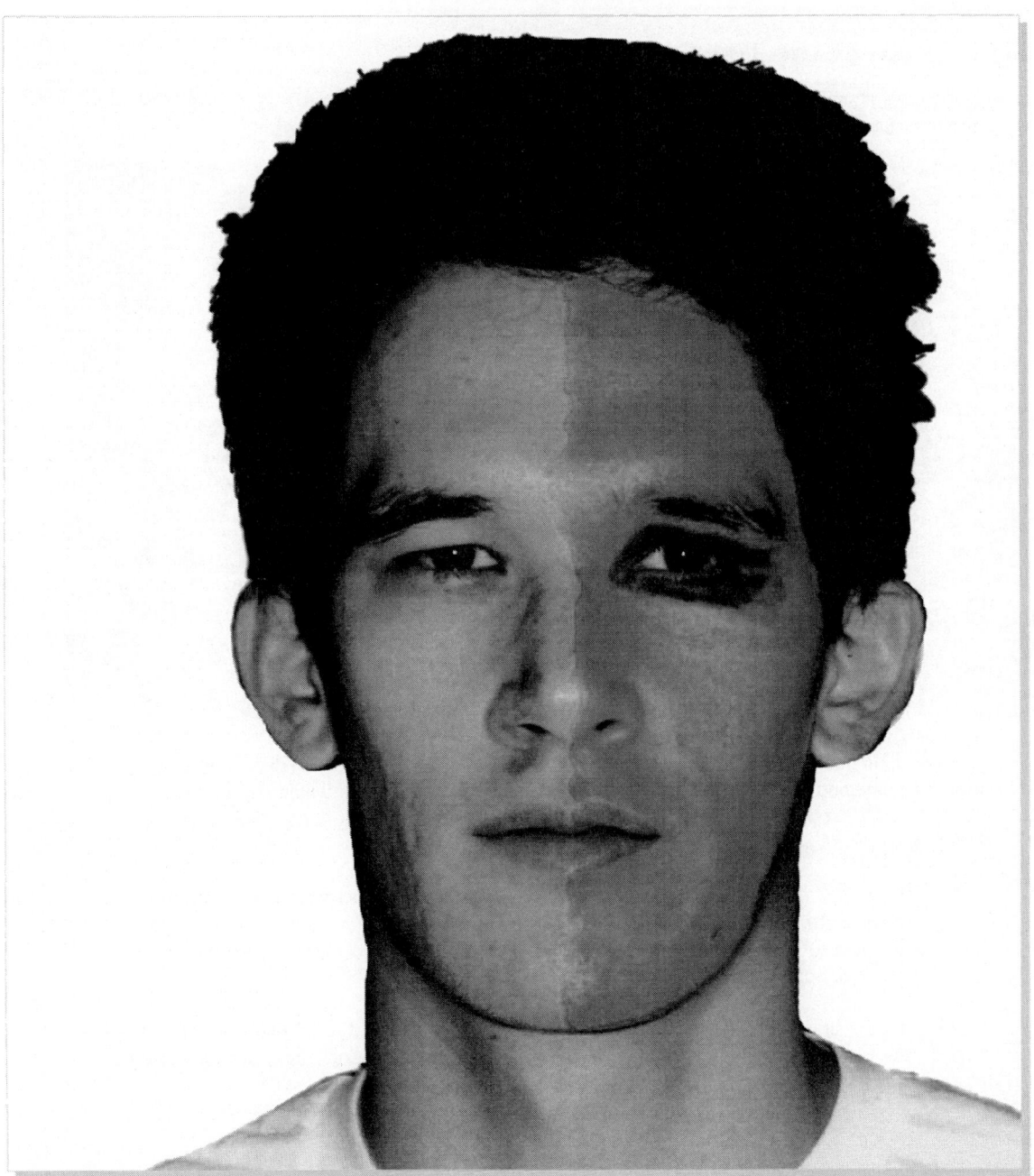

Miya – Face of the Tiger

For this portrait, my focus was on experimenting with transforming a female into a tigress. Aside from being associated as wild and exotic, tigers are also associated with glamour and wealth.

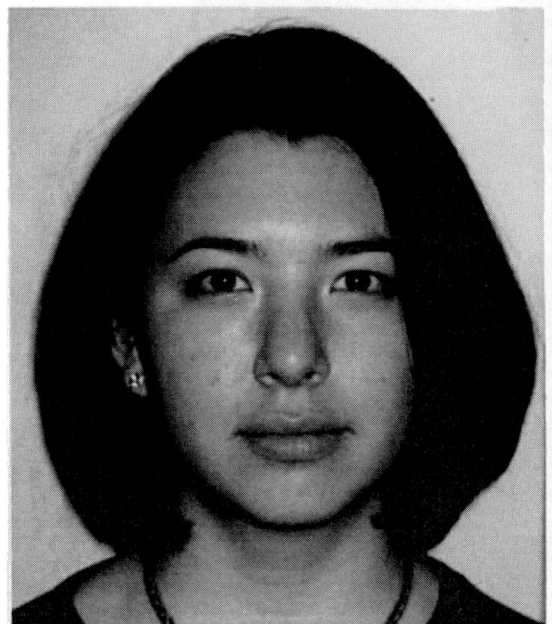

My main aim in this makeover was to combine the 'wild sides' of both women and tigers. The dramatic stripes and dark outlines that you see around the eyes and mouth of a tiger would also really help to enhance female facial features. The combination of soft white and orange furry texture, combined with stark black was a fun mix to experiment with.

1.   Open miya.jpg from this chapter's source files. Because the background to this portrait is pretty unattractive, we'll need to fill it in as we did in the previous exercise. Mask everything you want to keep (with the Selection Brush set to Mask), and on a new layer (background black) fill out the background with black.

2.   Once again, use the Selection Brush on the Background layer and select the area of the face you want to be painted. Click through Layer > New > Layer via Copy and place that layer at the top of the pile. Call it facemask.

3.   Now we're going to do what we did right at the end of the previous example – we're going to desaturate facemask so our colors look right. Click CTRL+U and set the Saturation level of the layer down to 0.

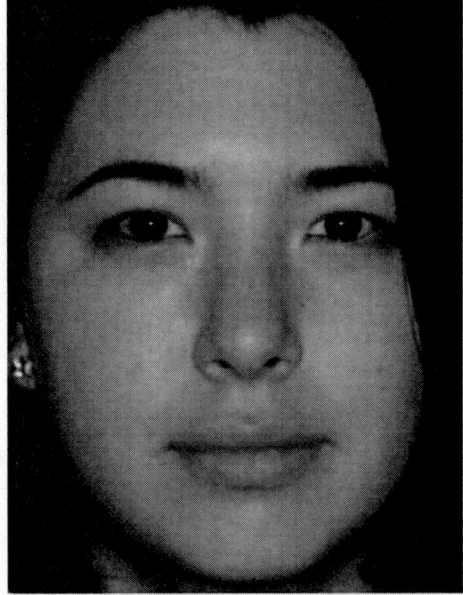

4.   Now, I find that a little flat, so in the spirit of getting everything right before proceeding, let's tweak the levels by pressing CTRL+L and entering the following values:

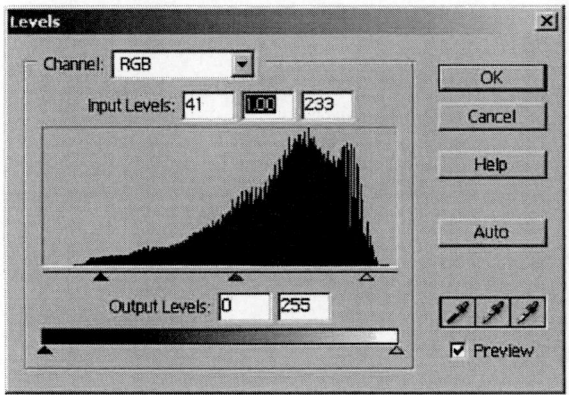

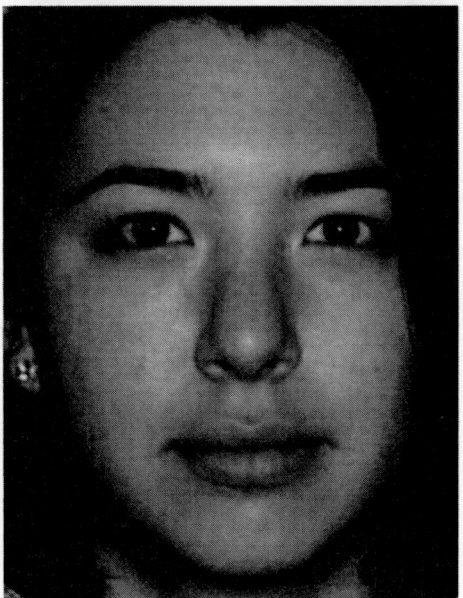

5. Now it's time to add a new layer for the paint. Call it paint – why not? Set its layer blending mode to Overlay.

    You'll remember we performed a very handy grouping of layers before in order to make that square blue and orange paint fall into line with the shape of the facemask layer. Well, let's do that again now – there's no reason to put it off!

6. While on the paint layer, click in the link box of the facemask layer and then click through Layers > Group Linked.

    Now for the paint. This face is much more about playing around with art styles and sketching, to produce what will hopefully be a fine feline – it's about building up paint, rather than wearing it away, as we did in the last exercise.

7. With a 50% Opacity Brush tool, start sketching with color, painting a faint undercoat shape of white and orange around the cheeks. Daub the lips with scarlet for the main part, and thin maroon edges. Remember your lip liner girls!

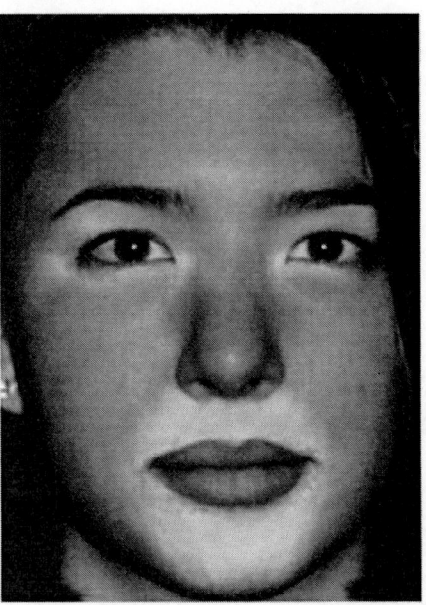

8. Now's the time to experiment with different shaped brushes. In the Brush menu, you have the facility to select Calligraphic Brushes.

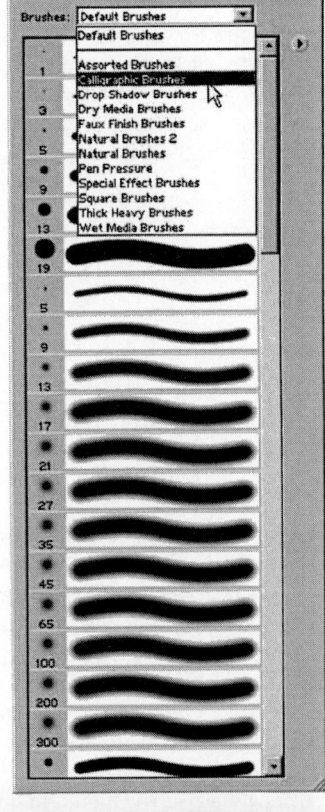

9. With a calligraphic brush – I've chosen the flat 235 px brush – brush 'eyeliner' around her eyes and start to lengthen her eyelashes by painting an exaggerated shape.

10. It's from here you can build your colors and blend the face to your own preferences. Personally, I darkened the existing orange and added more around her nose and forehead to help further define a tiger-like fuzzy chin. I also colored in the pink of her nose and outlined the top of the shape with a dark, warm brown.

    The design and impact of this makeover is mainly dependent on the placement and shape of the tiger stripes.

11. Use the Lasso tool to draw an outline of your planned pattern and fill it in black.

12. Using the Lasso tool and trying to work along the curve of the cheek, draw a jagged stripe, becoming thinner towards the nose. Paint the inside of the shape black using the Brush, and add some white with a soft white brush at a low opacity (10% or below) to help add softness to the pattern, and interrupt the flat black.

13. Next, add a new layer to the top of the layer stack and make a layer mask. We need to see what I was painting in the layer mask and at the same time, see the makeup to trace the stripes. Using SHIFT-CLICK, the new layer mask turns red and acts like a screen.

14. As the eyebrows are still showing through the Overlay layer, add a new layer (do not group it to the previous paint layer) and give it a Screen blending mode. Call it eyebrows. With a 30% opacity white brush, carefully paint over the eyebrows in white to reduce their presence on the face. This layer works as thick makeup to help cover over the eyebrows, but it looks natural because it is still possible to see the texture coming through.

I feel that was a pretty successful makeover.. Combinations of both striking and subtle effects bind really well together to help achieve the female tigress appearance. Of course, if you want to go beyond simulating makeup application and really incorporate a tiger appearance, you could look at manipulating the eyes and mouth so that they have more feline characteristics. Along with the addition of a few whiskers, you'd really have something far flung from the original portrait.

> *If you want to experiment with our finished file,* miyaTiger.psd, *you can find it on the accompanying CD-ROM!*

For now, though, let's get back to the realms of human beings (albeit silly ones) and look at a clown-style makeover.

Ava – Clown makeover

When I was a kid, my Mom would dress as a clown every year on Halloween. She was a drama teacher and very skilled at theater makeup. I always wanted her to paint my face like hers so I could see it transform. After seeing Ava's photo, I couldn't let the opportunity pass by to return to childhood memories.

Ava's expression in this photo was precious, how could I ever possibly improve on such a perfect photo?

We have to paint an even more endearing personality – that of a young hobo clown.

This makeover is based purely on greasepaint and love. I think the background looks great – sort of like a country setting that helps add a positive element to what should become a bittersweet character.

1. This time, we don't need to get rid of the background, we just need to create a facemask layer. So, as before, paint over the face with the selection brush and create a new layer out of it with Layer > New > Layer Via Copy. Call it facemask, and desaturate it.

2. Then create a new layer called paint, link it and Group Linked with the facemask layer. Give it an Overlay layer blending mode. We've done all this with the other pictures, so you should be pretty nifty at it now!

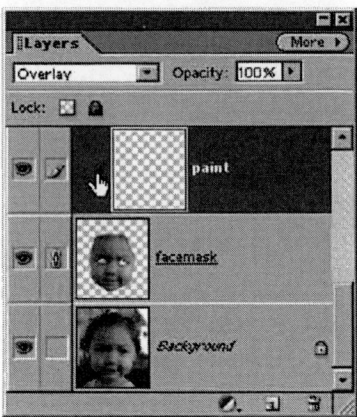

3. With a large 40% opacity brush, with its Hardness set to 0, start marking out where you want your colors to go. I began by marking out and filling in a peach color for her forehead.

4. Paint around her eyes with white, in order to give the makeup a powdery look. Start her beard by adding black under her nose with a soft brush at 40% Pressure, and continue the beard on her cheek and around the mouth. The appearance of the beard helps convey the look of a glum expression around the mouth area, which you can accentuate by painting the inside white.

5. Working in the color is 90% of the job with this picture. Paint over and over the picture with low opacity brushes until you have the color you want. For example, with the peach forehead, I added scarlet at a low opacity just to make everything look a bit more rosy.

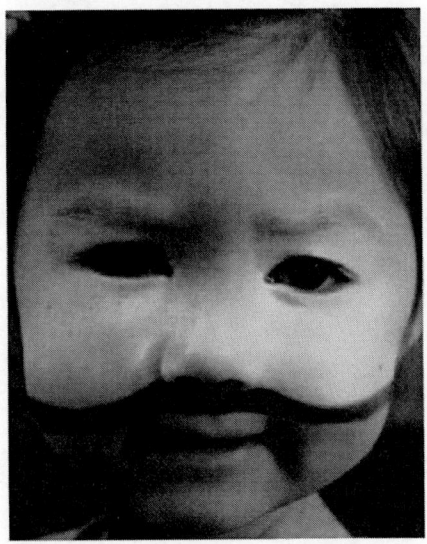
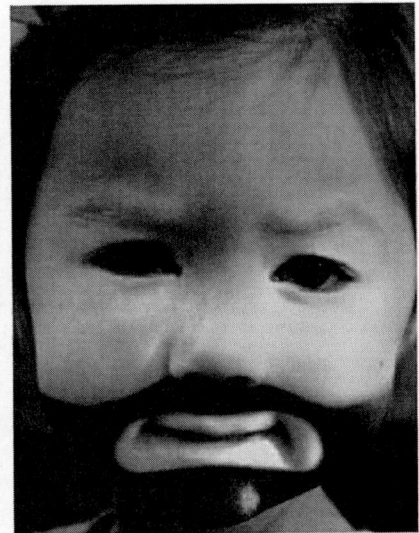

Her lips are still apparent in the Overlay mode, so we should disguise this.

6. Create a new layer (lips) and give it a Screen layer blending mode. Add more white to the area we've already earmarked (or *lipmarked*). Bear in mind, if the whiteness looks too opaque, you can always reduce the opacity of this layer, because it's independent!

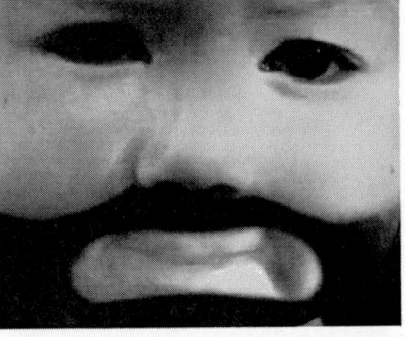

7. Back on the paint layer, draw a red line on her bottom lip to further accentuate the look of a frowning face. You may have to go back and erase some of the white on the lips layer to prevent it interfering with the red line.

8. Next, using a hard brush, paint her nose with the same deep red I used on her lips, before powdering her cheeks with a softer brush and a slightly more cool, rosy red.

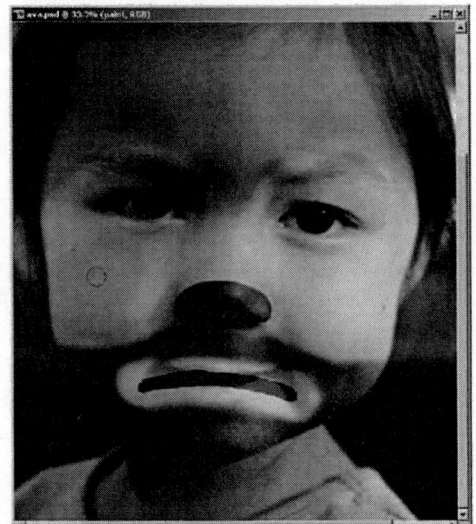

9. Finally, using a calligraphic brush, apply black around her eyes like eyeliner, and also add some long, stylized eyelashes to give her the special girl clown touch – we want to make sure we bring attention to the fact that she's a girl clown, even though she has a beard!

   After doing this, I realized I hadn't left room for the full color eyes when creating the facemask layer! Disaster! Not really – I just went to the facemask layer and deleted away the grayscale eyes to reveal color ones beneath.

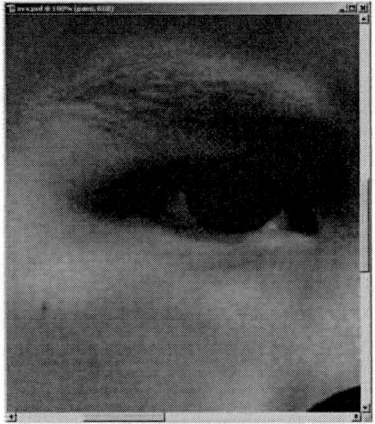

10. With the addition of some out-of-position eyebrows, our girl hobo clown is complete!

Ava's face now looks tinged with sadness, but is still captivating even though she's now wearing wacky clown makeup. The idea of wacky makeup leads us nicely into our next makeover.

> avaClown.psd *can be found in the* **Face Painting** *folder of the CD-ROM.*

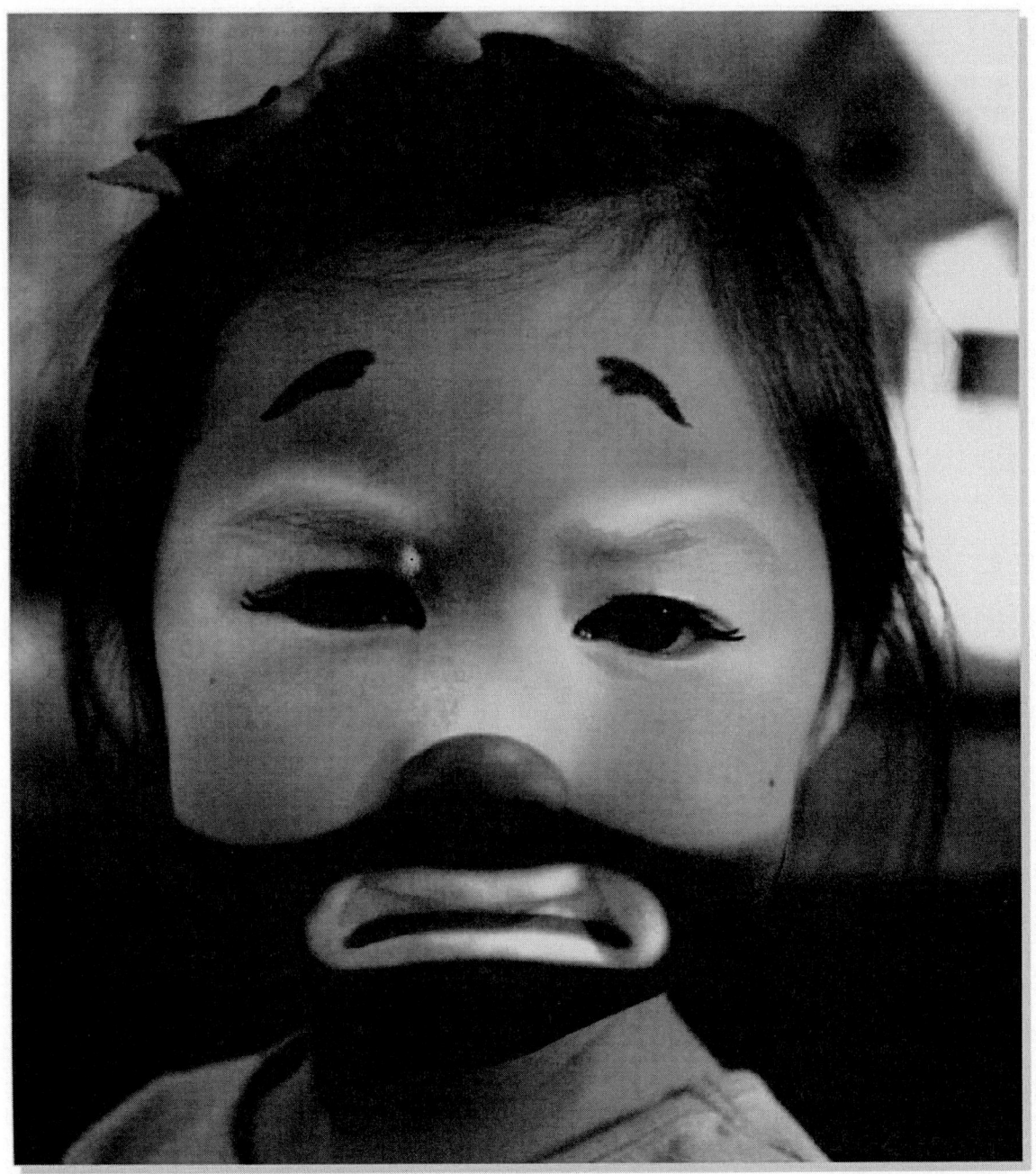

Kymar – a lightning bolt across the face

For the last makeover, let's work in Overlay mode as we have been all along, but with having to desaturate skin tone. Whereas paint applied in Overlay mode tends to over saturate on light skin, it is enhanced as it mixed with Kymar's darker skin tone. The makeover will be a vivid blend of colors that are very effective – and it's easy to do, with the right foreground color.

For this design, I wanted to replicate a makeover in the ilk of a 1970s glam rock star and looked at pictures of music artists such as David Bowie, Kiss and the New York Dolls.

As we've already experimented with thick paint, let's see how fluorescent color looks with a light application.

1. Block out the background in white, and create a facemask layer for old time's sake. Then, add a paint layer, grouped with the facemask layer, and set its blending mode to Overlay.

2. Using a brush at about 15% opacity, paint with red along the edges of his face. The glowing effect suits the concept for this makeover quite well, so use the same brush in facemask and draw a lightning bolt across his face at a greater opacity (about 50%).

3. Create a new Screen layer (paint2), and group it with **facemask** and place it underneath paint. Add some yellow through the lightning bolt at about 15% opacity, which transforms into more of a gold color and acts like a highlighter around the lightning bolt to help bring out its shape.

4. Create and group a Multiply layer (paint3), placing it at the top of the layer stack, and roughly outline the edge of the bolt with a navy blue, at around 20% opacity. Several strokes should see it dark enough.

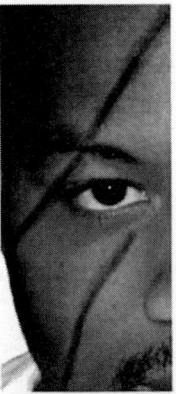

5. For the lipstick color, go for gold, which you can achieve by painting yellow back in the paint layer – the highlights in his lips really brought a glossy shine to the texture. Darken the edges of his lips a little by painting yellow in the paint3 layer.

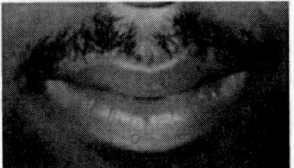

In a few short and simple steps, we have been able to give Kymar a lightning bolt like on David Bowie's *Aladdin Sane* album cover. When the approach is this straightforward, the effects are just as enjoyable as spending hours crafting a finished portrait.

See lightning strike twice by double-checking your version against our provided PSD — `kymarBolt.psd`.

Summary

Treating the face like a 3D canvas, Photoshop Elements' **blending modes** help us to focus on the photo and allow us to be expressive, while not straying too far from a level of realism.

It's worth experimenting with blending modes when using a photo as the beginning point for a portrait.

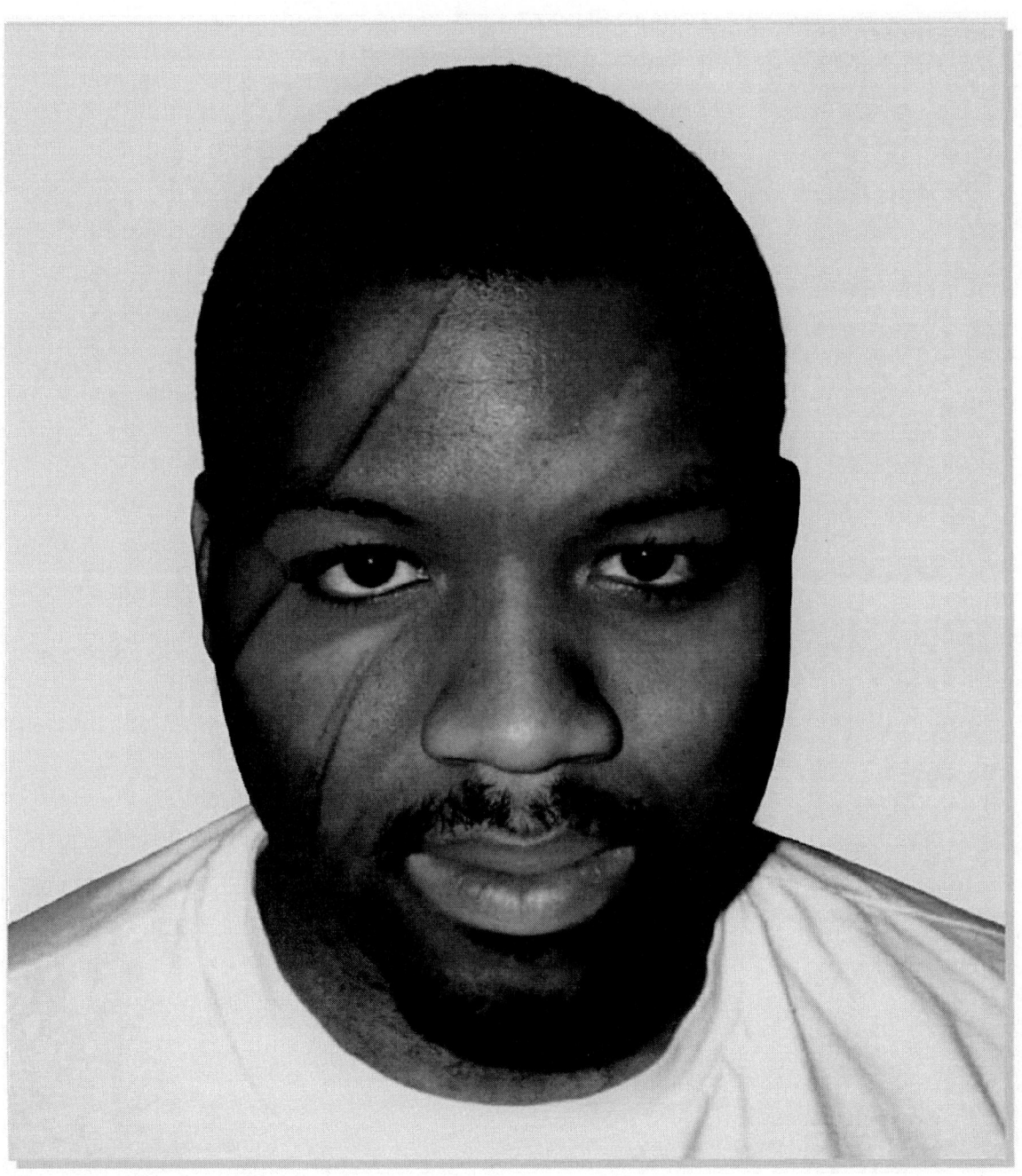

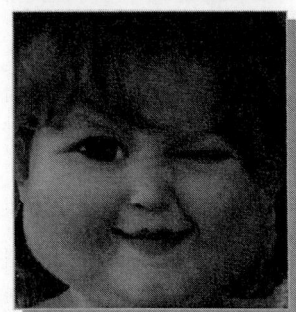

Chapter 5
Liquifying Faces

What you'll learn in this chapter

Tired of stuffy family portraits? Need some fun in your photos? Come this way and meet Elements' **Liquify** filter – the fast and easy way to mind-bending distortion effects. With a toolset including Warp, Bloat and Pucker it's a seriously fun way to liven up your photos. As we explore this cool tool we'll cover:

- The tools in the **Liquify filter** dialog.

- Using the Liquify filter to **create pixies** out of children and adults alike.

- **Warping**, **bloating** and **puckering** eyes, noses and ears to create instant amazing effects.

- Putting it all together in a cool **family puppetshow montage**; you'll never have a dull family portrait again.

In this chapter we'll explore Liquify's key tools. We'll liquify members of my very own family, with the overall aim of creating a unique family portrait of pixie puppets! Why pixies? Because unfortunately in the mid nineties I thought that *Magic Pixel House* would be a great name for a business, we've been called the 'magic pixies' ever since! Why puppets? I'm not entirely sure, but we do have a great homemade puppet theater that the girls love to play with.

Before beginning a composite image project such as this it's a good idea to list out the photographic elements required. In this example, these include:

- An empty puppet theater

- All members of the family against puppet theater backdrop

- Boy and girl puppets against puppet theater backdrop

A fun hour or two in the playroom, and the photos were in the bag! Our two daughters often dress up as fairies so required little encouragement – Selena my wife however was a little less co-operative, especially knowing what I had in mind. Let's get to work!

Holi – Pixie-liquifier

1. Open `holi.jpg` located in the **Liquifying Faces** folder on the Face Makeovers CD-ROM.

2. Select Filter > Distort > Liquify.

Elements' Liquify filter provides a real time what-you-see-is-what-you-get (WYSIWYG) environment for applying 'elastic' or 'melted' effects to your photos. Liquify's tools are located in a vertical bar on the left of the image space, tool options on the right.

People often comment on Holi's big dark brown eyes – let's use Elements' Liquify to give them something to really talk about!

> *A good strategy when attempting to create a caricature is to exaggerate the most noticeable aspects of a person's face.*

3. Select the Bloat tool (shortcut B) – it pushes pixels away from the center of the brush, effectively enlarging or creating a 'bloated' appearance. Set the Brush to a size that covers the main area of the eye. I've set mine to 100 and left Brush Pressure at the default setting of 50%.

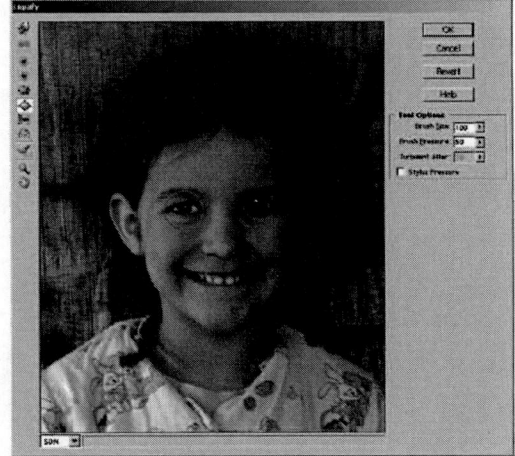

4. Click over each eye, applying the Bloat in short bursts by repeated clicking and releasing. I've chosen to apply the effect evenly to both eyes.

> *Heavy use of the Liquify tools can destroy detail in an image so unless that's part of your plan be sure to watch carefully as effects are applied, and stop while detail is visible.*

Every respectable pixie needs a fine set of ears! Now, Holi's aren't going to be as well-developed as Nalith's from the **Fantasy** chapter but they should still be pointy enough to poke an eye out.

5. With the Bloat tool still selected, increase the Brush Size to 200, and lower the Brush Pressure to 20. A lower pressure slows the rate the effect is applied at, giving us more control of the process.

6. Place the Bloat tool inside the left ear and click to gradually enlarge. You may need to apply the Bloat to several locations to evenly enlarge the ear.

We need to add a sharp tip to the ear. The Warp tool pushes pixels as it's dragged – sounds like the tool for the job!

7. Select the Zoom tool (Z) and zoom in to the ear as shown.

The Liquify filter dialog supports Elements Zoom shortcuts of CTRL+SPACE+CLICK to zoom in and CTRL+SPACE+ALT+CLICK to zoom out.

8. Select the Warp tool (W), and decrease the Brush Size – this will make creating a sharper point on the ear easier. Gradually push the ear up and out to the left, being careful to keep the outline of the ear smooth and flowing.

   Holi's other ear is obscured by her hair. However I've chosen to use the Bloat tool to enlarge the area to roughly match the size of the pixie ear we've just created, and have also used the Warp tool to add the beginnings of a pixie shape to the part of the ear that can be seen.

Elements' Liquify filter does not allow you to save intermediate states. If you've created a great effect but would like to keep liquifying the image without risking the effect, click OK to apply the effect to the image and exit Liquify. Then Save As giving the image a different filename, and CTRL+F to re-open the Liquify filter with your previous effect saved and in place.

OK, now our pixie needs a characteristically small nose!

9. Select the Pucker tool (P). The Pucker tool moves pixels towards the center of the image, effectively shrinking whatever is within the brush size area. Set the Brush Size to cover nose tip area. I've set mine to 150. Click to gradually reduce the size of the tip.

10. Switch back to the Warp tool (W). With the Brush Size at 150 work up and down both sides of the nose gradually pushing it in – a fine nose any self-conscious superstar would be proud of!

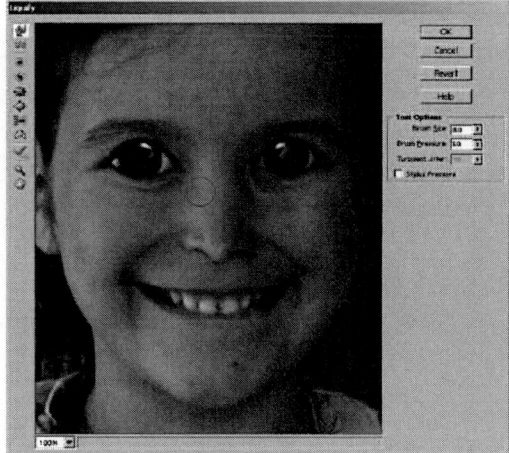

Holi's pixie face is coming along – a few minor touches and we'll be done. Let's make the bottom half of the face narrower.

11. Using the Bloat tool again, select a larger Brush Size – I've set mine to 300, and place the tool so the edge of the circle overlaps with the cheek and neck area we'd like to narrow as shown.

12. Apply the Bloat tool to both sides of the face, gradually pushing it in.

> *Be sure to leave ample room around your face to make Liquifying faces easy!*

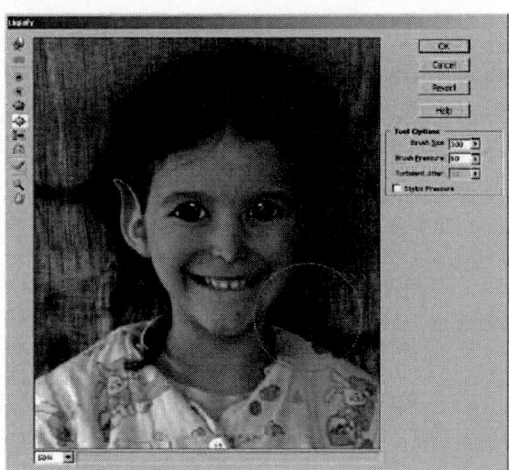

13. Now enlarge the forehead. Adjust the brush size as needed, being careful not to change the shape of the eyes.

Our final touch is cheeky eyebrows.

14. Set a small Brush Size on the Warp tool – I've set mine to 30 – and zoom in. Raise the eyebrows towards the outside, again being careful not to damage the eye shape.

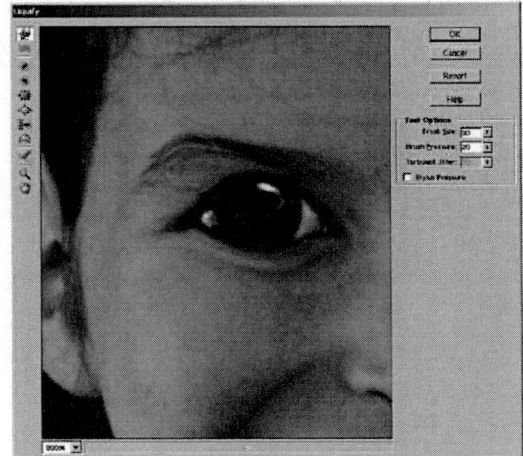

Our work here is done, one pixie caricature!

15. Click OK to apply the Liquify effects to your image in Elements and save your file.

> *You can find a JPG of my effect on the CD-ROM – it's called `holiPixie.jpg`. Why haven't we supplied the PSD – well, as Liquify effects are permanent once you close the dialog, the PSD would just be our finished picture anyway and wouldn't be editable!*

A pixie in only a few minutes – not a bad effort! Luckily for Holi her pyjamas won't live to haunt her in her teen years – later in the chapter we'll attach her pixie head to a puppet as a part of *The Greatest Puppet Show on Earth*.

> *Has your liquifying got out of control? Check out Liquify's* Reconstruct *tool (E) – it allows you to fully or partially reverse the Liquify effects you've applied to the image. Want to start over? Click* Revert.

Indi – More pixie tricks

From the day Indi was born, people have commented on her chubby cheeks. Even at three years old she's still growing into them – maybe we can add a few more years to that process for her!

1. Open indi.jpg from the **Liquifying Faces** folder of the CD-ROM.

2. Click through Filter > Distort > Liquify once again.

3. Select the Bloat tool with the brush set to a size that covers the cheek. I've set mine to 200 and have reduced the pressure to 20 to give me more control over the rate the effect is applied, as well as a better chance of stopping before too much pixel information becomes blurred and distorted.

4. Apply the Bloat gradually to each cheek. I've zoomed in a little for a better look at the effect being applied.

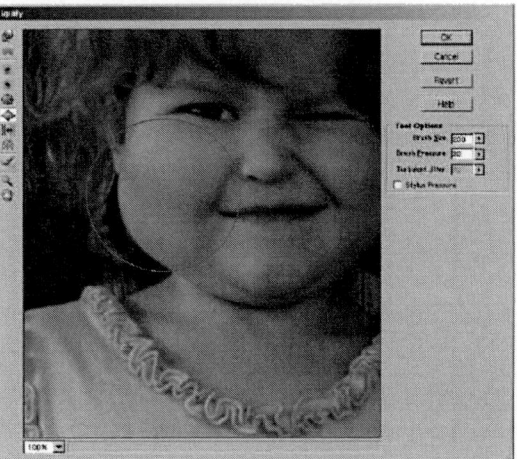

As you might guess from the photo I had a little trouble getting Indiana in front of the camera, let alone smile! With the cheeks out of the way what do we have to work with? An exaggerated right eyebrow could be fun.

5. Select the Warp tool. Set the Brush Size to 40.

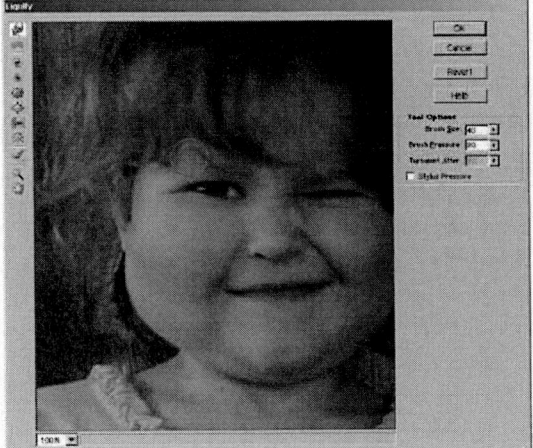

Our rambunctious pixie is coming together – some chubby lips should finish the job nicely!

6. CTRL+SPACE+Click to zoom in tight on the lips.

7. With the Warp tool still selected set the Brush Size to 20 – a small brush will help us with this finer work, as will a low pressure setting of 20.

8. Build out the shape of each lip gradually by repeated short 'click and drags' with the Warp tool. I've taken the opportunity to increase the smile a little too!

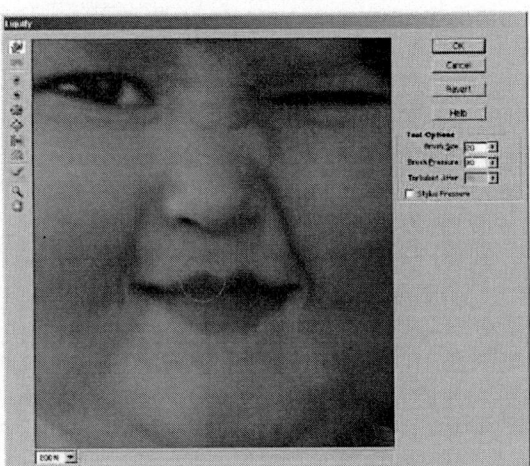

9. Keeping with the pixie theme I've chosen to apply the Bloat tool to Indi's eyes.

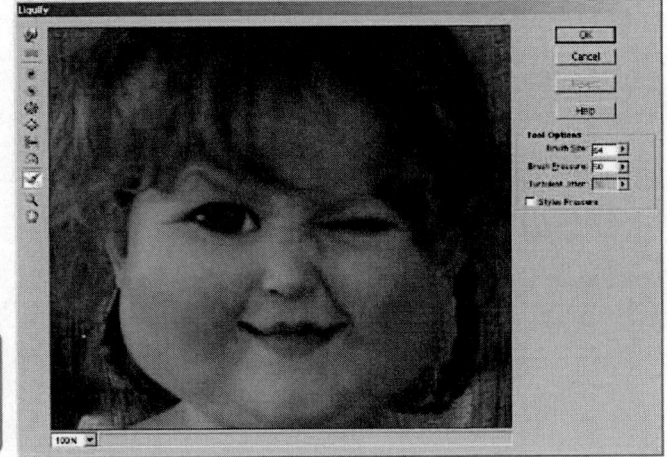

10. Click OK to apply the Liquify effects to your image and save your file.

> *As before, a JPG of my liquified offspring is on the CD-ROM as* indiPixie.jpg*.*

Pixie number two complete! Indi will be joining us in the puppet theater shortly.

Pete and Selena – Pixie parents

Aside from being great fun the Liquify tool can be also be great therapy – always wanted your partner to have pixie ears? Need a new look? The queue starts here!

1. Open pete.jpg and selena.jpg from the CD-ROM and liquify our faces, just don't mention it to my wife! Here's a few examples to get you started.

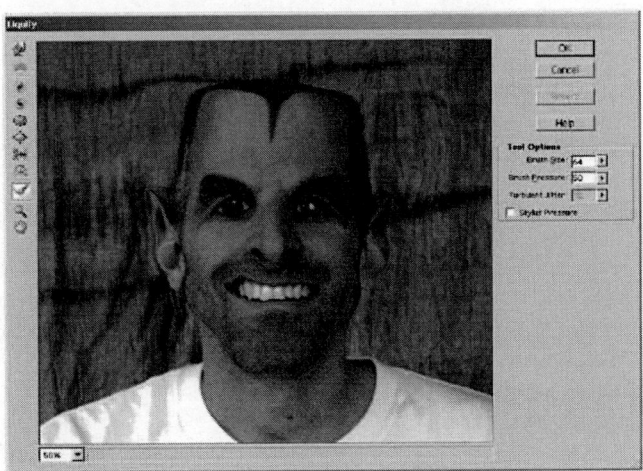

Self portrait – Max Headroom meets Mr Spock

I'll leave you to experiment in this stage of the tutorial; you know the tools and techniques by now – go have some fun!

> We've so far concentrated on the main Liquify filter tools, but there are more. Have a play around with the **Turbulence**, **Twirl** and **Shift Pixels** tools!

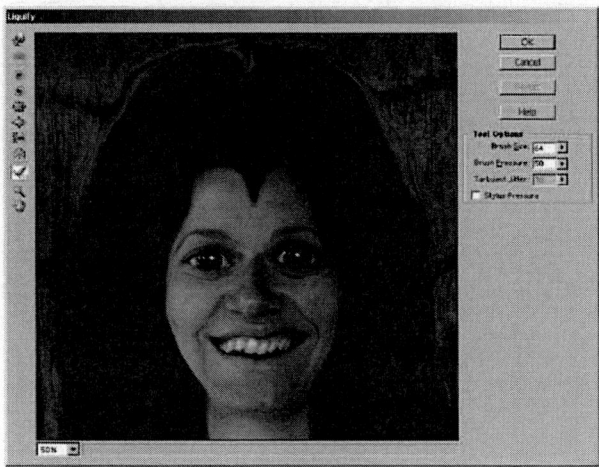

Selena meets Elvira

Puppet Assembly

With the family suitably liquified into pixies it's time to assemble the puppets! The puppet photos were taken in front of the same background as the family so merging them should be a snap.

1. Open girlPuppet.jpg and holiPixie.psd (the one you've saved!)

2. With holiPixie.psd active, select the Lasso tool and drag a rough marquee around the outside of Holi's head, leaving some of the background intact – we'll need some of it left to easily merge the two images.

3. With the Move tool (or holding down the CTRL key) drag the selected area into girlPuppet.jpg.

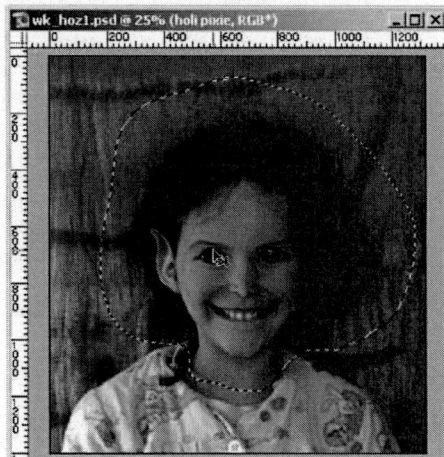

4. Name the layer head.

5. With the head layer active, select the Free Transform tool (CTRL+T) and rotate and resize Holi's head – the proportions are up to you. I want to replace the puppet's head with Holi's in approximately the same size.

6. Hit ENTER to apply the transformation.

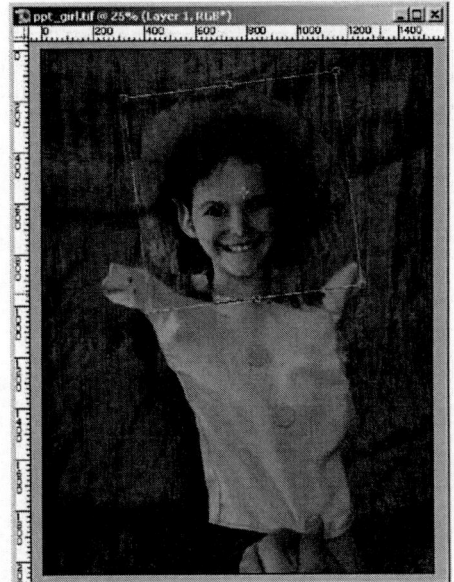

7. We need to merge the two images – the backgrounds are essentially the same, the only problem is the rough edge around Holi. A large soft brush at a reduced opacity will do the job.

8. Select the Eraser tool. I've set my Brush Size to 125, Opacity to 75%.

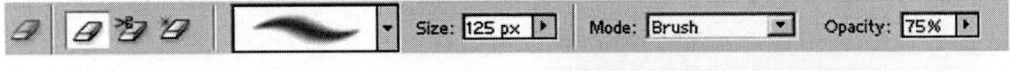

9. Work your way around Holi's head with the Eraser tool, removing the hard edge and making it appear the two images are one.

> Toggle the display of the Eraser cursor between Precise and Brush by using the CAPS LOCK key.

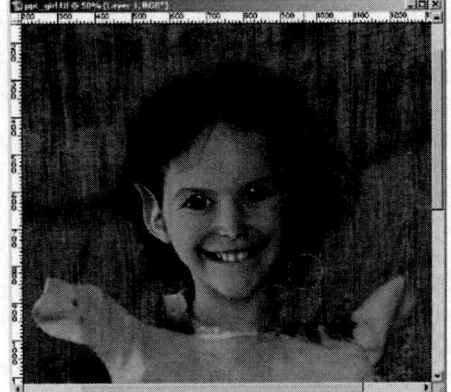

The neck area presents a problem – I'd like Holi's pixie head to replace the puppet's head cleanly, as if it had always been there! If only we could see through the head layer we'd know where to erase to reveal the decorative trim around the puppet's neck.

10. Change the blending mode of head to Multiply. This is only a temporary measure to allow us to see through the head layer to the puppet beneath.

11. Select the Eraser tool again, with a small soft brush at 100% opacity. I've set mine to 20 pixels.

12. With the head layer active carefully erase the pixel information immediately above the decorative trim.

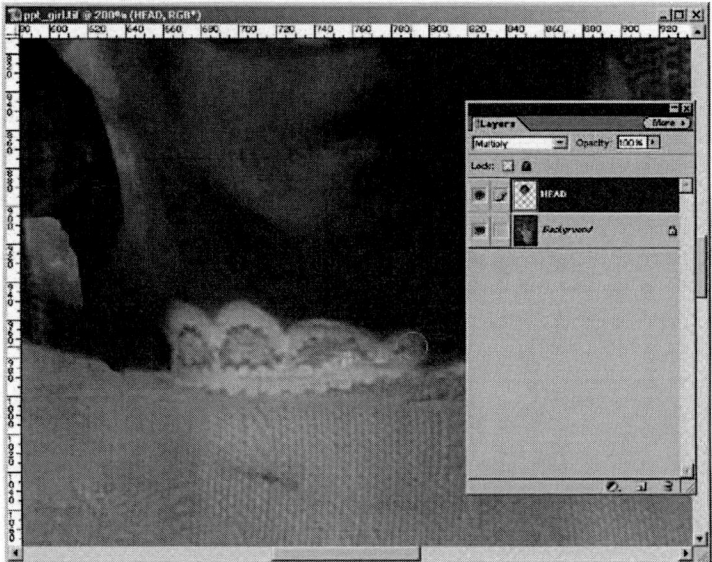

Some of the doll's head may now be visible around the lower part of Holi's head - time for the Clone Stamp tool.

13. Make the Background active.

14. Select the Clone Stamp tool. I've set my Brush Size to 75, yours may need to be larger or smaller depending on the resolution of the files you are working on. 75 should be fine if you're following along.

15. ALT+CLICK to sample fabric beside the doll's head and clone over any parts of the head visible behind Holi.

16. With the doll's head no longer visible, switch the blending mode of head back to Normal.

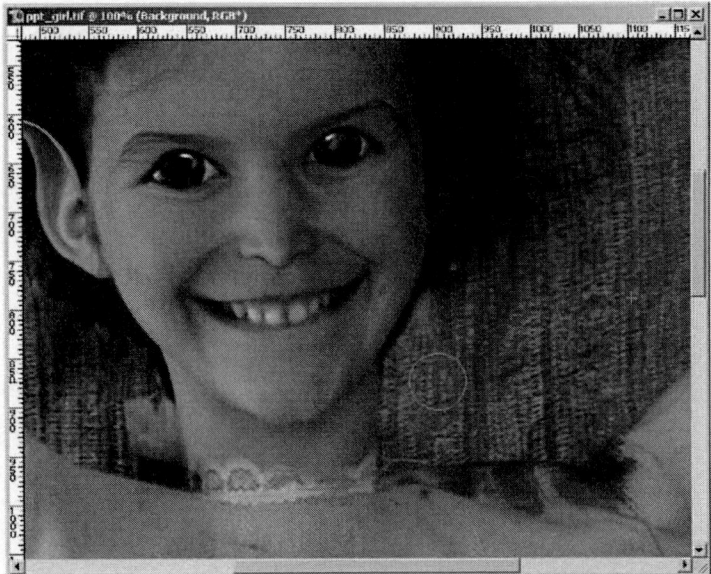

Our Pixie Holi puppet is now complete and ready for further use in the theater.

17. Save your file now and repeat the same process to create the Indi, Pete and Selena puppets. You can find a boy puppet image to use on the CD-ROM.

Puppet Show

Our pixie puppets are ready to move into their new puppet theater. Open `theater.psd` from the CD-ROM...

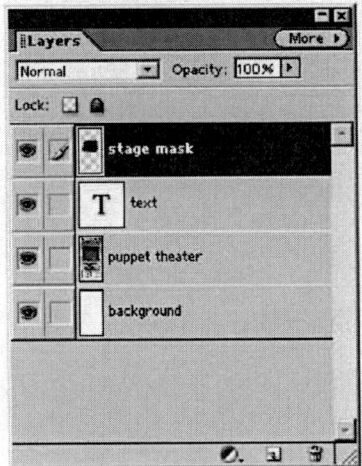

`Theater.psd` is a file I prepared earlier, based on a photo of the girl's puppet theater. It's made up of four layers:

- background (white)

- puppet theater

- text – for placing custom text over theater

- stage mask – the layer we'll clip the puppets too.

1. Switch to your Holi puppet PSD.

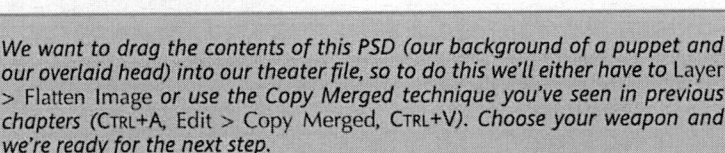

We want to drag the contents of this PSD (our background of a puppet and our overlaid head) into our theater file, so to do this we'll either have to Layer > Flatten Image *or use the Copy Merged technique you've seen in previous chapters (*CTRL+A, Edit > Copy Merged, CTRL+V). *Choose your weapon and we're ready for the next step.*

2. Select the Move Tool and drag the merged layer from the Holi puppet file into `theater.psd`. Place it at the top of the layer stack, directly above the stage mask layer and name it head.

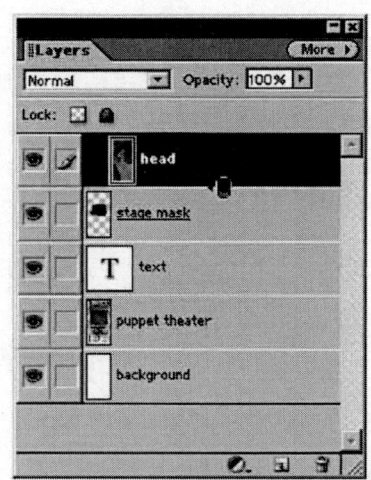

3. ALT+CLICK on the line dividing the stage mask and head:

   Holi's head is now clipped to the stage mask layer, but she is way too big!

4. Using the Free Transform tool, size the head layer down so the Holi puppet fits within the mask.

5. Select the Text tool, and add a title in the orange area using the existing text layer. I've named mine *pixie holi* using the Parry Hotter font, just right for pixies! If you haven't got this font, choose your next best.

I've continued to add the three other puppets I'd saved earlier using the same process, and finished off with a change of title and a tight crop, job done – *The Greatest Puppet Show on Earth*!

> You can find the finished article on the CD-ROM, saved as puppetsFinal.psd.

Summary

I hope this chapter has shown you how much creative fun you can have with Elements Liquify filter. As further projects, why not make a liquified portrait of a group of your own family or friends, or how about trying to liquify a photo of a cloud into the shape of a face!

Along the way I hope I've also demonstrated techniques you can use to combine liquified images with other photo objects. Remember with a tool like the Liquify filter there are absolutely no rules. Open your favorite images, explore each tool and settings and have fun – photos of your family and friends will never be safe again!

Chapter 6

Ageing a Face

What you'll learn in this chapter

In this chapter, we study the most fundamental face-shaping event any of us will ever encounter – ageing. Along the way, you'll pick up lots of tips about how to approach larger projects like this. Amongst the effects covered:

- Researching the ageing process and **preparing** your photos.

- Altering facial **colors** and skin **pigmentation** using **blending modes.**

- Changing the shape of the face using the **Liquify** tool.

- **Sampling** wrinkles and eye coloring from other photos.

The real power of a program like Elements lies in its ability to alter photographs. In this chapter, we're going to push this as far as we can. We've all seen how on magazine covers, wrinkles and spots are removed with the greatest of ease. Let's head off in the other direction: instead of reversing the ageing process, let's enhance it. Let's make someone actually look older than they really are.

Kirsten – has it really been 30 years?

Here's a picture of Kirsten – she's 25. We're going to spend the next 30 pages ageing Kirsten by about 30 years! Along the way we'll learn a lot about Elements, and a lot about the nature of the human face and how ageing affects our looks.

There is no Auto-Ageing tool for us to use here. Like all the previous chapters, we need to use a little ingenuity and some cool techniques to get Kirsten looking old enough to be her own mother. You'll be amazed at the results though.

Research and preparation

A good place to start when you're doing a project of this nature is to actually go and take a look at people who *are* 55. What's different about them? When we look at this person, how do we know they're in their fifties? We're going for maximum realism here, so let's make a list.

Perhaps the most important change in a person's face is the change of **elasticity** of the skin. As you get older, the skin begins to droop slightly. This isn't always the case, especially where the person is super thin and fit, but more often than not, this is a tell tale sign of ageing.

Next is the way the skin discolors. Older people have been in the sun more. Their skin has developed discoloration blemishes and such like. As the skin gets older, not only does it lose its elasticity, but also its continuous tone. Older people have more blotchy skin, as a general rule.

Obviously, because of the loss of elasticity, we start to see the appearance of wrinkles. Another major change in the actually morphology of the face is that people tend to put on a little weight as they get older. Also, as the skin relaxes, the face expands slightly. One last major change: the eyes discolor, especially the white areas.

Peripheral to the face are changes like hair color changes, teeth discoloration etc.

Obviously not all these changes happen to everybody. Everyone ages in a different way as we are all susceptible to different environmental conditions, life stresses etc. We are going to use these changes as a guideline, and make our way from there. For this project, we are going to attempt:

- Changes of face pigmentation

- Changes of face morphology

- Changes of eye color

- Changes in skin consistency

- A change of hair color

- Adding wrinkles

The face – pigmentation

Let's start by looking at Kirsten's face. Not much in the way of any pigmentation inconsistency, so we'll use Elements to introduce some!

1. Open up `kirsten.jpg` from the CD-ROM and take a look for yourself.

2. To get started, simply duplicate the Background layer and change the blending mode of this new layer to Linear Light.

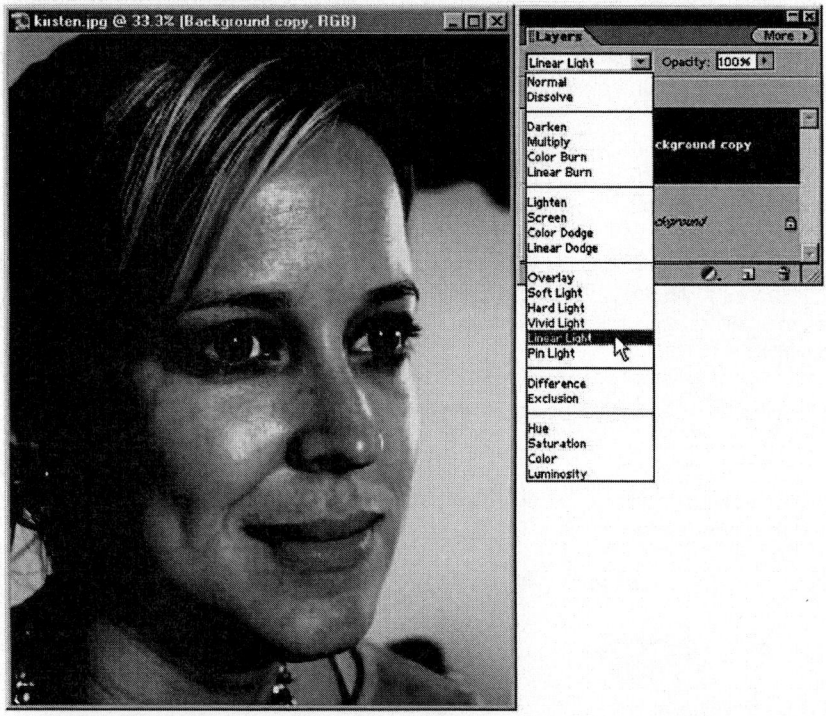

This changes the contrast of the photograph quite considerably. We're basically looking for high contrast here (you'll see why in a moment) and this blending mode is good for this.

3. Now let's make a merged copy of this layer (Select > All, Edit > Copy Merged, Edit > Paste) and change *its* blending mode to Luminosity. Again, we're looking for changes in the lighting, and nothing else. We can turn off the visibility of our original Linear Light blended layer now.

Remember that when we make a merged copy, it's like taking a photo of the way all the layers look together. If your blending mode is set to default for this layer (which would be the Normal setting), all the layers underneath this mode will no longer be doing anything to the image – they will be hidden by the merged layer. You can actually turn the visibility of all these layers off if you like. Just remember that this merged layer is replacing everything we've done up until this point – see it as a representative of our image so far.

Notice how the Luminosity blending mode picks up a lot of the contrast from our merged Linear Light layer, which is what we're going for.

We've already got some nice skin discoloration going, adding a year or two onto Kirsten's age. So now she's what, 27, 28? And we're just getting warmed up!

The contrast is a bit much however, especially around the eyes.

4. Make another merged copy of the image thus far, and change the blending mode of this layer to Lighten. Turn off the Luminosity merged layer we just made. We're just basically adding layers at this point to try, mess with the lighting on the skin – to break it up a bit. I also used the Eraser to remove the eyes on this layer, as I was just interested in affecting the skin at this point, and the effect was making the eyes way too dark. So we're compounding layers – each one we add is affecting all the others. Let's have a look at how this has gone so far:

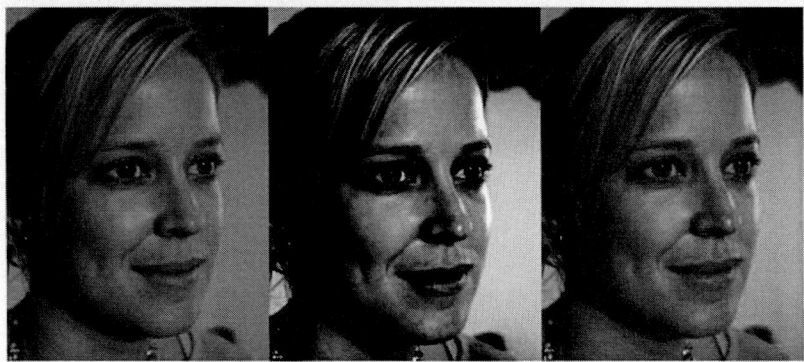

Notice that the difference between the first and third picture is fairly subtle. Have a look at the layers we've used:

A note about experimentation

We've used the second layer (labeled here as lum) which is our second picture, in order to create the lighting for the third picture. So actually, we can go ahead and delete the second layer – it's a piggyback to get the third. A fairly odd thing to do in a way – create a layer and then end up deleting it, but what we're doing here is looking for a specific type of lighting – we're trying to emphasize the discoloration in the face. In order to get to the third image, we need to really bring out the possible discoloration in the skin. Kirsten has good skin, so we needed to use a lighting effect that would totally exaggerate the tones of the skin – which is what we did with our luminosity layer. Once we had achieved this, we used this Luminosity merged layer as a springboard to get the lighting we wished to achieve.

This is easy enough for me to explain. But what about when you're sitting at home with your own projects? How will you know what layers to create and when? Break it down for yourself. First question: What do I need to achieve? Don't worry about the techniques you're going to use. Start just by answering this question: "I need to discolor the skin; I need to exaggerate skin blemishes". Then you can move on to: "How am I going to achieve this?"

Sometimes you will know the answer, sometimes you won't. Not to worry, there's a solution for both! In this specific instance I knew the answer – I knew what blending modes to use. But let's look at the situation where this isn't the case. Let's pretend I didn't have a clue which blending mode to use, or which layers to create.

If you're looking to create a lighting effect, the first thing to do is always duplicate the Background layer. Always do this. There are two reasons here:

Firstly, we're going to be messing with the image a lot. It pays to have the original handy as a frame of reference. Remember we're going for a subtle look – we want things to look realistic. If we make Kirsten look like a prune, no one is going to believe that she's really old. A good practice to get into is: whenever you make a change – in this case a lighting change – turn all your layers off leaving only the Background layer on – compare what you've done to the original. Is the enhancement you're making believable?

Secondly, the best and most natural way to make lighting changes that will be realistic is to use the existing lighting in the image. This means duplicating the background image and using that duplicate layer to enhance the lighting of the layer below it – which of course is our Background layer. We do this by changing the blending mode of the duplicated layer. This means that the two layers are going to combine in an interesting way. Blending modes affect the lighting of an image in all sorts of ways, and as I've said before, it pays to cycle through all the different modes just to see which ones work – even if you know before hand which mode you're going to use.

So what we've really done up until now is add a bit more lighting to the face, but at the same time highlighted areas of skin discoloration slightly. The change in lighting is less important than the fact that this change has caused the discoloration to become emphasized. Remember we're trying to be believable here, so we're going for a subtle approach.

That said, let's leave subtlety behind for the time being. We need to do something about the facial morphology before continuing.

The face - morphology

Let's have a look at a reference photo I dug out. Pictures of people who naturally are your target age are one of your best tools in creating a realistic looking face. This one can be found on the CD-ROM, entitled oldMouth.jpg:

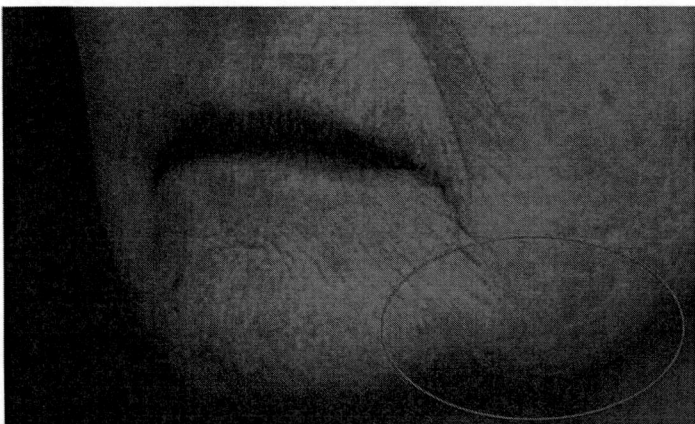

Notice the way the skin comes away from the jaw in the middle, and the cheeks have drooped a bit. Let's try emulating that.

1. Make a merged copy of everything (just as we've done before) and we'll get to work on the shape of the face with the **Liquify** tool (Filter > Distort > Liquify…).

> *Another copy-merging tip: the command works by taking a picture of the exact state of affairs, which allows you to paste this to a new layer – so hidden layers will obviously be ignored – it's just replicating exactly how things look at present. It won't work if you are on a hidden layer. If you're trying to use this command and it's not working, check to see if you currently have a hidden layer selected.*

2. I used a 260 sized brush with 70 brush pressure in order to pull the cheeks down and adjust the jaw slightly.

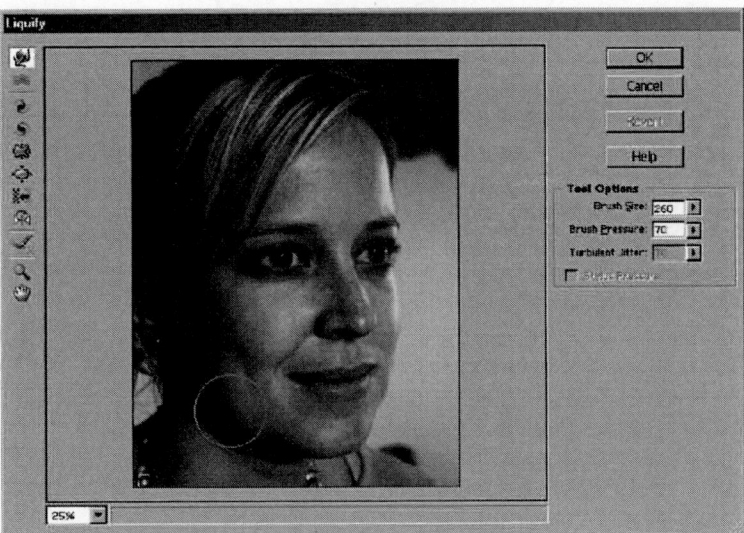

Your brush size depends on what you're trying to achieve here, obviously. I used a brush roughly the size of the oval in the above image of the old mouth so I could make a large yet subtle change. I also pulled the skin away from the right hand side of the mouth a little bit. In addition to this, I used our Transform tool to stretch the entire image a little bit horizontally – to make the face a little heavier. The morphology of the face tends to change a bit in this way as a person gets older, in addition to the skin sagging a bit:

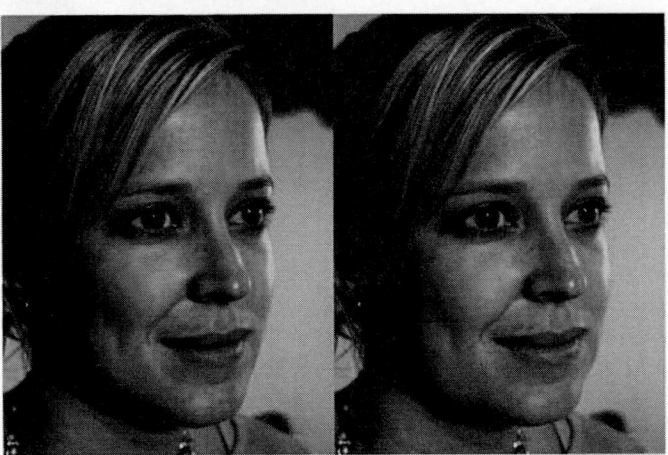

Wow, that really makes a major change to the look of the person! But they could have just put on weight. Let's start addressing the skin again.

In order to achieve this, we're going to borrow some of the skin from our study photo.

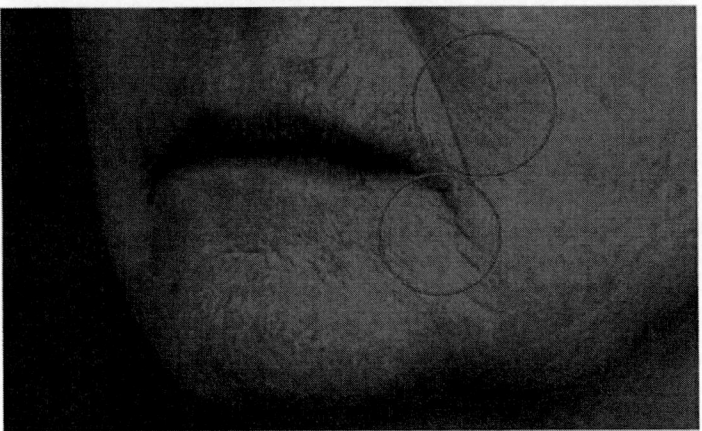

3.   Cut these areas out from our study image (oldMouth.jpg) and paste them onto new layers on our project. (I called these layers mouth wrinkle and cheek wrinkle). Notice that the orientation of the face is in the opposite direction, so we will have to flip the images around. (Image > Rotate > Flip Layer Horizontal).

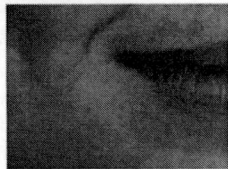

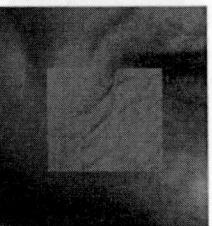

4.   For this piece, set the blending mode to Darken, which helps merge the piece into the background.

> Basically, this blending mode will merge the pixels together in such a way as to darken the resultant merge. So if you're merging a light piece onto a dark piece, the resultant will use the tone (how light or dark it is) of the darker layer and set the tone of the piece it's merging.

It's not totally consistent; as you can see the area to the left of the mouth is slightly lighter, but that's OK – we're going for a patchy skin look anyway!

The effect is perhaps a little bit too subtle. As you can see, I've cut the bottom circle area out of the raw material image and pasted it to a new layer (our mouth wrinkle layer).

I've used the Eraser around the edges to make the piece fit in with the image, but in doing so, we've lost quite a bit of the texturing. Let's go back and make a new layer and this time make sure that wrinkle at the corner of the mouth comes with it!

5. Head back to our raw material mouth image and use our Selection and Move tools to drag another piece of raw material across to our project. We'll keep the old layer, as it still adds a bit of a wrinkle which is good. We're going to call our new layer corner mouth wrinkle:

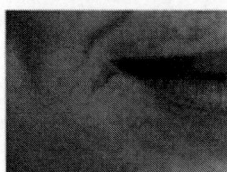

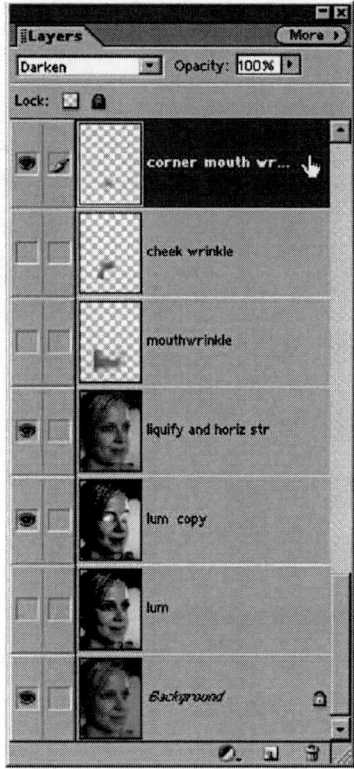

6. Much better. Do the same thing with the left cheek: paste from the original study piece (we're going to use oldCheek.jpg here), use the Marquee tool to select the area shown in the image on the following page.

7. Drag this to your project with the Move tool, flip the image around, set the blending mode to Darken and use a soft edged Eraser on the edges of the image to make it blend in better.

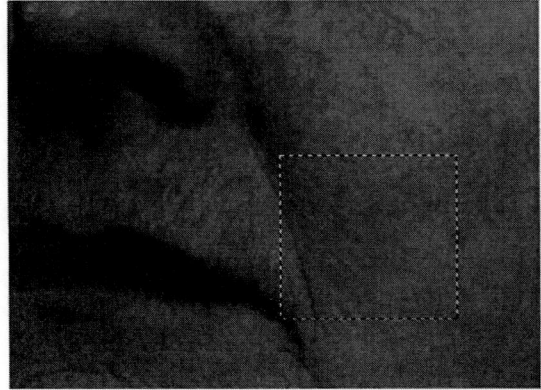 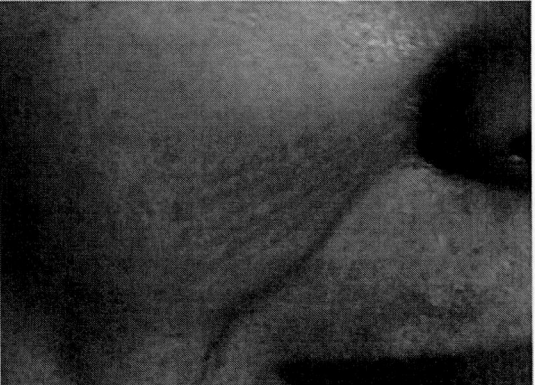

Cheeks as a general rule don't get too wrinkly, so don't go too over-board here.

Our image so far:

The Eyes

Time to get started on the eyes. What is it about old people that changes in the eyes? Let's have a look at a new study image, oldEyes1.jpg:

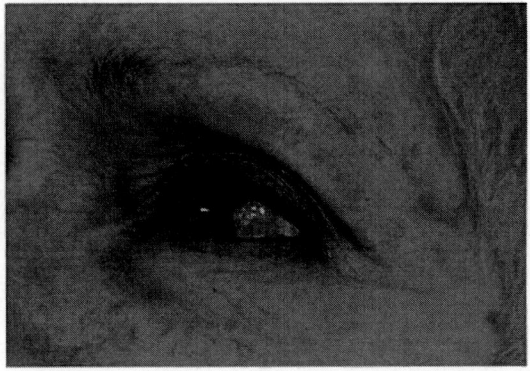

A number of things: firstly, the eye takes on a yellowish tinge. There's also a kind of build up of film on the eye that we need to take into account.

> *I was lucky in this instance – my source image and destination image (our project) were taken more or less at the same angle. If this isn't the case, you're probably going to have to make do with the Transform tool until you've got the perspective right.*

1. To get this right, cut the eye out of where it is, flip it around and shrink it so that it's more or less in the right place with the correct orientation. I used the Rectangular Marquee to select the piece I wanted (from my source image), then the Move tool to drag it across to our project (where it automatically becomes a new layer); then I flipped it (Image > Rotate > Flip Layer Horizontal) and used the Transform tool (CTRL+T) to resize it till I was happy that it fitted in properly.

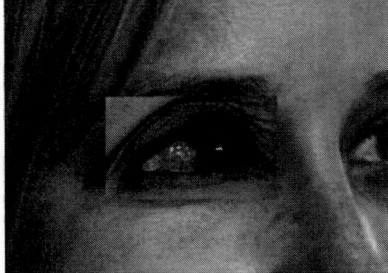

2. All we really want from this area is the white of the eye – or in this case, the *yellow*, so remove most of it using the Eraser tool once more.

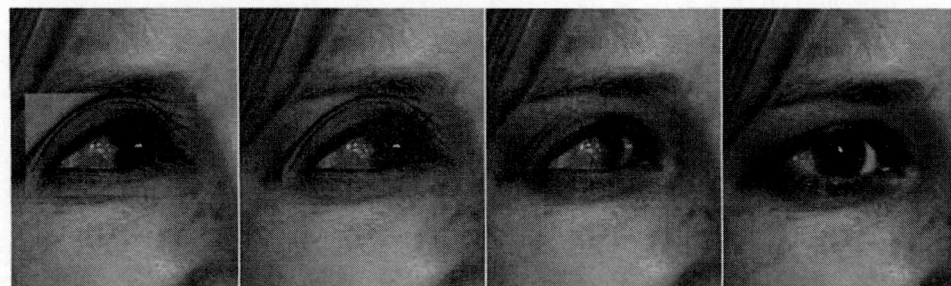

3. As you can see, all that actually remains from the source piece is the white of the eye on the left hand side of the pupil – I erased everything else around it from our source piece and just left that.

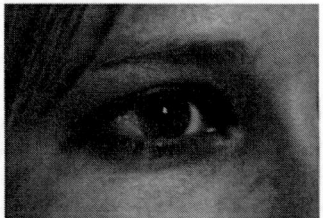

I ended up keeping a little piece of skin on the left of the eye too – a small fold that looked realistic to me. I called this layer left eye when I as done with it. Once again, a fairly subtle and therefore realistic change. We might need to address the right hand side of the eye, but let's move on for the time being.

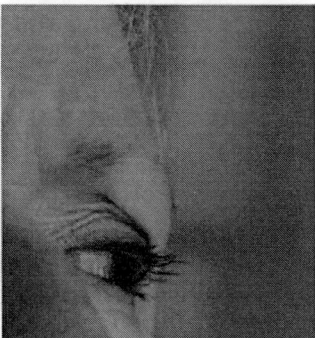

Here are some great wrinkles we can use for the right eye.

4. In exactly the same manner, cut and paste the area above the eye (source photo is oldEyes2.jpg on the CD) onto a new layer, then erase the bits around it:

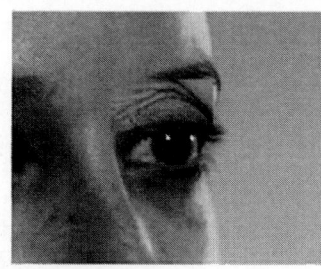

> *Because I shrank this piece to the right size (using the Transform tool), it was just a matter of using the eraser to blend it in properly.*

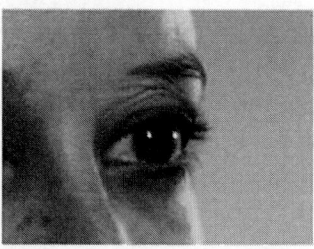

5. Use the Marquee tool on the source image and borrow wrinkles from just above the eye. Using the Move tool, drag this selected area from the source and drop it onto our project. Have the top layer of the project selected when you do this so that the piece we've stolen appears in a new layer at the top of the layer order.

6. Use your Move tool again to position the piece in the right place. Once done, you might need to resize the piece with CTRL+T, if it's too large or small to match the project appropriately. With this done, change the blending mode to Darken (if the piece you've pasted stands out too much) and use that Eraser tool (with a soft-edged brush) to blend the edges of the new piece in with the project beneath it.

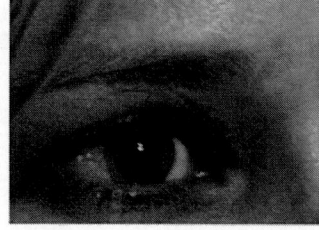

Skin consistency - forehead

We've been quite lucky with the skin in this project. Sometimes the difference in the skin tones is so great that you have to use a Hue/Saturation adjustment, or a different blending mode on the pasted piece in order to get things to match up. We're going for blotchy, but we're also going for realism. Take a step back: if you think the hues of the new piece and the project are too different, try adjusting the hue or changing the blending mode (I usually cycle through all of them to see what will work best).

Having finished the eyes, we need to move on upwards to the forehead. How about a nice wrinkle in this area? We could add lots of wrinkles here, but one should be enough. The person isn't frowning in the photograph, so introducing too many forehead wrinkles might be a tad unnatural.

Here's the image I used for the study, on the CD-ROM as `oldForehead.jpg`:

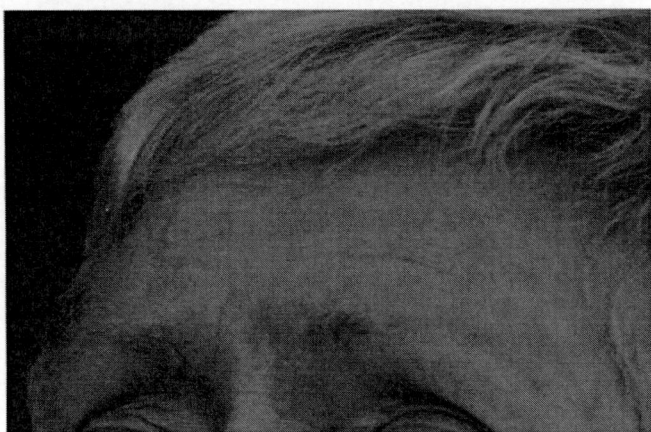

1. Not much in the way of wrinkles are there, so cut and paste the larger wrinkle on the right, then erase the edges.

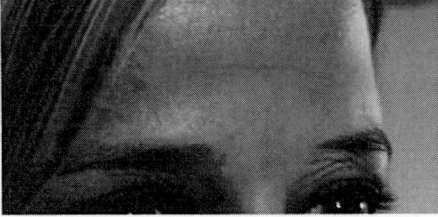

2. For this layer, use a Darken blending mode once more just to make things look more natural. The source image is quite light, using Darken means we get to blend this piece in better with our project.

3. Duplicate this layer, flip it around and shave some of it off to use as a wrinkle for the nose:

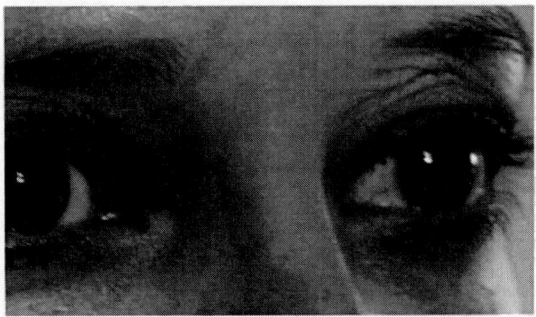

One major thing is bothering me. We've increased the sagging in the left cheek, but the skin in this region is really smooth.

4. To fix this, copy and paste from the original mouth study image, oldMouth.jpg:

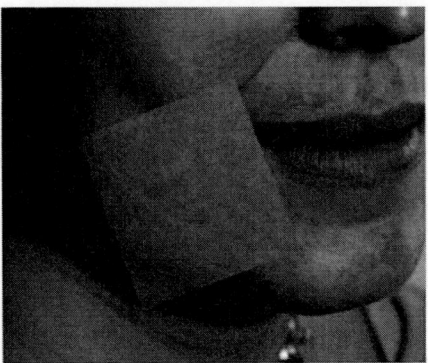

5. Use a Luminosity blending mode this time, since the tone is a little bit too off to just erase around the edges and be done.

Using the Darken blending mode doesn't work that well in this case as we're blending over a rather dark area. I first tried Darken but found that I lost almost all of the texture – which is what we're going for. This blending mode works well in this instance as the tone (light and dark) matches well, and we still get the texture coming through. So which blending mode do you use when? That's always a tough one. There are sometimes preferred blending modes to use in certain instances, but I find that it's always good to cycle through them all – it only takes a few seconds, and often you'll find a blending mode that works a lot better than the one you thought you needed to use. Overlay and Soft Light are often like this – I often think I want to use the Overlay blending mode, but Soft Light (which is actually very similar) sometimes gives me a softer effect which works better for the particular image I'm working on.

By this stage, we've covered so many blending modes in this book, that you will by now have a much better understanding of the effects each can have on a face!

In this instance, Luminosity works nicely to blend in with the skin tone, and once the edges have been erased, things look quite realistic:

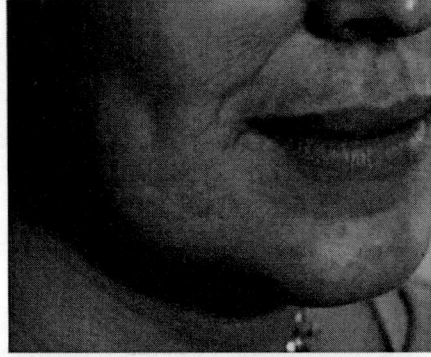

6. While in the area, we need to address the region just above the mouth – way too youthful still. Cut a piece from the original mouth study:

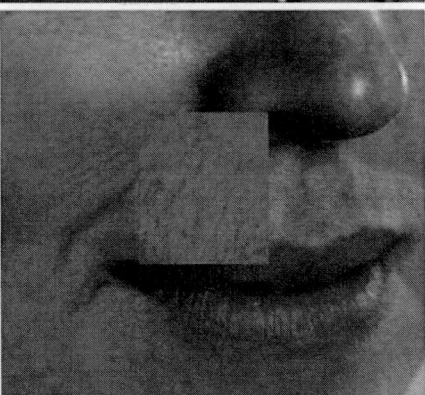

7. The Eraser tool will once again help you blend things in. Again, the effect is pretty subtle, but remember we're going for believable, not *creature from the black lagoon*....

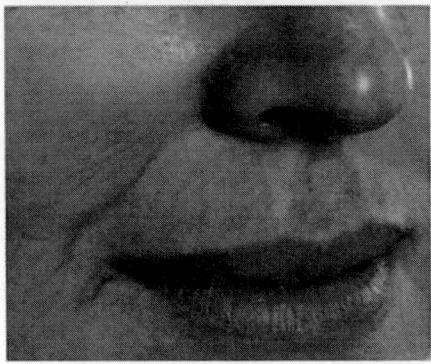

It's amazing how one thing just sparks everything else off. The area to the left of the left eye, and the region just underneath it bother me a little, up until this point. The area is just too smooth:

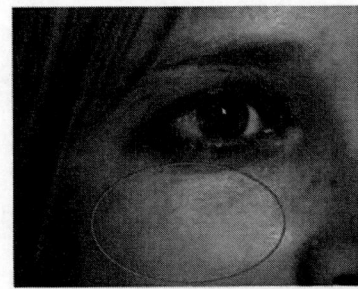

8. Once again borrowing from our eye study image (oldEyes.jpg), remedie the situation.

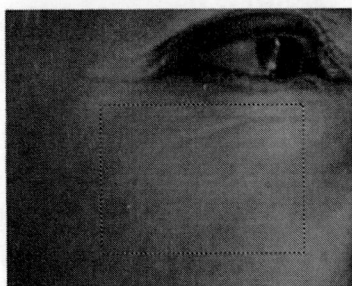

As you can see, we are applying the same methodology over and over again: sampling from our source image using the Marquee and Move tools, adding the piece to our project and then using the Eraser tool and blending mode change to make the new piece look natural.

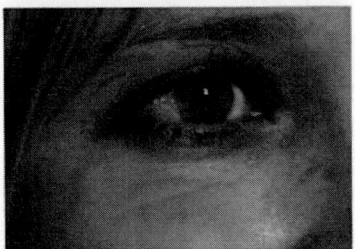

When I first applied this patch, I was a bit worried that it didn't fit in that well. In this instance however, I left things as is. I kind of liked the way the skin looked bloated/blotchy. I could use a blending mode to drop this patch in more naturally, but this doesn't seem necessary in this case.

Remember, all we're really doing at this point is borrowing material from our study images, and blending it into the project on separate layers. This isn't a particularly difficult task, but the important thing to keep in mind at this point is a sense of balance. Don't over-do one area and underdo another. People's faces tend to age fairly uniformly. Yes the skin gets unevenly discolored, but on the whole wrinkles appear over the entire face: if you've been a sun worshipper, you're bound for prunedom, if not, you're probably just going to get crow's feet and some mouth ley-lines.

Performing this part of the project is very much like painting in dabs. Apply a change, and then see what else needs to be done...

9. With this in mind, finish off the right-hand side of the left eye, which has been far too white:

    To do this, just went go and drag in more source material (from the same image), in the same way that we did before when handling the left region of this eye.

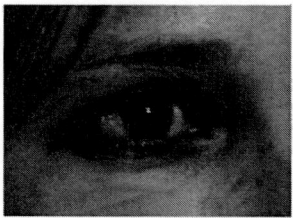

Finishing touches

When you're working on this kind of project, it's vital to constantly take a step back. Try and critically assess the image yourself. If someone told you this was a picture of an older person, what would give it away?

The *eyebrows*. This was the first thing that jumped out at me when I asked myself this question. Old people still have eyebrows; they just have much finer hair, and less of it.

1. To remove most of the eyebrows, use the Clone Stamp tool with a low opacity (20%) brush. Borrow the area just above the eyebrows and stamp this over the top of them. Because the brush is a fairly low opacity, they don't disappear completely; they just get a bit smothered:

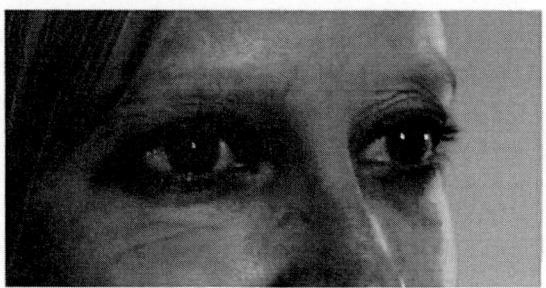

2. One final touch up to perform is addressing the line of the mouth. I use the same technique for obtaining source material as before. Because of the relaxing of the skin, the line of the lip wouldn't be so hard, so just borrow from our original mouth study image and fix this problem. I actually use a Normal blending mode on this one as the color and contrast of the skin match really well. Obviously, again I need to flip the borrowed image horizontally.

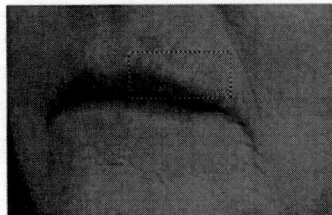 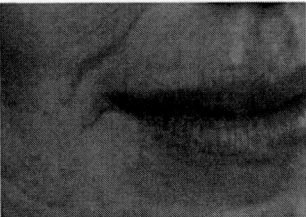

The Hair

Time to get cracking on the hair.

1. The first thing we need to do is select the hair using the Selection Brush tool.

2. Once done, copy the hair to a new layer and desaturate it using a Hue/Saturation adjustment (Enhance > Adjust Color > Hue/Saturation).

A little bit too harsh, don't you think?

3. To fix this, duplicate this layer, apply a slight Gaussian Blur to it (with a Radius of around 5-10), and then change the blending mode to Screen. Using screen means the light areas become lighter and the dark areas on the layer you're using to blend with (in this case, our duplicated hair layer) are discarded. So most of the gray stays the same, except for the light areas which become a lot lighter. This is useful to us because even people with whitish hair have darker grayer areas underneath.

4. As you can see, I've left a little bit of color in the hair here and there. Making it too uniform would be a little bit unrealistic, in my opinion. I achieve this by using a soft-edged Eraser on the edges of the gray hair layer – which means that some of the color of the original hair shine through from underneath. I could also not be so accurate with the Selection Brush and leave some of the hair unselected – but it's a lot easier to use the Eraser tool and you can at least see the effect taking shape. If I use the selection tool haphazardly, I won't see the effect at that point – because we were still selecting the area, so none of it will be gray at that stage!

More finishing touches

Hmmm. The eyebrows are looking a little bit underdone – perhaps we got a tad carried away with that Clone Stamp tool.

1. No problem. Just refer once more to our study (this time oldEyebrows.jpg) and borrow a few pieces of eyebrow:

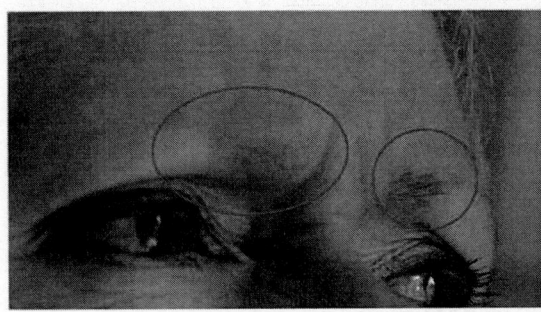

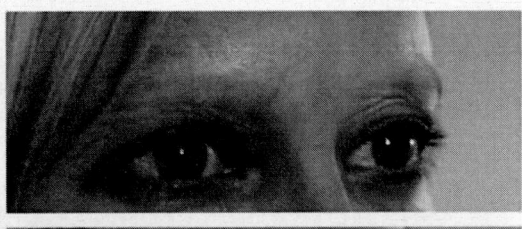

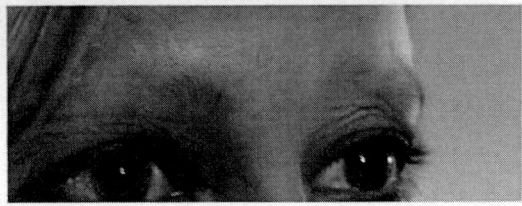

Taking a step back, the mouth is still looking a bit too youthful.

2. Add in more wrinkles just above the lips, by once again borrowing from the mouth study image and using the same procedure as in all the other adding of areas. This time, however, I stole a piece of the chin, rotated it 180 degrees and blended it in. No one will know when you're done!

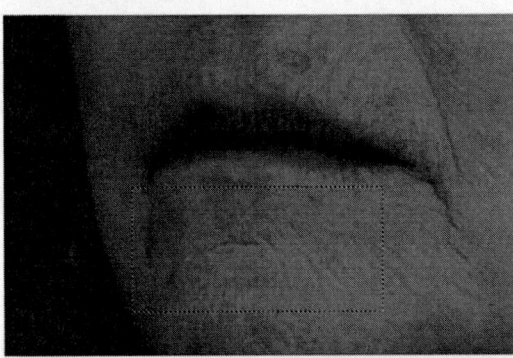

Much better! One last look around the image and I notice one really important thing. Old people do not really have shiny skin. The skin is rougher, and not as good a reflector of light.

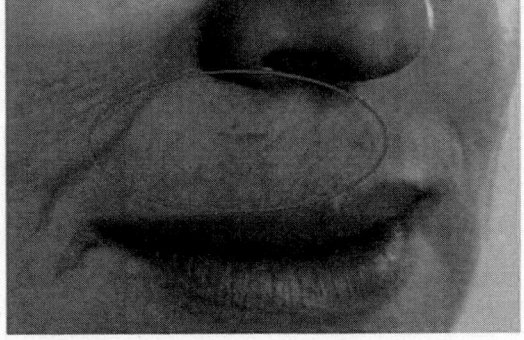

3. So, add another layer, using the Darken blending mode, and this time use the Airbrush (with a brush about the size of the pupil of the left eye) to just paint some matt skin over the shiny areas.

4. Use the Eyedropper tool to select a fairly average color (a color that to your mind represents an average of the skin tone for the whole image) and use this as your paint. Use the brush at fairly low opacity (15%) so you can apply the paint evenly and carefully.

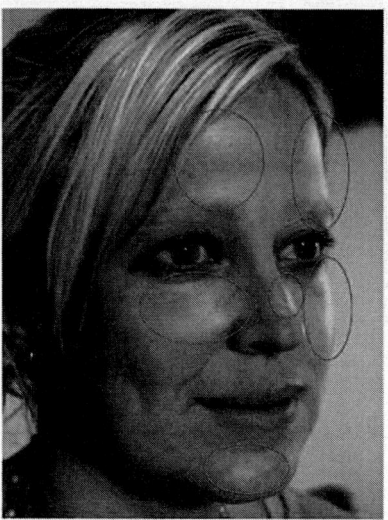

Well, Kirsten certainly looks a lot older:

> You can deconstruct my final PSD by opening it up from the CD-ROM; it's called `kirstenOld.psd`.

Further ideas

There are still a few areas that we could work on. Firstly, as you can see I haven't touched the neck. Necks often get wrinkles pretty much before any other area. This would need to be addressed. Secondly, the left cheek has lost quite a bit of texture, so we might want to fix that. Sometimes things don't go quite as planned and you will need to step back, critically assess the work you've done, and decide which (if any) areas need redoing. While we're at it, the right eye needs to be a bit duller. So who's going to fix all this?

Well, why don't *you* have a crack at it? All the files are available to you. Try a bit of cut and pasting yourself. When you're done, show someone the image and see if they believe this to be a 55-year-old woman. As you can see from the images below, you can go in either direction. In the first image, I used lighting and airbrushing to make Kirsten look really pretty (not much of a task as she's already really pretty!). I think you'll agree that the difference between the two images is certainly substantial. Have a look at `kirstenYoung.psd` on the CD to see how I created this glossy image.

Is this really the same person?

Photoshop Elements gives you the power to go in any direction you want with your photography. Tasks that would have been impossible (or at least very expensive) using traditional methods are now just a few hours away. The things you can achieve are virtually limitless with a little planning and a little time.

Chapter 7

Fantasy Faces

What we'll learn in this chapter

In this chapter, we leave reality behind and set out to create some truly stunning fantasy figures out of our faces. We'll show you how to turn ordinary people into fairies, witches, vampires, and more, giving each a thorough and out-of-this-world transformation that leaves no facial features untouched. Among the techniques we'll cover:

- Using the **Clone Stamp**, **Dodge** tool and more to create fantasy facial features.

- Creating other-worldly **lighting** and **layer blending** effects to complement our faces.

- Using the **Liquify** filter to **enhance** and **warp** facial features.

- Create **fairies**, **witches**, **devils**, **sirens** and **vampires** in no time at all.

From *Star Wars* to *Lord of the Rings*, the appetite for fantasy figures has gone through the roof. In this chapter, we're going to work over some of the most effective techniques for turning your photographs into fantasy masterpieces that wouldn't look out of place on any movie poster, or for that matter in any other world or mystic realm.

The techniques we're after are occasionally subtle, but always effective. Along the way, we're going to be touching on some techniques that the professionals use – so buckle yourself in!

Of course, **fantasy** is a pretty abstract concept, so we have to make sure we're focused on what we're doing. We have to find some kind of way to generate ideas for each picture.

You'll quickly realize, fantasy can be pretty much anything – it can be the abstract, the bizarre or even the unbelievable. It's a good idea to generate some kind of backstory to your picture in order to realize exactly what will be needed. If it's fantasy you want, you'd better start fantasizing!

If you're looking to create the complete composition, as well as focusing on the faces, it's a good idea to work on their environments too. Remember back in **Chapter 1** when we saw how the surroundings managed to alter the way we interpreted Elizabeth's cute (or was that mischievous) smile? To that end, we'll be adjusting the backgrounds of the images to help contribute towards the overall effect, and create a realistic setting for our fantasy characters.

Nalith – the fairy

Unlike previous tutorials, for this chapter we're going to be working with shots that I've thought a bit about beforehand. I had my intentions for the picture in mind when I took the photo, and also when I chose the model. What I've done here is make efforts to use a person who looks a bit like they might suit the role ... *Nalith the Fairy*.

On top of that, the subject is wearing distinctive eye make-up, and has brushed her hair in an interesting style so that her ears are showing a little. A white blouse seems like a good idea too, as this seemed to correspond with the classic vision of what a fairy might wear. So you see, it's not rocket science, and it's not Hollywood make-up design, but it's just employing a little thought *before* you get the image into Elements.

Preparation

By way of preparation, I've made up the following image for a background, which is created by various 3D elements layered on top of one another using different blending modes such as Screen and Multiply. The image is included with the source files, entitled nalithBackground.jpg.

1. First off, let's open nalith.jpg and put the figure on a new layer. We've visited various ways of doing this in previous chapters, so choose your weapon, select the head and body, and copy them to a higher level. If you can't make your mind up, I suggest just lassoing around her and clicking through Layer > New > Layer via Copy! Call the new layer nalith.

2. Copy the nalithBackground.jpg image and paste it onto a new layer in your new PSD. Alternatively, just drag the image from its window into your Nailith window and it will automatically paste in.

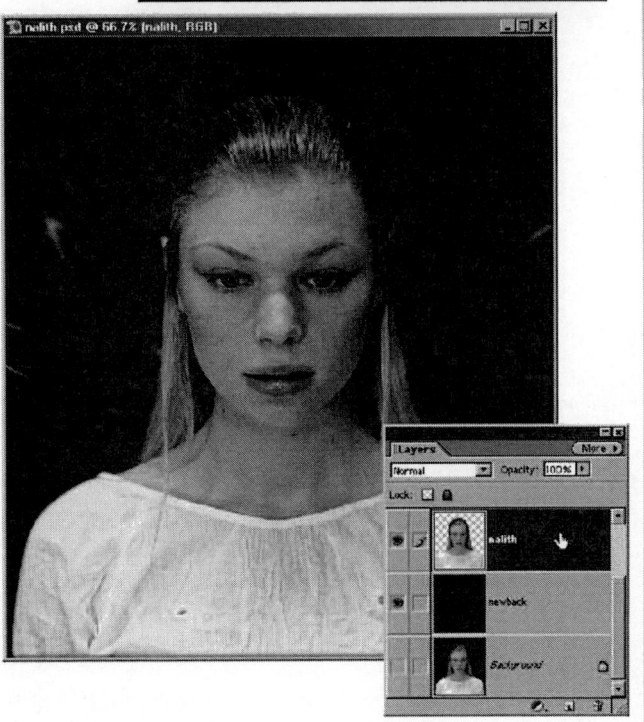

Retouching

OK, so this is no snapshot, but the photo's poor quality has given us a bad lighting and ugly grain. If you look at the original photo, she appears not to have a chin because there isn't enough light to cast a sufficient shadow. Fairies have a range of unique physical characteristics, but being chinless isn't one of them. So we have to make one!

1. Make a selection underneath her chin using the Lasso tool with a feather value equivalent to the rest of the photo's edges (about 4). Ensure Anti-aliased is checked. The selection should cover about half of her neck so we have enough space on which to add shadows.

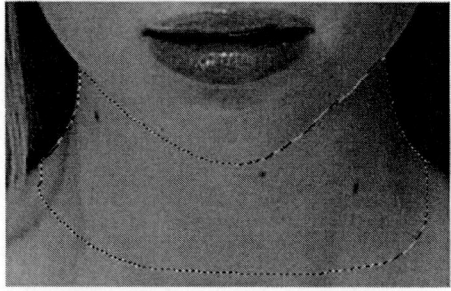

2. Create a new layer (CTRL+SHIFT+N) and call it chin shadow. Select a dark matching shadow color from a suitable area of her skin with the Eyedropper tool – I selected from her cheek/jaw on the right half of the image.

3. Select the Brush tool with quite a large brush with hardness set to 0, and between 10% and 30% opacity.

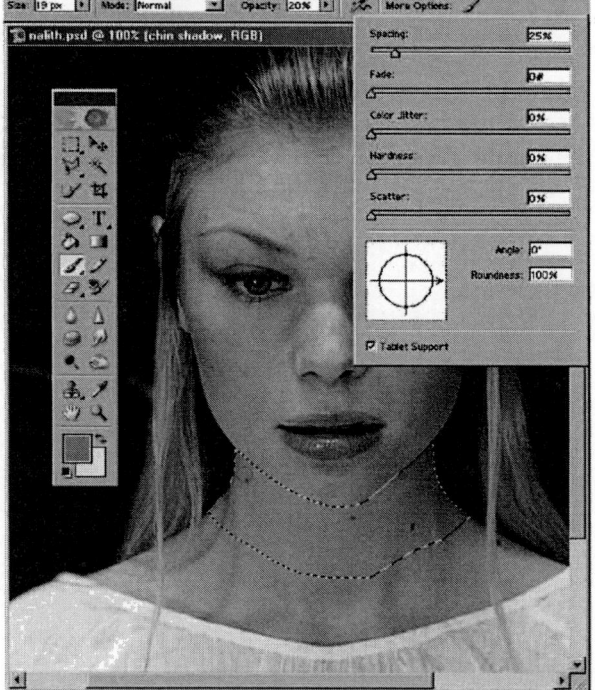

4. The best way to go about this is to brush quite intensely near her chin, and ease off further down to create a realistic fade. Finally, select a layer blending mode of Multiply to help the shadow blend more seamlessly with her skin.

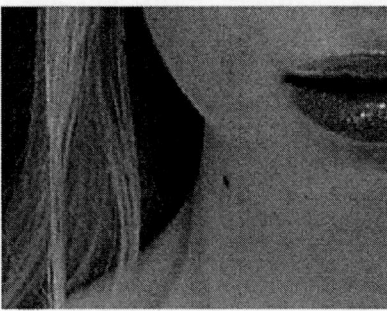 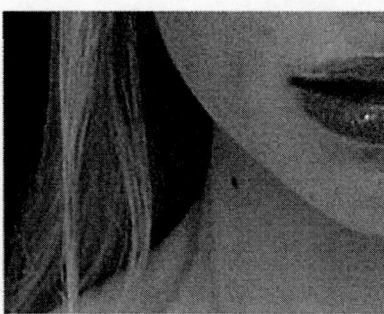

Now we've sorted that out, we need to give her some supermodel skin like the images in glossy magazines.

5. With the Clone Stamp tool, select the areas of her skin that appear more clean/smooth and apply these to the areas that need improvement. You learned how to do this in **Retouching Photos**.

Pretend Nalith is going to be on the front cover of *Glamour* and be ruthless with every fickle imperfection!

6. To provide a little extra facial definition, create a new layer (contrast) and use the same techniques we used on her chin to add more contrast — apply to her cheekbones, neck and hair. Once again, use a Multiply blending mode.

7. Now we've darkened areas, the logical thing to do would be to bring some out into the light. To achieve this, create a new layer (highlight) and this time brush with a brighter color. When you've highlighted the areas you want to, apply a Screen blending mode in the Layers palette. This should bring those areas out a treat!

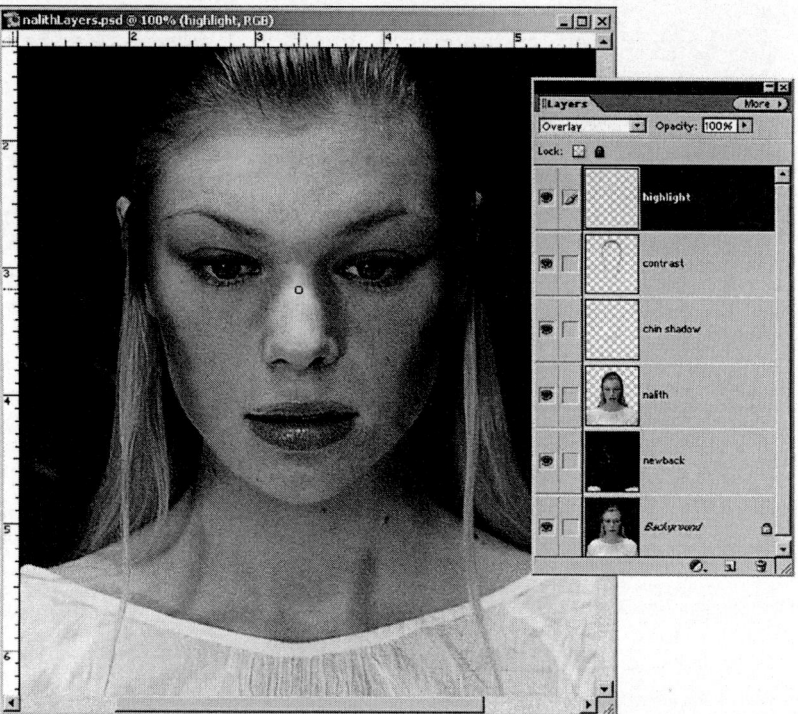

8. Finally, to give her that semi-shiny look, hide the background layer so the image becomes transparent. Next, choose the Select > All and Edit > Copy Merged menu options, and paste it at the top of the layer stack before switching the background layer back on. On the new merged layer, select Filter > Noise > Median with a radius of about 8.

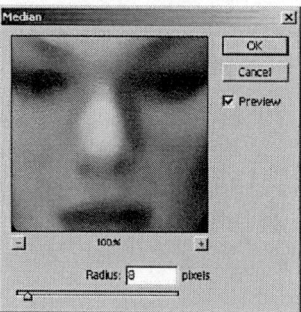

9. Next, apply a Soft Light blending mode and bring up the Hue/Saturation window (CTRL+U) to reduce the saturation to –60 so that it doesn't look too color burned.

10. You may be wanting to use Levels to perform this kind of skin-glowing task, but Median does a better job because it makes the skin look even smoother.

The four stages of facial retouching

Ears

Now it's time to turn our attention to the ears.

1. Choose the Lasso tool to make a selection for her sexy new ear shape. Make sure the selection overlaps the real ear so we can make a nice blend between them.

2. Create a new layer called ear fill, choose a color close to that of the existing ear and fill the selection.

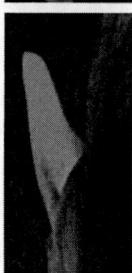

3. Next, copy a selection of skin from her face (from the nalith layer) and paste it on top of the ear fill as a new layer. Then, link it with the ear fill layer and group the layers via CTRL+G. This crops it to the required shape. Apply a Multiply blending mode for a subtle blend.

4. To finish off, use the Dodge tool to make the ear look more realistic – brushing the edges for lighting or holding down ALT for shading to give it a more beveled look. Once you are happy with the ear's appearance, merge the skin with the ear fill layer.

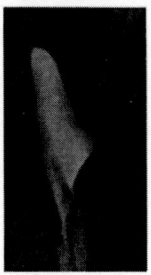

5. Fortunately, her other ear looks the same, so we can just copy the new ear extension and flip it horizontally before positioning it correctly. Now doesn't that look sweet!

Wings

Now, it's a fact that Photoshop Elements makes you want to fly before you can walk. Resist this! Before I started making the wings, I sat looking at the image for maybe an hour – planning on how to make fairy wings that are translucent, and of course how to make them look convincing.

First I created a base and added several textures and translucency effects before simply duplicating what I'd created. When I had finished with the wings I was laughing a bit, because it was easier than I had imagined it to be. I can now make wings! I'm sure the techniques and approach that I took will be replicated in some way in my future projects. Well, there we have it, a finished fairy! No, only joking … let's make those wings.

The base

The base is built up in almost the same way as the extended ear.

1. On a new layer (left wing base) create a shape for the left wing. I found using the Line tool is best for this delicate operation. You'll have to link all the eventual shape layers and press CTRL+E to Merge Linked. Make sure you create a closed shape, so you can fill it in with color (I chose beige).

The opacity should be fairly low so we can see through to the background.

2. In the Layer palette, drag them down to below the nalith layer. Repeat this action for all of the wings (left and lower left, right and lower right), so you end up with four layers:

Next, for each wing, we're going to create a gradient layer. Let's run through it once.

3. On left wing base, select all the beige with the Magic Wand tool. Create a new layer called left wing gradient.

4. Using the Gradient tool, create a white linear gradient (white to transparent) that starts near her back and fades off about a third in on the wing.

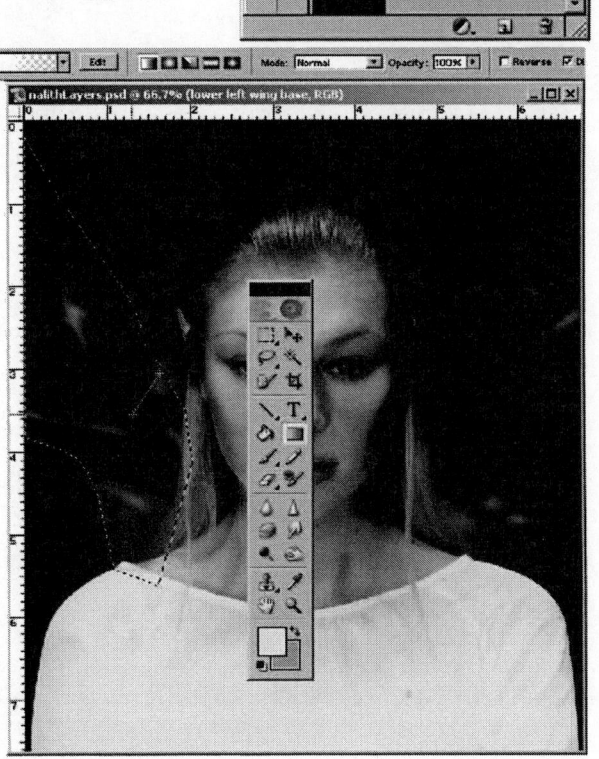

5. Give the gradient a Soft Light blending mode so that the wing is brighter close to her body and becomes darker towards the top, helping make the wing look as if it is slightly pointing backwards into the image.

6. Repeat for all wings.

7. To add more strength to the wing, select the Edit > Stroke option (while you're on each **base** level) with a Center Location on a few pixels (I've used 3) to give the wing an outline. This makes the wing look more contained and stronger for flying — even though we all know fairies fly off of pure magical energy, and according to studies their wings are just a distraction from keeping their secret of controlling energy!

The texture

The texture for the wing was a product of pure experimentation.

8. Create a new layer called wing lines, and make a pattern with a thin brush, adding random diagonal lines all over the wing. Then apply Filter > Distort > Wave to give the wing a more organic look and feel. You can, of course, play with the settings (this is a very versatile tool), but I used these:

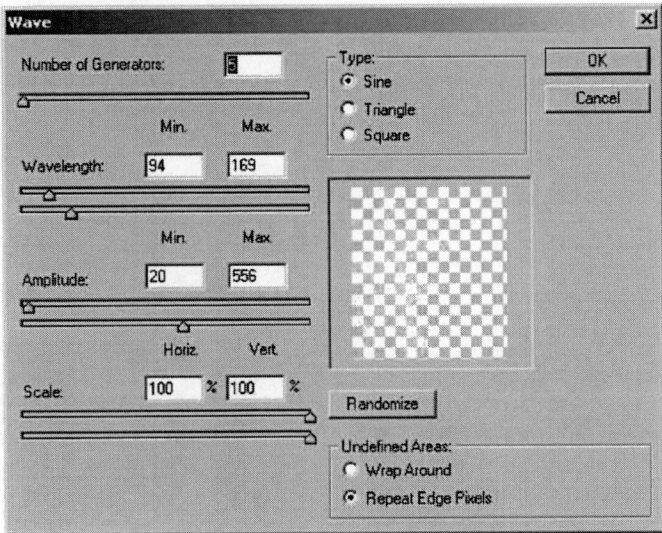

You can see the lines here, before and after the filter has been applied:

9. Keep the result of the texture inside of the wing canvas and erase where required using the Lasso tool. Blend it in using the Soft Light blending mode again.

10. For depth of effect, you may like to duplicate the texture several times and give each of them different opacity percentages and color hues, putting them on different areas within the wing canvas.

11. OK, so let's add a little more texture here. Use a brush to make random curvy patterns all over the wing. The overall effect suits the wing rather well. It's best to use an Overlay blending mode on this layer, to make it glow a little bit. Again, it's totally up to you, but to make the effect a little more subtle, I used a 30% Eraser tool on the lines, just to work them into the wing membrane.

   It would be brilliant to add a little translucency to the wings.

12. On the Layer palette, CTRL-CLICK on the base layer for each wing. This selects everything in that layer. Next, select the newback layer and apply a Gaussian Blur (Filter > Blur > Gaussian Blur). I used a strongish blur of about 10.

Final touches

1. On top of all the layers, create a new one and add a linear gradient in the bottom (white to transparent) to give the sense that she's glowing a little bit out of pure magic.

2. It's popular among fairies to use glowing makeup that attracts more attention to the eyes so, using the Brush tool with no hardness and full opacity, make a combination of dots next to her eye. Give them a glowing appearance using an Overlay blending mode. Put the additional makeup on the other eye by duplicating it and flipping it horizontally. Personally, I decided to put 40% opacity on the left-hand side and 30% opacity on the right, since her face is slightly darker on that side.

3. At this stage, I wanted to see a little bit more glow in the whole image. I merged the image into a new layer called diffuse glow (Select > All then Edit > Copy Merged before pasting on top of the layer stack), and then applied a Diffuse Glow (Filter > Distort > Diffuse Glow) with a Graininess factor of 0, Glow Amount of 2, and Clear Amount of 6. Finally, I set the opacity for the layer to 15%.

Focal depth

Lastly is a variation on the technique used in the chapter **Freaky Faces**. We're going to do fake the depth perception a little bit by erasing Blur.

1. First, duplicate the diffuse glow layer and then apply a Gaussian Blur with a factor of 9. Using the Eraser tool with a low opacity brush (about 20%), start erasing the areas in the image you want to keep sharp and in focus.

> *Personally, I tend to use a fairly short focal depth because it makes the image more interesting. This helps to more easily emphasize where I want the view focused and which areas are more or less important.*

I also wanted her eyes, and most of the face to look sharper. The upper wings are supposed to be pointing a bit backwards, so I didn't erase the Gaussian Blur further out on the wings because they are further into the image (less in focus). I divided the image into five depths:

Foreground – for the glowing energy balls which we'll add in a moment
Middleground – her face
1st set of wings
2nd set of wings
Actual background – least focus

2. The final touch is to add some glowing magic balls, which will surround Nalith. They were simply achieved by distributing several white dots of varying sizes using the Brush tool in a new layer. I then simply applied an Outer Glow layer effect with a slight red tinge.

And there we have the finished portrait. Talk about someone whose beauty is out of this world. Now go find some friends or family to experiment on!

> *As ever, our PSD file on our special CD-ROM. You'll find it in the* ***Fantasy*** *folder, entitled* `nalithFairy.psd`*!*

Délonia – the siren

I'm still unsure what Délonia is, but that furry coat makes me think of a bird; I think she'd definitely pass as some sort of **siren**.

You can find Delonia's original portrait on the CD-ROM.

Retouching

To begin retouching the image, we need to paste her onto a new layer. With that hair, I must admit, this is a bit of a chore, but follow this advice, and you'll be grand:

1. Use the Selection Brush to select her face and shoulders, leaving only that troublesome blonde hair.

2. Then, pick the Magic Wand tool and set its Tolerance level to around 10. Make sure Contiguous is unchecked so that *all* instances of the color are selected – not just the color immediately adjacent to your clicking point.

3. Holding down the SHIFT key, select her hair, tone by tone, until the whole barnet is surrounded by a crawling marquee.

> *Note – if you accidentally select a load of the background, just Undo until you've got back to a safer position.*

This took me about 10 minutes to achieve.

4. Create a new layer via copy (call it delonia).
Create another new layer *below* it, fill it with
white (Edit > Fill... > White), and call it white.

5. Now, start selecting the ugly areas and edges (containing grain and elements that you couldn't
select) with the Lasso tool, and then fill them with white. Where the hair is still blocky and
pixilated, use the Dodge tool to burn out the hair to blend with the white, making the edges
less prominent.

6. Add a Radial Gradient (white to transparent) on a new fill
layer to create a sense of depth in the image.

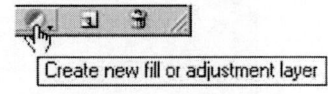

Create new fill or adjustment layer

*Now we're going to change a few colors. We'll do this
by adding adjustment layers. To find the color you want
is very much a process of experimentation, and I tend
to add lots of them and change them until I'm happy
with the result.*

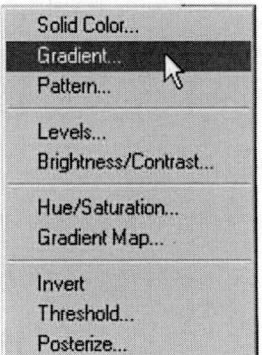

Solid Color...
Gradient...
Pattern...

Levels...
Brightness/Contrast...

Hue/Saturation...
Gradient Map...

Invert
Threshold...
Posterize...

7. Using the New Adjustment Layer button again, add a Hue/Saturation layer. In the reds, set the Hue to −20. In the yellows, set it to −40. Then, create a new Levels adjustment layer, and set it to the following:

Of course, it's up to you what sort of tint you're after, but that about suits me.

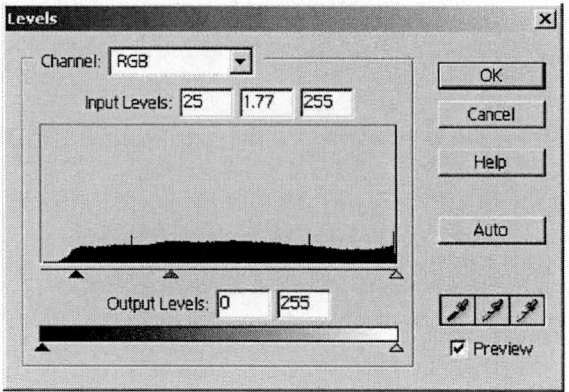

8. While we're at it, delete the shoulders with the Eraser tool, and be careful to go easy around the neck area to help create a nice tone.

9. Delonia's skin doesn't need much retouching since the lighting was rather good from the beginning. However, you might want to do some cloning with the Clone Stamp tool, as we did with Nalith, applying the finer areas of her skin to where the less fine areas are.

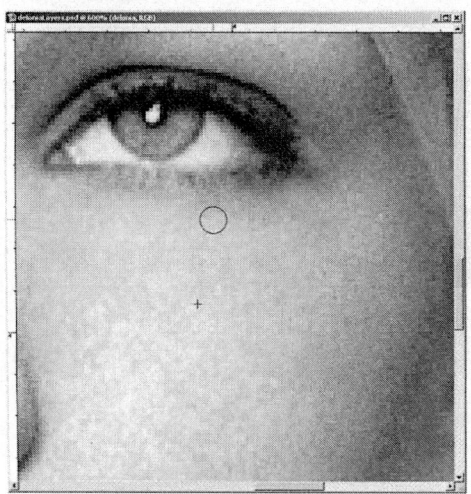

Fur Coat

The next step is to create her furry coat – imitation of course!

10. Start by creating a new layer (coat) and making a selection with the Lasso tool for the base, and then click through the Filter > Render > Clouds menu option to get some texture.

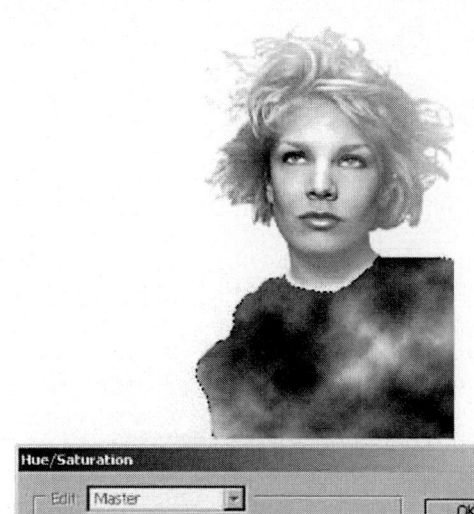

11. Press CTRL+U to open the Hue/Saturation dialog. Colorize the coat to a suitable pink:

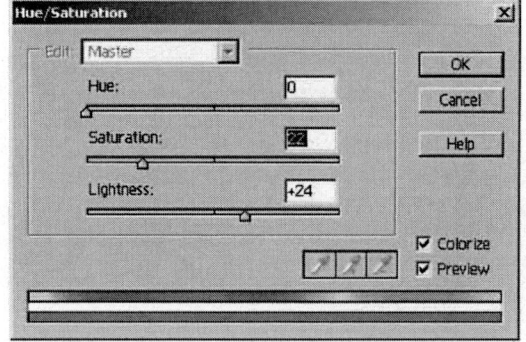

12. A few delicate deletes around the edges, and then a few brushstrokes across the shoulders should turn that blocky outline into something more tactile. In addition, try using the Smudge tool to create an extra furry outline!

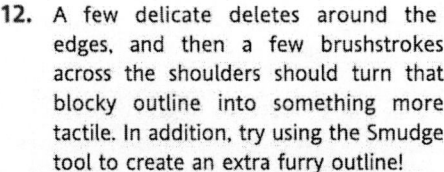

As you can see, we're wading through these tools, but as you've found in this book, even the most complex and amazing effects can be achieved with the right combination of tools and a bit of imagination!

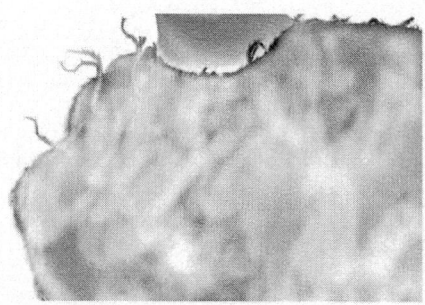

13. Next, with a number of different brushes of a number of different sizes, work up the texture on the coat to refine the effect some more:

14. Link all the adjustment layers together, and merge them so you have just the coat, delonia, white and Background layers. We're about to perform the masterstroke on Delonia's coat. Man, you'd want to buy this if you saw it in the local store!

15. Copy pieces of her actual hair, resize them, duplicate them and place them randomly over her body to create the fur. Simple eh? And so effective! It's a good idea to distribute the pieces we copy very randomly, and also flip or rotate them so it's less visible that it was taken from her hair. A careful going-over with the Clone Stamp tool will also improve the subtlety of the effect.

16. Finally, use the Eraser tool to remove any ugly edges that were copied across with the hair. What I chose to do was singe a few of the edges a little using the Dodge tool. It is also a good idea to put some hair behind her (on a new layer behind coat), so she looks like she is actually wearing the fur.

17. As a final final touch, I adjusted the Saturation of the image so that it had only a 50% value. This makes a little color difference between the coat and the hair.

Amazing huh? The things learned here have so many applications; I'll leave you to discover all the wondrous new tricks you can perform.

> *If you want to check your version against mine, the final PSD is available for inspection on the CD-ROM — it's called deloniaFur.psd! Zoom in on it and let us know at what % zoom the fur starts looking fake!*

OK, now I know what you're thinking – *"enough with the beauties, where's the monsters!?"*

Let's play Dr Frankenstein and create us a monster...

Dakar – the devilish fiend

With this image, I wanted to create an ugly, devilish being. Once again, I've just applied a little bit of thought to the picture before I took it: having him start off making that really ugly face made it all so much easier, while his hair and clothes enforce the whole look.

Hey, what do you mean I've got weird friends?

> It's important, and a great time-saver, to do as much as you can before taking the picture, saving Photoshop Elements for the truly impossible stuff. It's very easy to style your model's hair beforehand, but a little trickier to paint that hair on in Elements!

Here's what we want to end up with:

Our motivation here is to take one bad boy and just *emphasize* him a little into a genuinely *evil*, bad boy.

Now, I'm going to employ a little bit of cutting to the chase here – you'll need to prepare the image in exactly the same way as we did the others.

1. Open dakar.jpg and cut the image out on to a new layer (call it devil, and then create a black background for him called black). You'll have to be pretty careful around that hair, but it's defined enough to use the Selection Brush.

2. Next, it's time to add a bit of color. Make a selection encompassing all the exposed parts of skin – going deep into his hair roots to cover that area as well. Create a new adjustment layer and apply the coloring of your choice. I've used the following settings:

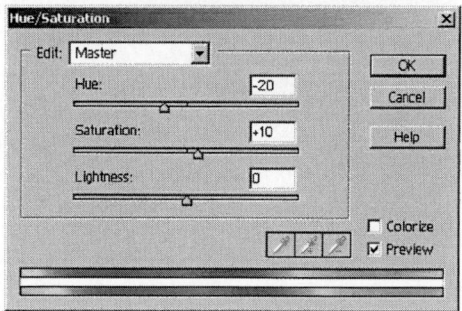

3. To make it smooth and to remove the sharp edges by his hair, simply erase smoothly from his hair towards his face, using a low opacity Eraser.

4. The rest should be easy now we've seen it in action with Nalith and Délonia. The most obvious changes are the ear, which we learned how to do with Nalith, and I removed his eyebrow using the Clone Stamp tool. You'll remember we did this in the earlier chapter on **Freaky Faces**.

   Next, if I say so myself, comes the moment of prime inspiration – that oddly spinal-looking construction down his throat, which is made up solely of Adam's Apples. Man, it shows you how wicked this guy must be if he swallowed three of the things!

5. All you have to do is, on the devil layer, lasso and copy the lump and a circumference of skin. Then simply paste it onto a new layer above devil and maneuver it into position. (Note you may have to switch off the Hue/Saturation layer to avoid moving that around). Use a soft Eraser to calm those edges down a little. See! Textbook Elements! Simple and effective!

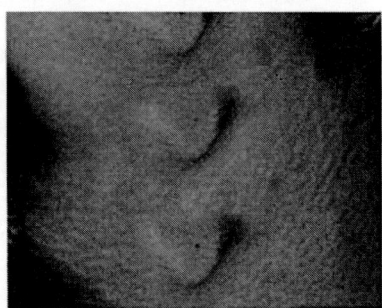

6. To create the sharp teeth, use the Lasso tool to select areas where you anticipate the gaps to be. Then, on a new layer (teeth gaps), use the Eyedropper and Fill tools to select the dark color inside his mouth before using it to fill the gaps.

To increase the nostril size, simple apply a bit of Clone Stamping on the devil layer.

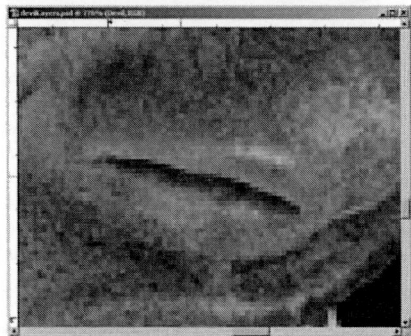

7. Of course, you can't pass up using an ace line like that defining his cheek, so on the devil layer, copy it, and paste it to its own layer (cheek line). Rotate, resize and move it to follow on from the existing line. As with the Adam's Apples, employ a soft Eraser to ease the obvious join.

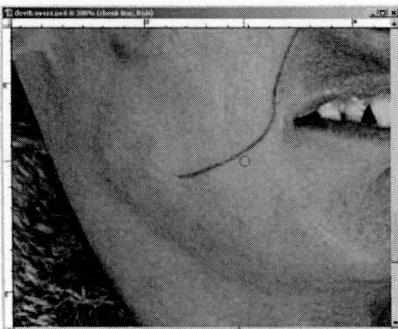

8.   Now it's down to nit-picking. Select all (CTRL+A) and Copy Merged (CTRL+SHIFT+C), before pasting onto a new layer. Set the layer's blending mode to Multiply, which just darkens everything up a little, and makes it look more sinister.

9.   To finish things off, tint his wide eye yellow (just with a low-opacity yellow paintbrush), and further seal his other eye with the Clone Stamp tool, by drawing a few flaps of skin over it to semi-seal it.

> *You can find our finished Dakar on the CD-ROM, called* `dakarFiend.psd`.

There we go, I think we have ourselves one bad fantasy dude! Enough to make Nailith and Delonia hide behind the sofa! Without bothering to wonder whether fairies and sirens have sofas, let's move on to make another bad boy, and this one's fangtastic...

Vampiel – the vampire leader

With this image, I had no idea of the outcome, except that I wanted to make a sort of **vampire**-like figure. This was just pure experimentation from layer to layer, which is something you'll learn to do more and more successfully the more you get comfortable with Elements.

...and here's what I ended up with:

I like to think it's got some kind of back story to it – there's certainly oodles of dramatic tension going on there – an idea which is harking back to what we did with the little girl's face in **Chapter 1**. We've added *context*. So, let's give this one a go

1. Open the image vampiel.jpg from the CD-ROM, duplicate the Background layer, and call the new layer vampiel.

2. Start by distorting the face using the Filter > Distort > Spherize menu option over the entire new layer, making it inflate. Set the palette options to create an inverse sphere:

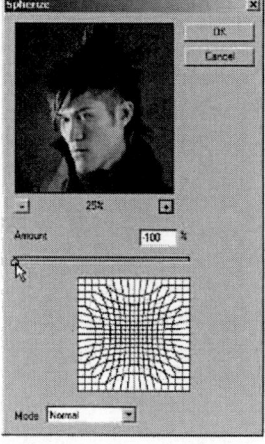

3. The face has grown some spikes and the chin is now pointing out a bit.

4. Through a little use of the Liquify filter and using the Warp tool, tweak the nose tip and make the eyebrow look a bit meaner.

5. To pursue the look in the eyes, simply use the Dodge tool to burn out the colors – giving them a very cold and intense look. The ear was done by ... well, you know by now!

6. Next, take the time to mask the face and put it on a new layer (vampiel2), and then introduce a black background, as we did in the previous examples.

7. To thunder it up a bit, add a Levels adjustment layer and set it to the following:

8. To alter the coloring, create a new layer and fill it with a color similar to that of Vampiel's eyes – a sort of yellowy green. Then, switch the layer's blending mode to Multiply. This should give Vampiel an unhealthy yellow tinge. Good for night vision!

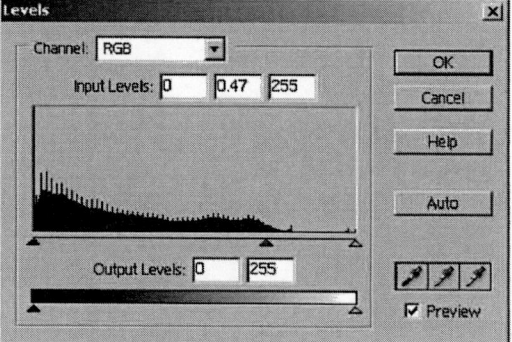

9. Create a Hue/Saturation adjustment layer and make the Hue +13. This should add a red, murderous feel to everything.

10. OK, let's flip the image horizontally to make it look like he's going out for the hunt rather than coming home for his supper (Image > Rotate > Flip Horizontal).

11. Once again, apply Filter > Distort > Spherize over the entire vampiel2 layer to make it inflate even more. Carefully delete any area of the coat that gives away our Spherize shenanigans, leaving his body in gloom.

12. Duplicate the figure, and paste it on a layer just above the background. A quick resize, a slight rotate and a Gaussian Blur create a little different character – a vampire brother.

> *You can look up* vampielTwins.psd *on the CD-ROM – just don't look at him the wrong way!*

Lothirade – the evil witch

Now we're going to look at a way of repurposing a picture with the utmost simplicity. Believe it or not, it's an *evil* remix of Nalith using simple edits to create a whole different character. There are no special techniques involved, so this will be relatively easy.

1. Our starting point is the image of **Nalith** without the distracting energy balls, and without wings. The source file is included, called lothiradeStart.psd, if you don't want to use your own.

2. Start by darkening the whole of Nalith's image using Levels. I used these settings:

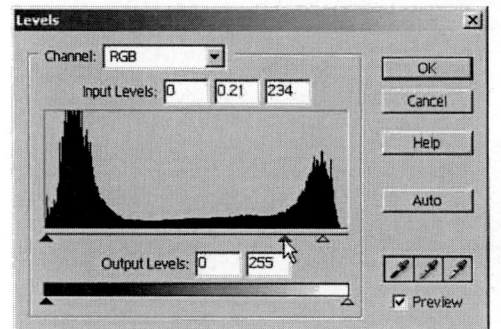
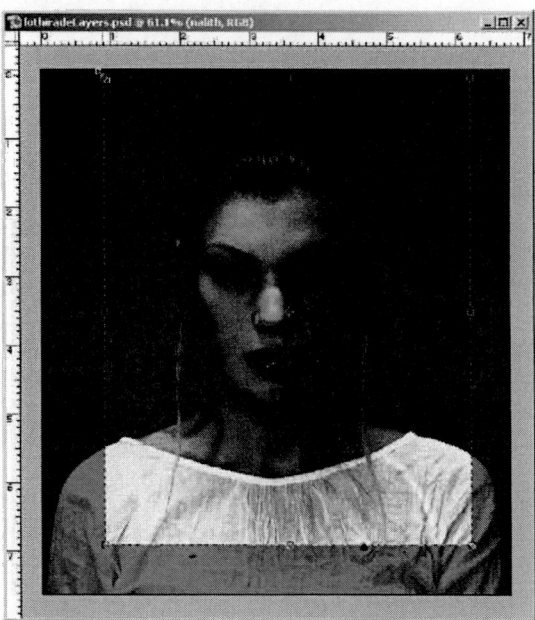

3. Next, crop the whole thing to focus a bit more on her face and apply Filter > Distort > Spherize to her head, using the familiar –100 setting. Maybe we could start calling the Spherize filter the *evil* filter, as it seems to do the trick for us every time!

4. To easily change the expressions in her face, use the Warp tool in Filter > Distort > Liquify... to do the following:

■ Drag the outsides of her eyebrows upwards:

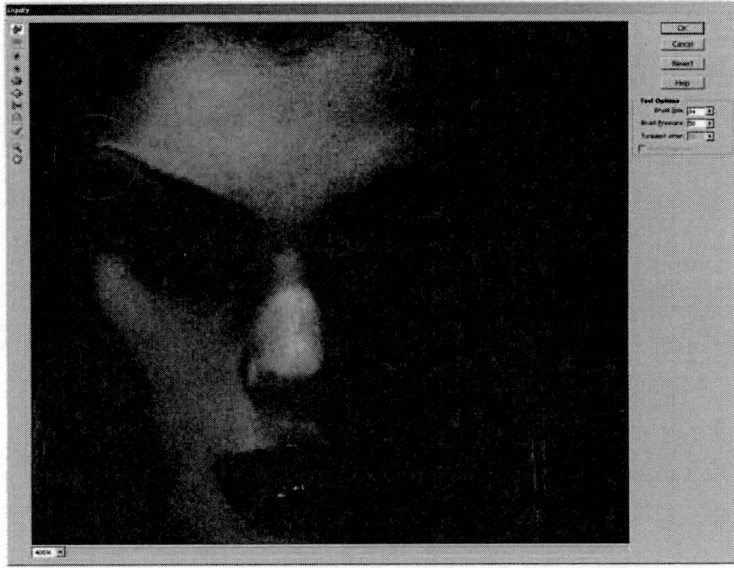

■ Push her brow down:

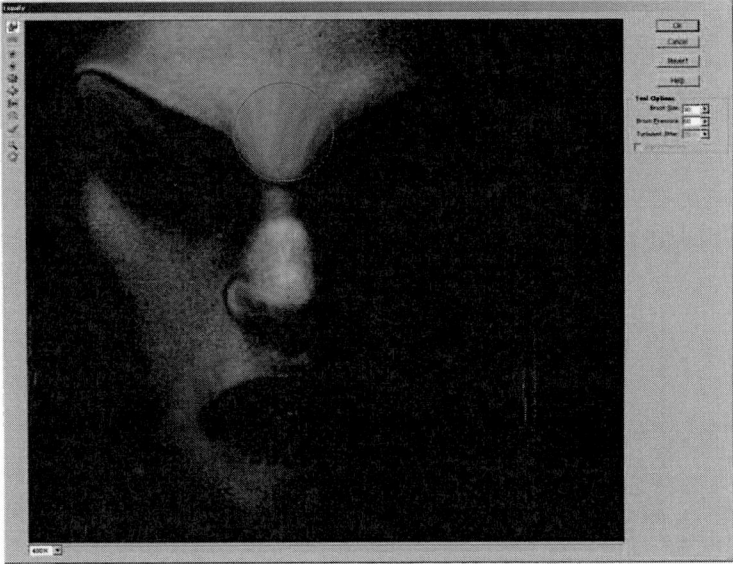

■ Make her nose pointy:

■ Give her mouth that sour look:

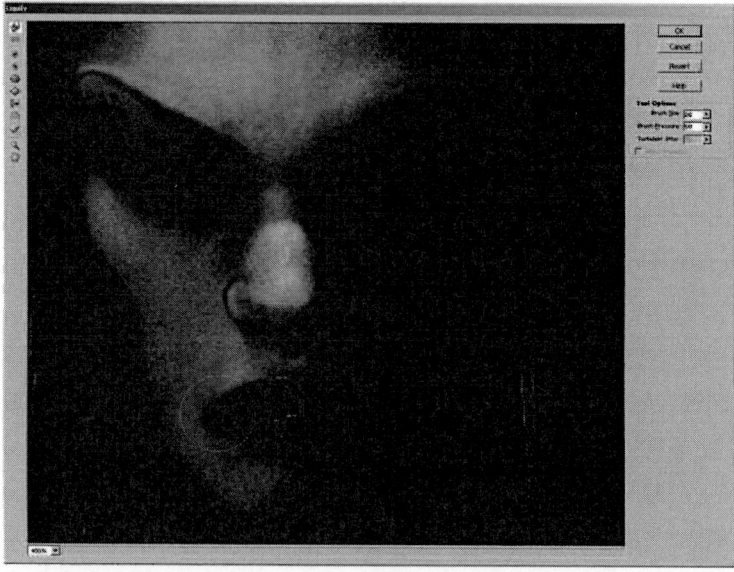

> *Now remember, Liquify may be a wondertool, but that doesn't mean you should shirk on being careful. You can mess things up very easily with a shoddy liquification!*

5. Additionally, gradually fill her eyes with black, using the paintbrush at a 10% opacity.

6. Next, select her face using the Lasso tool with a Feather value of 10 and paste it into a new layer (ghost) before applying the Screen blending mode. Using the Move tool, stretch the copy quite a bit towards the top right-hand corner to make it look as if it's her demonic soul flying out.

7. A motion blur should add the finishing touch.

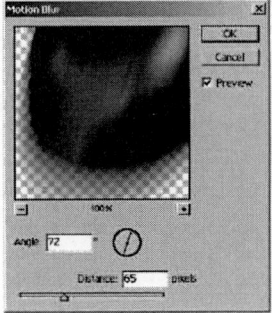

8. Paint a quick black mask on a new layer (black mask) to blot out that virginal looking blouse, and to add a little evil drama to the bottom of her face.

9. Finally, add a Hue/Saturation adjustment layer on top of everything, and reduce the saturation to around -50. You might also choose to add a greeny tinge by creating a new layer (tinge) and filling it with a greeny color, and applying a Multiply blending mode.

And there we have it – *Lothirade*. Nalith's sister, who didn't get the best bicycle and wasn't allowed to go out to play when she wanted.

That's how easy it can sometimes be when re-using material. Bear it in mind!

> `lothiradeWitch.psd` *on the CD-ROM has all the steps above, performed to perfection.*

Dæva – Enchanted!

For the next portrait, I wanted to give model Megan horns and distort her features somewhat. I also put some sticks in her hair. Sure, we could have spent a few hours doing this in Elements, but this is another example where a little preparation on the original photo can save you time in front of your computer!

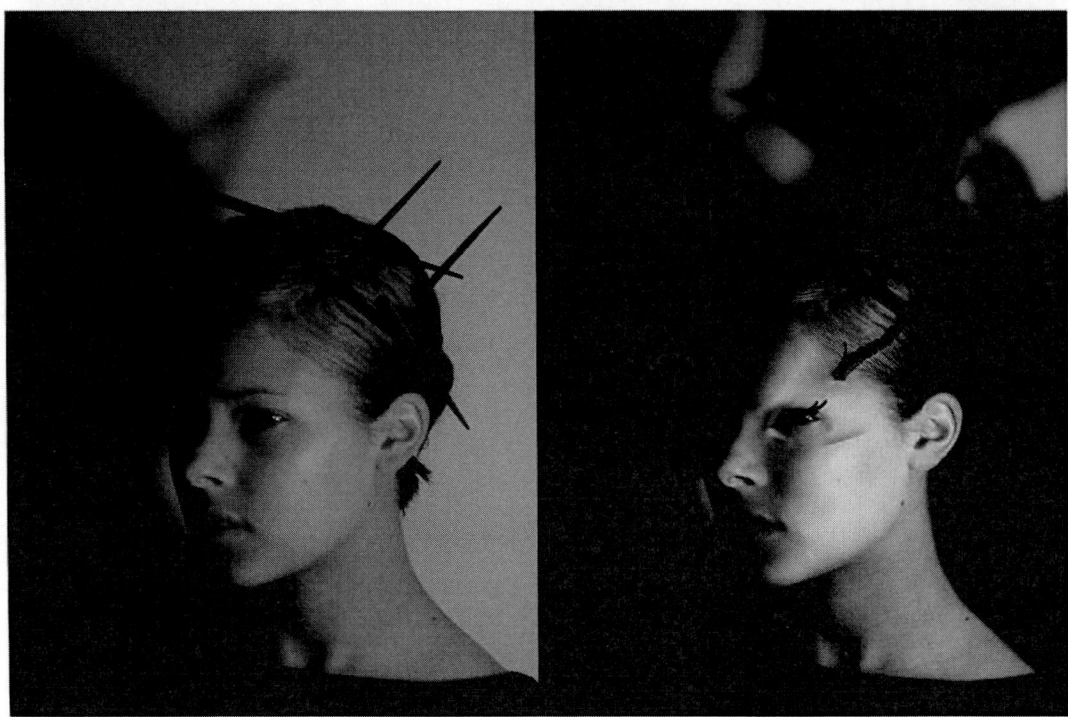

1. First off, after opening daeva.jpg, duplicating the layer and calling it daeva, add a Hue/Saturation layer and apply the following values:

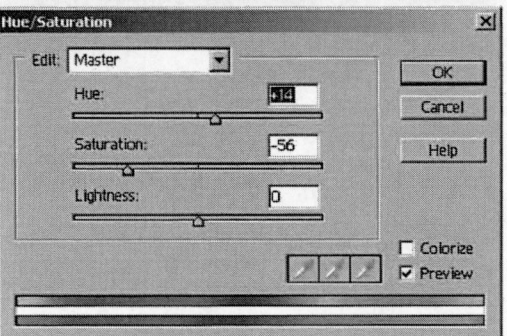

2. Next up, use the Color Burn tool to remove her teeth.

3. Now, let's have a go at her eyes. On a new layer (eye skin), using the Clone Stamp tool, copy parts from her face, place them on her eye, and then use the Eraser tool to remove any surplus parts.

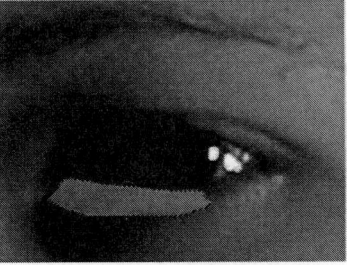

4. Then, using the Color Burn tool, darken areas to help the eye modifications blend more seamlessly into the rest of the face. This is a question of *feel*.

5. It's time to put something that looks freaky under her skin. Add a new layer, scar. I think it looks like an embedded needle, but I don't want to think about that too much. The basic technique is to make a selection with the Lasso tool, using as your first line the *exact* line you want the needle to go along. Then, clone some light skin right up to that line. Next, pick up the Inverse selection and clone dark skin along the top, all the way up to the line. Softly erase around the ugly edges, and you're laughing!

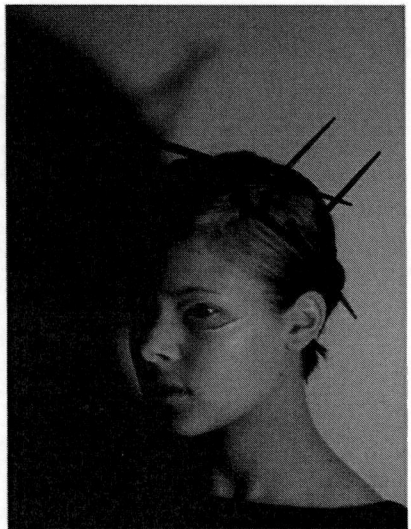

OK, so lets get busy implanting some horns in her head!

6. With the Lasso tool, draw the base shape of what you want the horn to look like, and paint it black.

7. Then, using the Brush, with the Airbrush box checked in the menu bar, brush in some highlights in white. Add some Noise through the Filter > Noise > Add Noise menu option. Add more highlights and darken to taste, using the Dodge tool as we did on the previous skin effects.

8. Another exciting texture can come out of the bag here – add a slight Craquelure to the horns through the Filter > Texture > Craquelure menu option.

9. When you're happy with the result, duplicate it, flip it horizontally and then distort it slightly using the Move tool before scaling it down. Finally, use the Image > Adjustments > Hue/Saturation menu option to make the horn darker by adjusting the Lightness setting.

10. Once you're happy with the look of the horn, it's time to make it look like it's coming out of the skin. Using the Clone Stamp tool, grab some parts of the face and started painting some skin over the horn. Using the Burn and Dodge tools, shade the skin.

11. Aw, go on then. Just to finish off, paint on some dramatic eyelashes using the Brush/Airbrush tool, not forgetting to add a couple of highlights to make them look cool! The Calligraphic brushes are best for this sort of thing, and I used the Flat 10 px brush.

It's now time to change the colors to give the image a more fantasy feel.

12. Again, using Color Balance, change the piece to a purple color, and add in a background containing a similar color. Reverting once again to the Airbrush and Dodge tools, continue to add further elements of light and dark to her face.

13. Try a new technique to add a little drama to the lighting. Add a Gradient Map adjustment layer, and select a black and white gradient to go over the top of the picture. Then set the layer blending mode to Overlay.

This should give you a moody sepia-toned picture, and the finale to a perfect effect. We're not quite sure what Daeva is, but she's sure got a past!

> *Check out our final PSD,* daevaHorns.psd, *on the CD-ROM.*

Summary

So, there you have it! We've made some pretty beautiful and some pretty horrendous creations! Did you notice how quickly we got on to the horrendous side...? Sorry about that. Still, I'm sure you'll have some delightful masterpieces cooking before you know it!

Hopefully, you'll have learned to raise your game, and think with a professional-level standard, while agreeing that it really doesn't take that much effort. It's all easy, if you've got the right ideas!

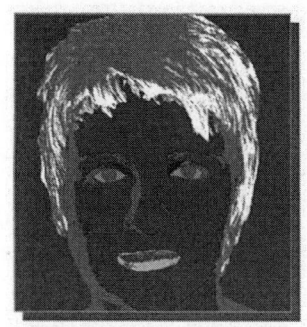
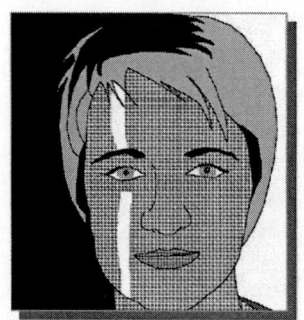
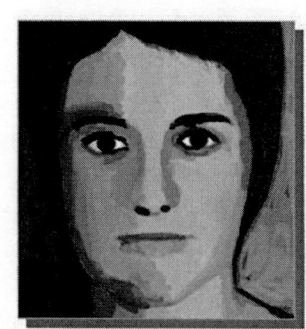

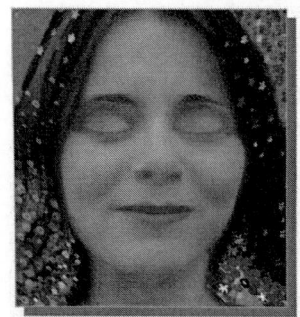

Chapter 8
Imitating Artists

What we'll learn in this chapter

By now we've covered most of the basics of face transformations in Photoshop Elements 2. It's now time to get a bit more artistic and draw some inspiration from some classical artists and art styles. From Andy Warhol to Van Gogh, this chapter will show you how to reproduce the familiar styles and unique flair of your favorite artists. We'll cover:

- Simple **layer** and **selection** techniques that can produce amazing effects in a snap.

- Creating **patterns** for overlays or backgrounds.

- **Stretching** faces and **smudging** the complexion to create the perfect forgery.

- Imitate **Warhol**, **Lichtenstein**, **Van Gogh**, **Klimt**, **Matisse**, **Modigliani**, and even **Manga**!

Imitation is the sincerest form of flattery. And, it makes things a whole lot easier when you're trying to take control of your image manipulation techniques! What better than to have a finished product before you begin? Seriously, it's a really useful tool to aspire to existing artistic styles, because you can gauge exactly how sensitive your Elements touch is becoming. Moreover, it's an excellent opportunity to create image gifts for cards and presents! It's a sure-fire winner to render your nearest and dearest into an *objet d'art*!

It would be amazing if we could modify a picture so that it looked like a Warhol or a Van Gogh. Then we'd really be able to see exactly how far digital art has come in the last 20 years. This book is about taking Elements to the limits, so let's not feel overwhelmed by the task ahead. Let's just do it.

We'll take a look at a single snapshot and attempt to work it into a convincing rendition of various artistic styles. It's the same snapshot used in **Chapter 1** when we had a quick whiz around the Impressionist brush. Now it's really time to imitate some other artists.

Jolly – painted by a dozen artists

At the behest of the model, I should point out that this snapshot was taken in a kitchen with a single fluorescent tube for lighting, the night after a very heavy party. This will ensure the maximum wow quality from our Photoshoppery.

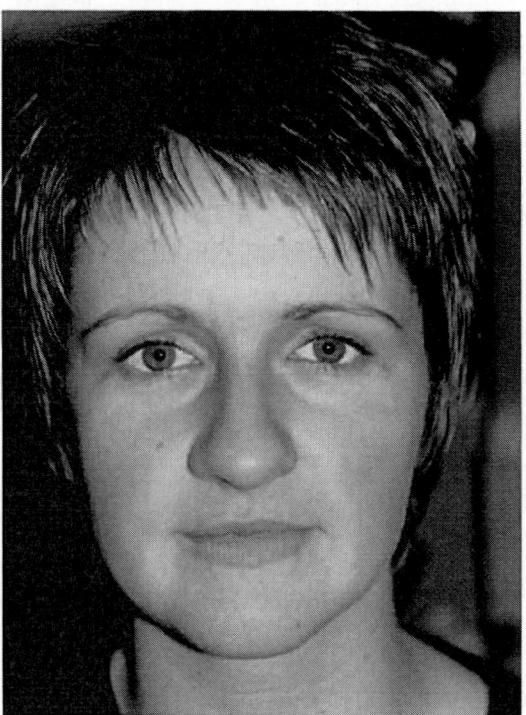

Pop goes the easel

A good style to begin with is **Pop Art**. The whole point of Pop Art was to create easily-copied and mass-producible images. It's not about excellence; it's all about image. Better still, it's about relatively easy things to do in Photoshop Elements. Flat colors, simple shapes – all things that are going to be easy for us to approach.

If you're unfamiliar with Andy Warhol and Roy Lichtenstein, I'm sure you're familiar with their pictures, as they are some of the most imitated around. Advertising uses them a lot – but the basic breakdown is: Warhol used Xeroxed photographs in psychedelic colors, and Lichtenstein created comic strip-like paintings, colored in with little dots.

Warhol

It's no surprise **Andy Warhol** is the easiest artist to mimic. He was all about convenience, which suits me down to the ground! It also means we're going to have to chuck subtlety out the window. We're on a production line here.

If you look at Warhol's most famous paintings (like his famous picture of Marilyn Monroe), you'll see that the photographs he uses are of very bad quality. They're newspaper snaps, basically, using the newspaper technology of the 1960s. That's the first thing we're going to have to mimic. It's black and white for a start – and I don't mean grayscale. BLACK or WHITE.

1. Open up `jolly.jpg` from the **Imitating Artists** folder on the CD-ROM.

2. To mimic the Marilyn picture, we're only interested in the head and face, so select all of the head and click through Layer > New > Layer via Copy. Call it Warhol. On this new layer, fill the background in with pure white using the Paint Bucket.

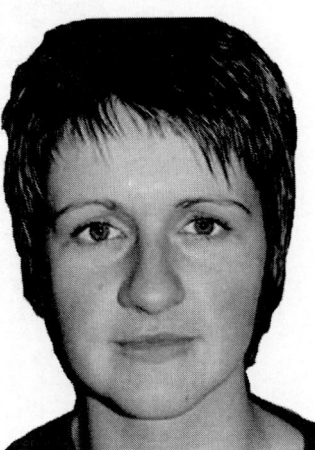

5. In your Layers palette, C<small>TRL</small>-click the right-hand icon (which has a black and white image of the threshold you've just created).

> *This will select everything in the layer. It's a handy tip for lots of occasions!*

6. Press C<small>TRL</small>+A<small>LT</small>+I, which will invert the selection. From the Warhol layer, create another Threshold adjustment layer, and fix the face's levels. I used 170.

Strangely enough, it gives the image that Warhol-hair look! The rest is easy – this is where we whack in the colors!

What we need to do is create a new layer for each color we're going to use. We will fill each layer with exactly the color we want, and then set its mode so that the black shows through.

7. Create a new layer and call it lips. With the Lasso tool, select around the lips and then choose the color you want to turn them into. I'd say scarlet is pretty much within Warhol's subtle palette!

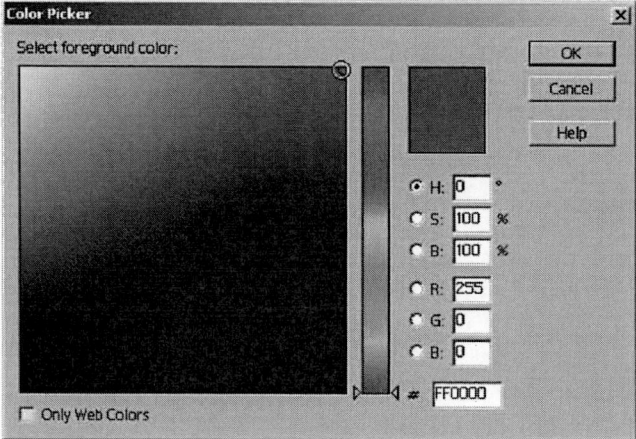

5. In your Layers palette, CTRL-click the right-hand icon (which has a black and white image of the threshold you've just created).

This will select everything in the layer. It's a handy tip for lots of occasions!

6. Press CTRL+ALT+I, which will invert the selection. From the Warhol layer, create another Threshold adjustment layer, and fix the face's levels. I used 170.

Strangely enough, it gives the image that Warhol-hair look! The rest is easy – this is where we whack in the colors!

What we need to do is create a new layer for each color we're going to use. We will fill each layer with exactly the color we want, and then set its mode so that the black shows through.

7. Create a new layer and call it lips. With the Lasso tool, select around the lips and then choose the color you want to turn them into. I'd say scarlet is pretty much within Warhol's subtle palette!

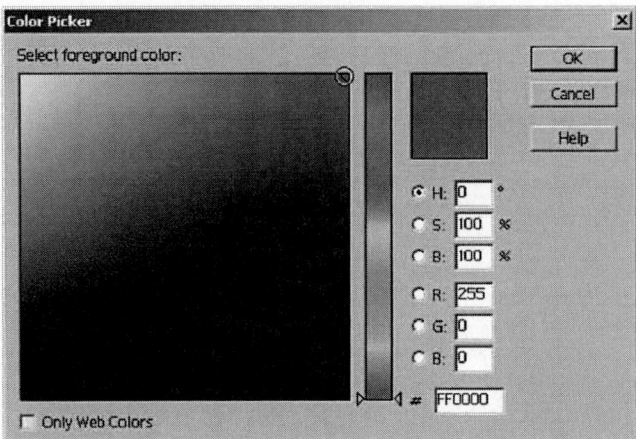

8. Click through Edit > Fill and fill the selection with the foreground color. Finally, set the blending mode of the lips layer to Multiply.

There we have it! Colored lips! You can adjust the potency of the red by messing around with the layer's Opacity setting.

A quick note: You may find, when you make selections like those for the skin, you end up overlapping colors on other levels. This makes for a very weird and unsatisfactory color mix. To get rid of this, use the technique of CTRL-Clicking on each Layer palette icon (to make a selection) and deleting away that selection from the skin layer.

9. The rest is just mechanical – move on to the eyelids, eyeballs, hair, face and background.

And, I'm ashamed to say, that's about it. But using that technique, you can create as many variations as you like!

Both of these variations are based on Warhol's own colors. His classic Marilyn image used something close to human tones – pink skin, yellow hair and so on. Later versions became a little more psychedelic, with even the black being replaced. You could try a few variations of your own, to see how random Warhol could get – or was he being very careful? You decide!

The final PSD for this effect in on the CD-ROM, and is called `jollyWarhol.psd`

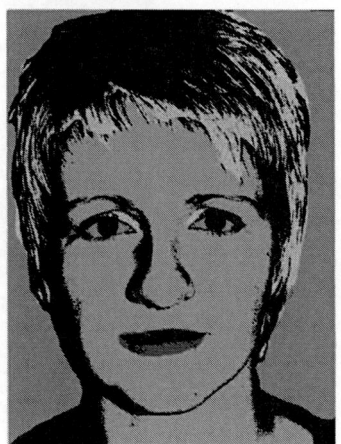

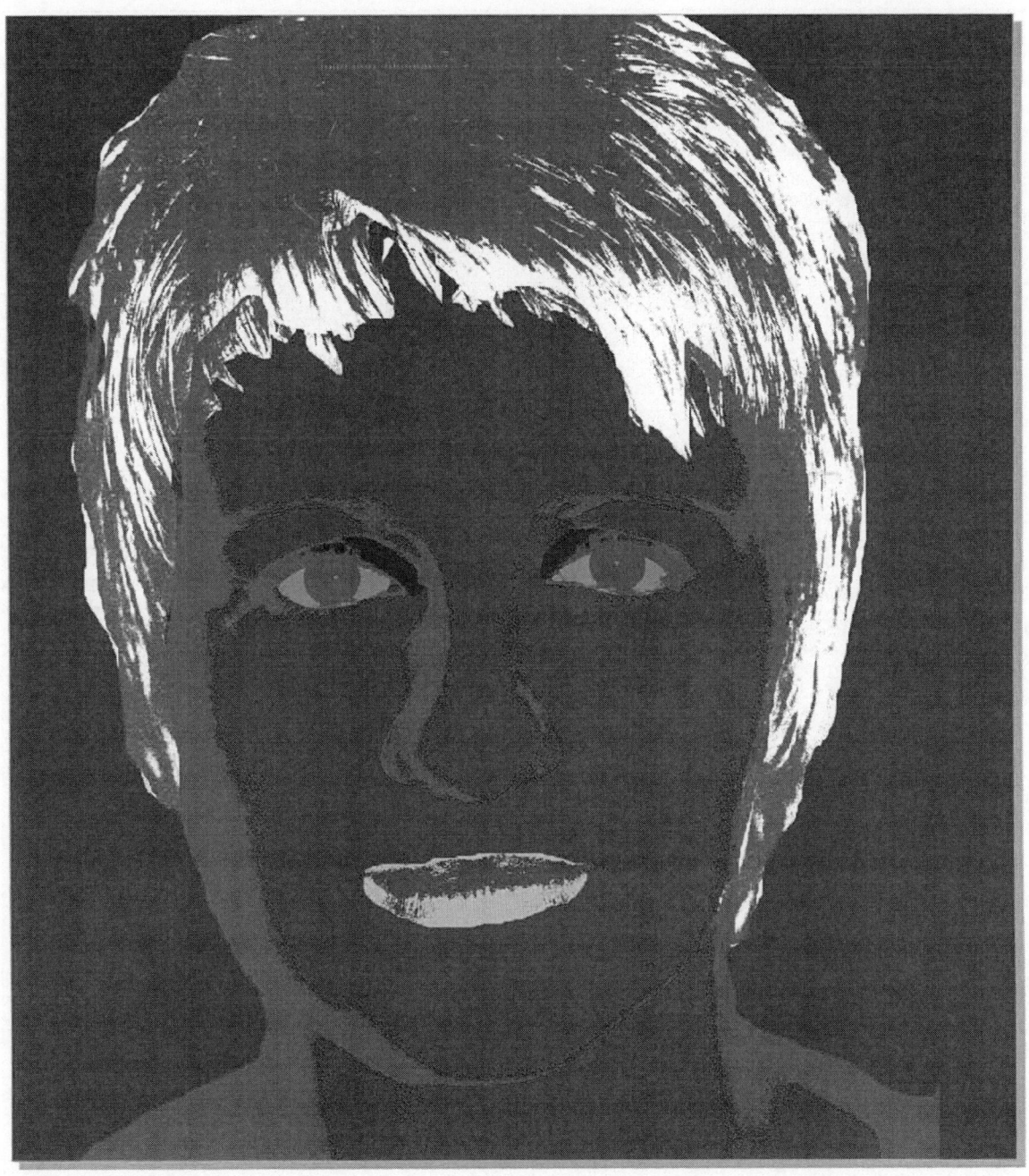

Chapter 8

Lichtenstein

OK, that was just too easy, and I don't feel like I've earned my fee yet. I tried explaining that I'm only contracted for 15 minutes of fame, but...

Let's move on to that other great icon of 1960s Pop Art, **Roy Lichtenstein**. Compared to Warhol, he seems a whole lot less cynical – there is craft to his art, so we can begin pushing the subtlety up a little bit.

Reverie by Roy Lichtenstein
© Christie's Images/CORBIS

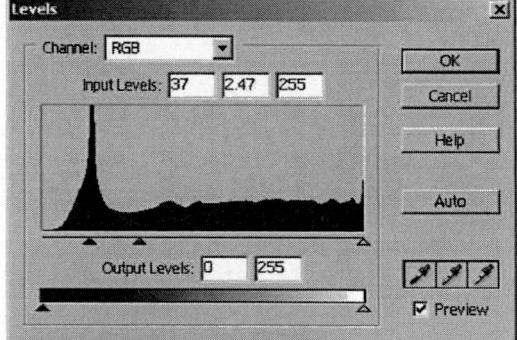

1. Once again, the utter hopelessness of my photography threatens to make this a difficult task, so we'd better play around with the mid-tones in the Levels palette (CTRL+L) until we have quite a flat-colored image.

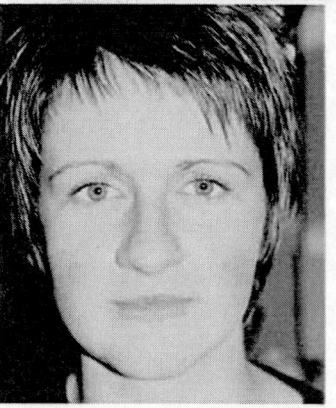

2. Fortunately, we can bring out some hair color to work with, while leaving those eyes still nicely defined.

The Eyes

Let's isolate the eyes. It's much better to get them onto their own layer so we can work on them without worrying about everything else.

3. Draw around them with the Lasso tool and copy them onto a new layer. Call it *eyes*. It's all in the eyes with Lichtenstein. The eyes are the focal point (as with lots of art styles), and are often the most beautifully crafted part of a Lichtenstein print.

Here they are with the background layer turned off:

4. For the time being, simplify the eyes with a small paintbrush, making the whites all white (quite a task after such a heavy party), the blues all blue, and the blacks all black. The blue should be chosen using the Eyedropper (!) and selecting from the existing blues.

5. Then, with a small-brush size on the Eraser, get rid of as much of the residual skin pink.

Lines

The next thing we need to do is draw in some lines to define the face. Now, I'll be honest with you, Elements just isn't that good at lines. Even full-fat Photoshop (the $600 variety) has trouble.

We can't draw curved lines (unless we do them freehand which, in this instance, takes some phenomenal talent), so we're going to have to draw lots and lots of straight lines.

6. Select the Line tool:

7. Set its thickness to 3 px. Note – don't forget to actually type the px, or this tool is liable to throw a wobbler and give you a 3 cm line!

Now, we want to draw in those main places of definition on the face.

8. Start off down the length of the nose. Click and drag a short line. Then, holding down the SHIFT key, click and drag again. The reason you have to hold down SHIFT is so you stay on the same layer. Otherwise, Elements would give you a new layer every time you drew a single little line, which is just too impractical.

9. In this fashion, line by line, work your way down the length of the nose.

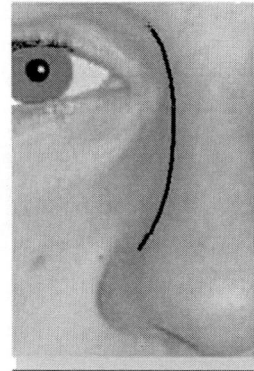

If you've successfully managed to get through that test, it's time to pick out all the other defined areas of the face.

10. Draw a series of lines to mark out the eyelashes, eyebrows, nose, lips, edges of the face and the neck.

11. Once you're satisfied you have every line you need, simplify the layer via the Layers palette. This basically unites every line you've drawn into one big pattern.

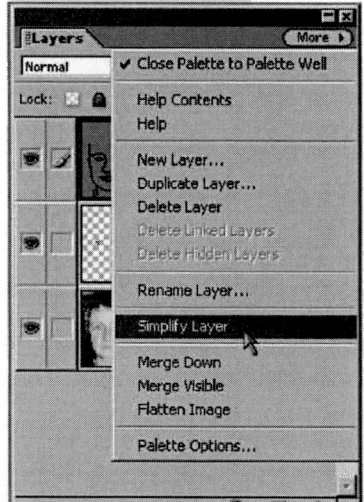

Here's what my image looks like after having drawn in the lines, filled the eyebrows in with black and brushed in some eyelashes using the Brush (set to a Calligraphic brush to bring out a stylized lash shape).

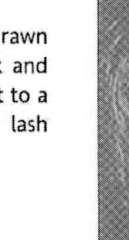

Next, we have to set about using the same technique to draw in the hair. This is the first place where artistic interpretation really comes into play. The hair has got to look good and comicbook-like, so you should simplify the fringe somewhat and think about how you're going to shade everything.

> It's probably best to turn off the Background layer while you're working from now, so you can troubleshoot any gaps between lines. We're working at filling in whole areas with the Paint Bucket tool, so gaps between the lines can become a real problem. If you find gaps that let the paint leak through and fill an inappropriate area, just fill it in with a small black paintbrush.

OK, let's get going on that hair. Now, Lichtenstein doesn't do shade. Like Warhol, he's an **absolute colors** man. Moreover, he's an **absolute primary colors** man. So, this hair is going to have to be flat yellow, and flat black.

12. To this end, start drawing Paths with the Pen tool in black, and then using the Paint Bucket tool to fill them with yellow highlights or black lowlights.

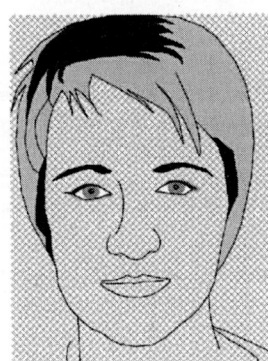

13. To make the hair look better, fill in the background – one side white, the other black.

Dots

Aside from the clarity of lines, the other main problem this artistic style throws up is how exactly to get the familiar Lichtenstein newsprint dots. As I've already stated, there is no room for shades in this picture, and we have to get the right kind of pink by using a very regular pattern of pure red dots. So what do we do?

Well, uniform dots are actually pretty easy to come by. What we're going to do is create a pattern! They've got to be the right size, and the right color. It might take a couple of goes, but this is what you do.

14. Select the Brush tool, with a circular brush. Resize it to roughly the size you want your dots to be. The brush size I've selected is 10 px.

15. Create an entirely new file in Elements and size it to a few pixels larger than your chosen brush (so mine was 14 x 14 px). Then, paint a single blob in the middle of the canvas. This is our sample spot! From this we're going to make our pattern!

16. Click through Edit > Define Pattern. It takes everything on your canvas (namely, one spot) and turns it into a pattern. Name it spot1. OK, you can happily close that small file without saving it; our pattern is created!

17. Next, on your main canvas, select the Paint Bucket tool. In the Options bar, change the fill from Foreground to Pattern. Then, fill the area you like!

And that is more or less it. The only subtle difference is the lips, for which I created a new brush. It's an 8 px white brush on a 12 px red background. It's a subtle change, but it does make the lips a darker tone of pink.

Final touches

So, how do we give it that authentic look? Well, the face as I originally had it looked a bit flat, and when it comes to highlighting, Lichtenstein goes for the dramatic.

18. There isn't a great deal of drama to the original image, so we'll have to make it up – lassoing a section of the skin and filling it with white.

It also might be quite nice to make the eyes a bit bigger, to go for that real comicbook proportions routine.

19. To achieve this, go to the lines layer and select the black of the eyelashes with the Magic Wand tool. Then, with the SHIFT key pressed, select the insides of the eyes (these should be transparent, looking through to the eyes layer below).

20. Click through Edit > Copy Merged, and press CTRL+V to paste them onto a new layer. This was so you can happily select and resize each eye with ease.

So there we go – one genuine lost Lichtenstein. Form a queue, please!

jollyLick.psd *is provided on the CD-ROM so you can look over it.*

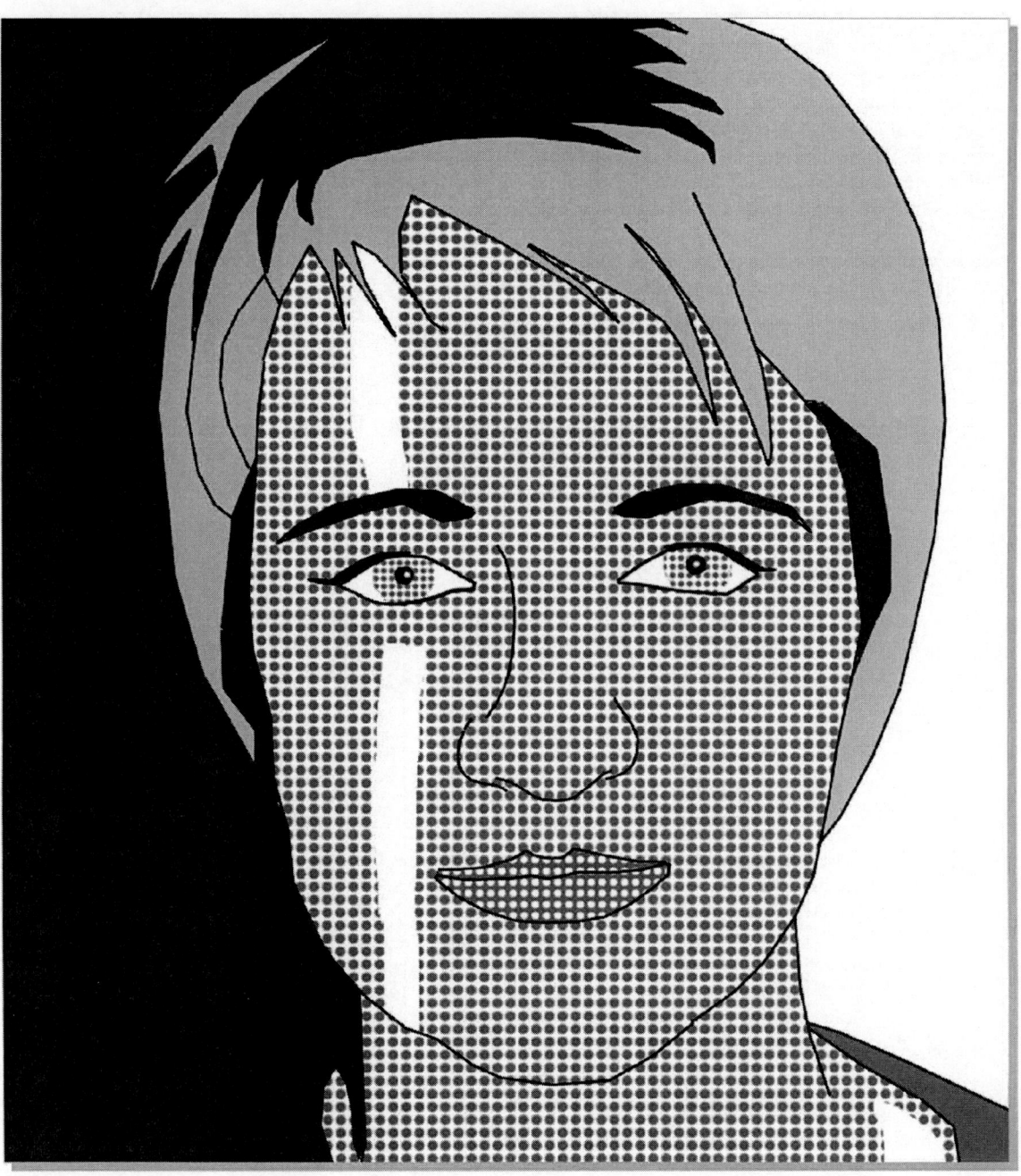

Matisse

If we're looking to move on from Pop Art, then we're going to have to move backwards (historically speaking, of course). The challenges thrown up by an artistic style such as that employed by Matisse are significant. He uses more than just primary colors, for one. What is our palette going to be? With this image we're going to look at how to narrow our colors down, and how to develop to brushing styles which will give us some nice oil paint textures.

So how do we cut down the photorealistic colors? One way is through the simple addition of a **Posterize** adjustment layer.

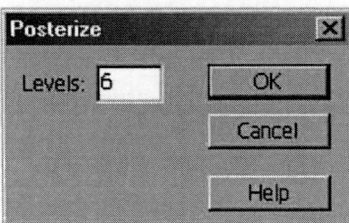

1. Take the original photo, and add a Posterize layer – allowing for six levels of color. Select all and Copy Merged, before pasting into a new layer and renaming it base.

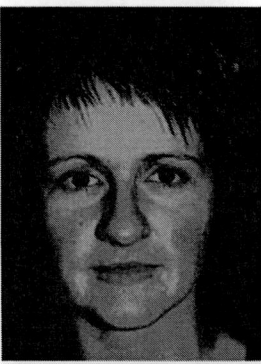

2. The next significant problem is that of brushstrokes. Now, we have some Artistic filters to play with, such as Paint Daubs and Palette Knife. So, let's go for Palette Knife. I used a Stroke Size of 10, Stroke Detail of 3 and Softness of 5. I really smear those oils around:

   So – at least we have some shadows to play with. It doesn't really give a sense of thick dirty paint, but maybe that will come later. The next thing to do is get going with some brushwork.

3. To get us in the mood get rid of the face shine. Select a pink from the face using the Eyedropper tool. On a new layer (flat matting) use the Brush to just fill in the white areas, so we've got a flatter, less photographic canvas to work with.

4. The Matisse painting that formed my touchstone for this project was *The Green Stripe* (1905), which has very unusual colors in well-defined facial areas.

The Green Stripe by Henri Matisse
© Archivo Iconografico, S.A./CORBIS

Given the photograph I was working with, the color to choose for that central streak would be bright white, but I figure that's not *Matisse* enough. So, let's go with yellow and brush it down the center of the face using a medium-sized soft brush at a fairly strong opacity (60% for me!).

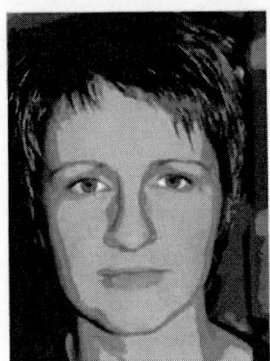

5. The next thing to do is divide the face into two pinks – we should go for a light side and a dark side. Fortunately we've already sorted the light side of the face (on the right), so let's just paint in a darker color for the shadier side of our model. I used quite an orangey shade (not sampled from the face itself). Again, I had the brush at 60% opacity to provide evidence of some brushwork.

You'll note there is an extra lowlight down the left side of the face – that is created through exactly the same technique, using a darker, more orange shade. The rule is basic: if you see anything that looks like a photograph, paint over it! The shape of the shadow on this picture is totally dictated by daubing over the photographic shading.

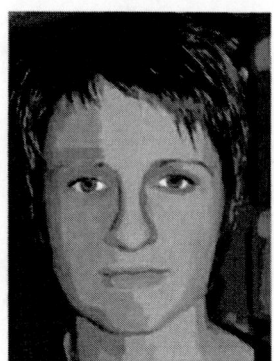

6. Now we want to move on to the hair. On a new layer (hair), fill in the darkest areas in black. For the more defined, highlighted areas, select a brown color and fill in. It's all simple stuff! The real trick is to be patient and allow your black paints to go over your brown paints, and your brown paints to go over your black paints. The more you switch between the two colors, the better. While we're here we may as well daub in the background:

As you'll see, I've had another go down that left side of the face, because I like the brown of the hair. This is a picture of experimentation!

7. Now it's time to do the eyebrows and eye definition. This is a place for *black*! Use a small brush and highlight the eyebrows and the definition of the eyelids and so forth. You can also take the chance to fill in the colors of the eyes. So, Lichtenstein saw the face with blue eyes, Matisse with black. Go figure.

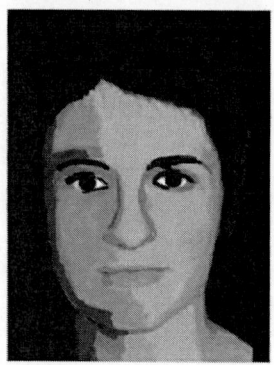

8. To finish off the image, it's a question of working at the flat matt colors until you're happy with the blend. Personally, I worked to make the left side of the face more convincing – less a line of color, more a whole shaded area. It was all done by selecting the colors that were already there and painting back over them with a 60% opacity brush.

9. I also emphasized the lips by selecting a scarlet versus a pale pink and picking them out.

    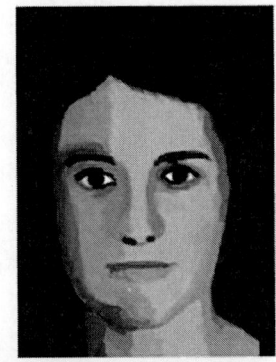

    The resulting image is a combination of the colors that were in the original photograph, and the colors that you might expect to see from Matisse. It is, after all, his style we're after, and as we had to bend to Lichtenstein's use of primary colors, so we have to bend to Matisse's subdued hues.

    Now it's time to get that dingy background sorted out, so let's experiment with some brush shapes.

10. Create a new layer (new background). From the Default Brush menu, select the Chalk brush. I chose the 36 pixel sized one. Oddly enough, this gives us a very good oil paint effect. Select a completely fake looking red and daub around the head on the left side of the picture. Do the same on the right side of the picture with a completely fake looking blue. Why fake? Well, that's how it is with Matisse!

    The background on this version is I think excellent, but that's mostly because I utilized reduced opacity brushes over the top of other colors.

    > *Check out* `jollyMatisse.psd` *from the CD-ROM.*

Modigliani

Modigliani didn't tend to paint Western-style pictures. He was very keen on incorporating African influences into his art, which makes for some very distinctive faces, usually elongated (like some African masks) with simplified features. He was driven largely by shape rather than texture, and he had a fascination with reds and russets.

It's fascinating to tweak a picture and see exactly when it attains a recognizable quality of the artist in question.

To gain that Modigliani look, we're going to have to expand the canvas, to allow for that stylized elongation, so open `jolly.jpg` again and let's get going.

Head of a Woman by Modigliani
© *Christie's Images/CORBIS*

1. Click through Image > Resize > Canvas Size, and increase both the width and height by 125%, anchoring it at the bottom left hand corner.

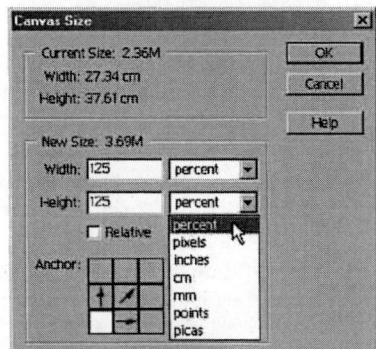

2. Make a selection around the head with the Lasso tool and, with the Move tool, elongate it, and then rotate it until you have a satisfactory result. Then, fill in the resultant gap with a black Paint Bucket, and employ the Clone Stamp to extend the neck. Don't worry if it looks a bit duplicated, because we'll be spattering it with paint before you know it!

   In a sense, that's it – job done. The rest is just going through the paces. Well, more or less.

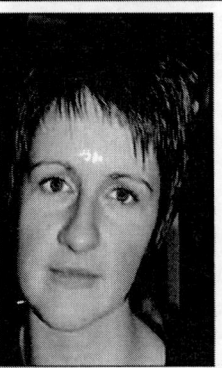

3. Blocking the colors in is simple enough, by clicking through Image > Adjustments > Posterize, and giving it a six.

4. Then, fix the color so it has more of a russet feel. Elements has a simple tool for this, Enhance > Adjust Color > Color Variations. Using the default settings (namely, midtones changing at a medium amount), I hit the following sequence:

   Increase red x 7
   Decrease blue x 2
   Lighten x 2

5. Press OK, and watch the picture gain that autumnal hue!

6. On a new layer (daub) choose the most apt color with the Eyedropper tool, and daub the whole face with it. The basic idea is to get rid of the white, thereby flattening the whole image, and making it look less obviously digital.

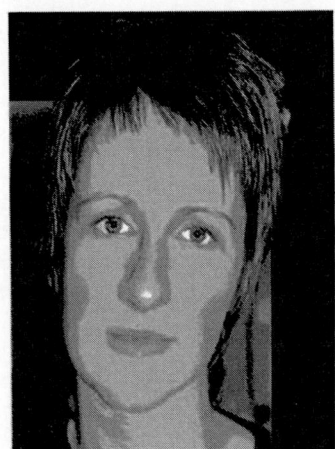

This time though, the need is for further elongation.

7. From the Default Brushes, use the Chalk brush (any of them!) to get a good texture going at this point – fix it to 50% opacity in order to get some sense of paint thickness. Where you have a choice while painting over shadows, go for long and thin. The nose is the most obvious instance where we can "up the Modigliani".

> *As with Lichtenstein, this artist is very particular about eyes. Quite often in his paintings they are reduced to dark hollows, or even closed altogether.*

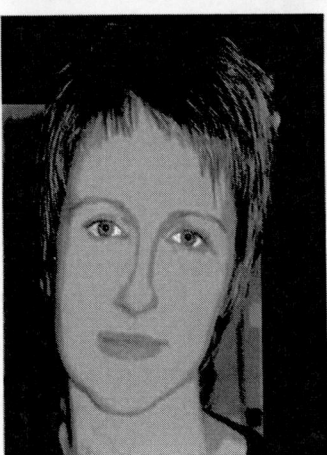

For a little variation on this portrait we're going to opt for the latter. For the time being, let's just rough it in.

8. Zoom in and carefully paint over the eyes with a small paintbrush. Leave the existing eyelashes to mark where shadows should go later on. Add a few daubs to shade the eyelids and give a rounded feel.

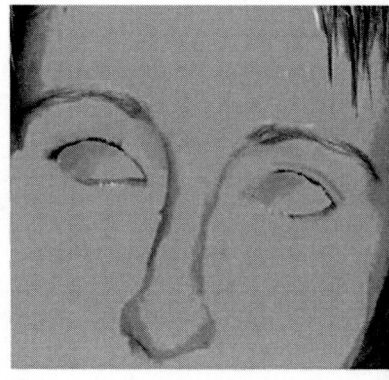 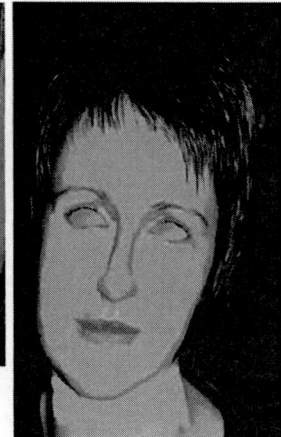

As with Matisse, Modigliani tends to keep shadow and shading fairly muted in his pictures, preferring instead to emphasize the fascinating shapes that go to make up his subjects. So, in this picture we're concentrating on the shape of the jaw, the neck, the nose, lips and eyes, while keeping shading and shadow to a minimum.

So, now for some heavy brushwork. Remember to keep those brushes quite small.

9. You should begin the task of replacing that orangey shading around the periphery of the face (left over from the Posterize) with something more appropriate – a reduced opacity (about 10%) gray seems to do the trick, particularly around the eyes.

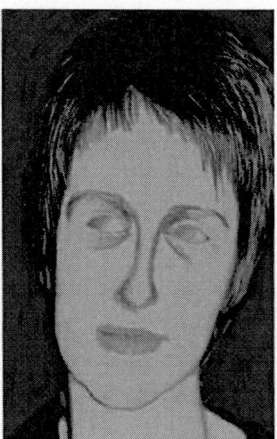

The lips are important – Modigliani favored scarlet, pouting mouths.

10. To achieve this, use red lines (like the black ones in Lichtenstein) to accurately emphasize the features of the lips that are already there.

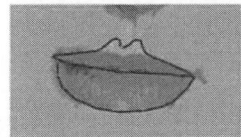

11. The result is a kind of caricature, with a really emphasized Cupid's bow. Fill them in with a scarlet brush, at about 20% opacity. Really work it in to the center and corners of the mouth to build up the red.

There's a running theme in Modigliani: there's a romance and sexuality about them, which is really emphasized by the lips and the faintly sensual poses. I guess we're learning to read art!

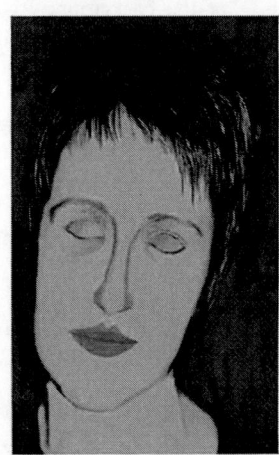

12. Next, let's turn our attention to the blacks. Create a new layer named blacks.

13. Draw in black lines for the eyebrows – I suggest using a soft paintbrush at about half the width of the brows themselves. Pick out the eyelashes also. You may wish to blur these a little with the Blur tool so as not to make everything look too severe.

> *As these things are on a new layer, you can take the opportunity to clean up underneath them if your black line is slightly off the mark. Forward thinking!*

14. Now it's time to go 19th Century on the hair – something to counterbalance that brewing sexuality. Simply *paint it black*, as Mick Jagger once said. Use a 70% opacity brush to give a nice sloppy paint appearance.

Filthying it up

Once again, a problem we encounter with this picture is the regular old digital problem – clean colors. Everything is bright and beautiful, and wholly un-Modigliani-like.

15. To dirty up the face a little, create a new layer (filth). Using the Eyedropper tool, select some of the darker tones from the face and paint back over the face with a reduced opacity paintbrush.

16. For the background, select a dark green and work away with a reduced opacity and a tiny little brush until you have something you're pleased with. I used the green and a little white.

17. This is the perfect place to get out your Impressionist Brush of course – so long as you have the right color blend. Whack the Impressionist Brush around for a nice filth.

Finally, and very importantly, we have a signature Modigliani style: rosy cheeks!

Now, you're going to have to trust me on this. I spent *ages* trying to get the rosy cheeks right. I tried soft brushes, pinks at 100%, reds at 10%, I tried marqueeing and changing the color balance and also tried the Burn tool. However, I just kept getting washed-out or circular cheeks or obviously shoehorned-in cheeks, or black cheeks.

The final answer for this subtle effect comes from an unexpected source. It's a brush yes, but it's a weird brush.

18. If you go to the Faux Finish Brushes option, you'll find the Mesh brushes. They're really square and blocky, but they deliver exactly the right amount of color for these purposes. I guess in a strange way it's the same as doing what Lichtenstein did – using uniform dots to get the right blend of color.

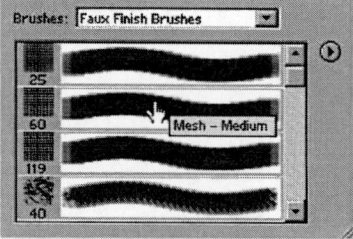

19. Anyway, choose red, and get this brush to do the business for you:

If you want to compare yours to mine, check out `jollyMod.psd` on the CD-ROM.

Manga

The amazing thing about globalization in the latter half of the 20th century is that we can now get some amazing art from cultures that have previously been totally isolated from one another. The artists I've looked at up to now have been Western masters, but how will our face look with an Oriental look? **Manga** is probably the most exciting form of figurative art around, and it is the result of hundreds of years of Eastern thinking being twanged onto a Western pop culture. The result is some pretty amazing faces – so let's see how and why.

Manga is a cartoon format (note to self – one day you must work out what differentiates cartoon styles from non-cartoon styles) and so the face should be based on a single flat shade of pink.

1.   There are subtle shades to be added, but for a base color start by posterizing the face and choosing one of the most pleasing pinks to paint over much of the face.

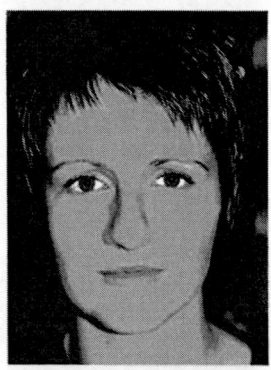

Proportions

The first thing people said to me when I suggested doing a Manga remix of someone's face was, 'big eyes'. And they were dead right. The most notable thing about a Manga picture is eyes the size of saucers. In fact, the Manga face has proportions roughly equivalent to those of a baby or young child: Big eyes, small nose, and tiny mouth.

Here the Liquify tool comes into its own.

2.   To capture the eyes, hop into the Filter > Distort > Liquify interface, and apply the Bloat tool to each eye. The real trick is making sure the tool is dead center on the eye, otherwise you could end up with some pretty warped looking eyes.

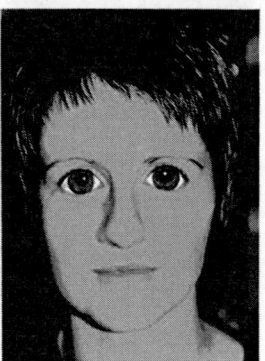

As I found, it's probably best not to let the subject of your picture walk in at this point. The result was pretty pleasing more or less straight away. That's where Elements' strength lies – excellent results in seconds. You've just got to know where to start!

Manga eyes can be seen as very beautiful or grotesque – it's a fine line. What I find amazing is that they're almost photorealistic in a comic book world. I won't be doing anything to the pupils from now on. That's pretty amazing to me.

3. So, what's next? Well, the background of this picture is hopeless. Really dark, and we're in a cartoon world, so we'd better choose one of the greens that are just perceptible back there, and paint the background in with the Brush tool, making up any outlines we can't see.

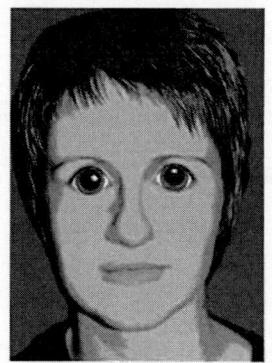

Then I turned my attentions to the other essential Manga feature: the small nose. Manga noses have no width to them at all.

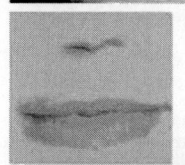

4. Begin by blotting out the bridge with your chosen shade of pink, and head back to the Liquify interface. Use the Pucker tool to reduce the size of the end of the nose, leaving it no width at all. Press OK to return to the main Elements interface.

5. Next, let's turn our attention to the mouth. This is real chop shop time. What we're going to do is basically pull the corners of the mouth inwards, to make the whole thing smaller. Lasso a marquee around the corners of the mouth and copy them onto a new layer, mouth. Drag each half into the center, and slap pink over any telltale holes left on the layer below:

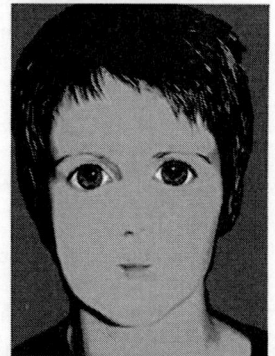

6. It's best to Copy all this onto a new layer, so Select All (CTRL+A) and then Edit > Copy Merged (or CTRL+SHIFT+C), before pasting all onto a new layer.

The final move to make in order to get the proportions right is to shrink the head. If you look, the head's just too adult-shaped. The nose-space is too long for a cutesy Manga face.

7. Draw a marquee around the bottom half of the face, making sure to include the nose, and drag the whole thing up with the Move tool until the facial proportions say Manga. Of course, the sides of the face won't fit, so stretch those out using the side handles. Fix the shading by daubing everything in pink.

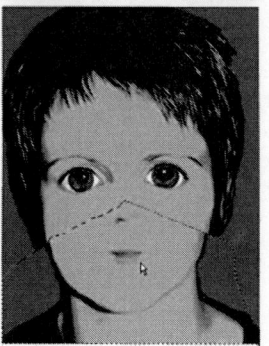

If you've got the proportions right, the rest is just style. So, what we should look for from now on is to get the final look of everything right. We've got to get the delicate shading right, get the expression of those features right, and for heaven's sake do something with that *hair*. Then we should be done.

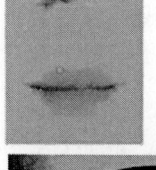

8. First off, reduce the lips somewhat with our trusty pink – using a smallish brush with about 50% opacity. Then choose another pink directly from the lips and paint them in a bit for that slightly vague watercolor look.

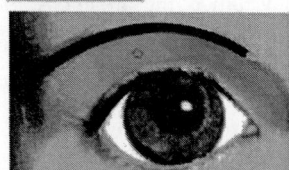

9. Next draw lines over the existing eyebrows, taking your color from the dark head hair. Take the opportunity also to draw lines for the eyelashes and lines for the chin.

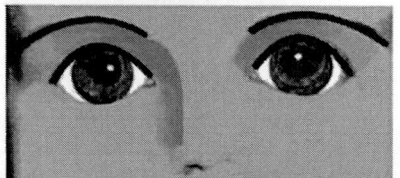

10. To shade the eyelids, select some of the eyeshade that is already there and, using a 30% opacity brush, begin to fill in. The more you work, the further down the nose you'll find yourself going!

11. Finally, get rid of any dark pink that remains from the initial image, using the stock pink we chose at the start.

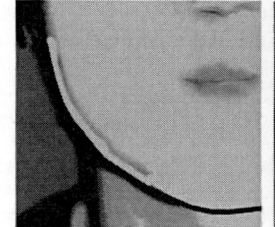

So – time to take care of the hair. Manga hair varies. Some of it is really wispy and time-intensive, and some is quite blocky and 2D, like vector graphics. We'll go for the latter, in order to achieve the maximum effect in the minimum time.

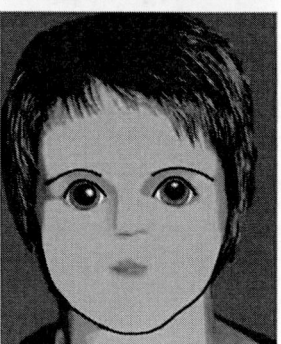

As with the Lichtenstein image, outline the hair using black lines, and then fill it in using a flat black. For some reason, black works better with Manga hairdos – it's just more dramatic.

12. Carve out a suitable looking area (using lines again) and fill it in a blonde shade, just to give the 'do a bit of shape. The addition of a white gleam adds to the dramatic impact, and a few spidery locks will blow beautifully in the Manga wind.

> *My final PSD is saved on the CD-ROM as* jollyManga.psd.

OK, so I think we've made the point about this one very badly taken photograph. Let's branch out and see how else Photoshop Elements is going to springboard us towards the masters.

Van Gogh

One artist who's really going to put Elements to the test is Vincent van Gogh. His paintings are full of vivid colors and rich textures. He painted landscapes, still life, people – anything. He produced a huge volume of work, but sold only two paintings before taking his own life. His brushstrokes and paintings are full of the inner torment he felt throughout his turbulent life, and if you look carefully you can see his technique and his palette change and develop as his life progresses.

Open `ollie.jpg` from the **Imitating Artists** folder of the CD-ROM and we'll try to make our own Van Gogh...

Self-Portrait (1889) by Vincent van Gogh
© *Gianni Dagli Orti/CORBIS*

Ollie – Van Gogh's long lost brother

One of the most important things to do is to give a bit of texture to the image. I did this to serve as the base onto which I could add paint strokes.

1. To do this, we'll have a go at using the Angled Strokes filter (Filter > Brush Strokes > Angled Strokes). Use the settings shown – a Direction value of 50, Stroke Length 30, and Sharpness 3.

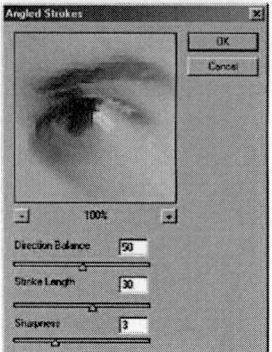

    OK, so we're narrowing the face down a bit so its flat planes are easier to work with.

2. The face at the moment has too many planes of color. Rather than Posterizing as before, click through Image > Mode > Indexed Color to limit it to 256 colors. Then once again click through Image > Mode > RGB Color to carry on working on it. This gives us a much flatter base to start the real work on.

We also want to make the background more like the Van Gogh self portrait above – this was his last self-portrait, and his palette had become much calmer, and more toned down.

3. Select only the background and using the Hue/Saturation dialog box (CTRL+U), change the Hue to +40 to make it a greener blue.

4. Then, invert the selection (CTRL+SHIFT+I) and change the Hue of that to +40 and the Saturation to +75. There you'll find we're getting closer to Van Gogh already! Genius indeed...

5. Invert the selection again (CTRL+SHIFT+I) for our next trick...

> *One major part of Van Gogh's work is his erratic brushstroke technique. The key to making the photo resemble a Van Gogh is delivered to us in the form of the Impressionist Brush.*

6. With the background selected, create a new Layer via Copy. Ha! Putting the background in the foreground! Maybe he *was* a genius...

7. On the Layers palette, click the little checkered icon to lock the transparent pixels. This means our brush won't dare spew paint all over the space where the face is showing through.

8. Get the normal paintbrush and, selecting colors from across the background, put in little daubs of dark on the light and light on the dark – just squiggles will do, to get us an interesting pattern.

9. Then, use the Impressionist Brush to your heart's content! I set mine to Loose Curl Long using an area of 50 px. Be sure to stay on the background, because if you stray on to the face area a whole load of white will be entered into your Impressionist palette. Give it a try if you don't believe me...

10. The next part we'll move on to is the sweater. What we need to do is put the figure on to its own layer. You can easily select the figure by applying a magic wand to the empty space in the Impressionist layer. This selects exactly the right shape. Then simply move down to the layer containing the actual image, and create a new layer via copy.

    Looking at some Van Gogh portraits, he used short stubby downward strokes for the clothes. So, what we're going to do is create a brush! This is very much like the pattern creation we used for Lichtenstein.

11. Using a fresh canvas (by creating a brand new file), create a new layer, and then make the background layer invisible (via the eye icon on the Layers palette). This will help us define the brush/pattern from the background.

12. Make a series of short, stubby downstrokes. When you're happy with your pattern, click through Edit > Define Brush. Call it VanGogh1. While we're here, let's define a pattern and call that VanGogh1 as well. This will save us a bit of time!

13. Back on the main canvas, use the Lasso to select the sweater. Then on a new layer (brushing), use the Paint Bucket tool (selecting the newly-created pattern from the drop down menu) to fill it in. The problem with patterns is you have to create them in the color you want to use, but with brushes we don't have the same problem.

14. Offset this by using the new brush to mess things up a bit with variant colors. Use the brush most heavily where the material folds.

Definition

Looking at a Van Gogh portrait, you'll see a deep cobalt blue (almost black) around the clothing.

15. On a new layer (jumpDef) using a small round brush, trace around the outlines and folds of the sweater with a nice blue cover. Don't worry about making these lines perfect — in fact they look better the rougher they are. Reduce the opacity of the brushing layer if you can't see the original sweater.

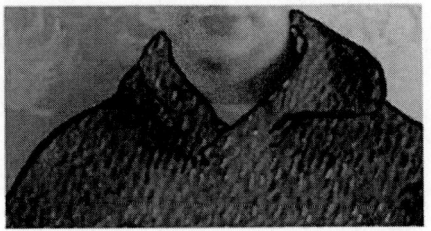

Now to concentrate on the hair and face.

16. On a new layer (facePaint) use the Eyedropper tool to select colors, and paint specks in using our VanGogh1 brush. It's just a question of getting the paint mix right. The model doesn't need to look like he's got measles, or to look too much like a photograph. After you've painted to your heart's content, set the layer blending mode to *Soft Light*, which will give you a much subtler blend of colors.

The last thing to do is to bring it all together by adding definition to the nose, neck and chin. With the nose, you can see a natural division of color, so what we need to do is emphasize that.

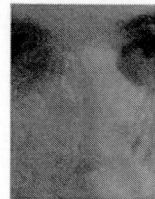

17. Under the chin, draw in a soft brown line to provide a bit of shadow and to show the jaw line.

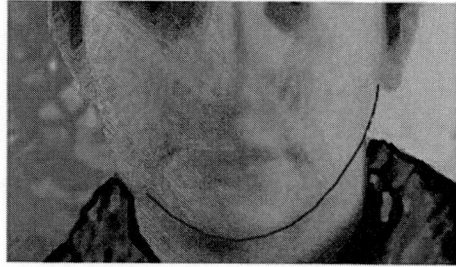

18. Work this in by simplifying the layer and smudging it with the Blur tool and a soft eraser.

19. On the lips add a less passionate color than the rosy smacker that has evolved. Looking back at Van Gogh's painting, his lips look as if they're already dead. Green and yellow should be used to subtly flatten their effect.

20. On the hair, do what you did on the skin, introducing just three or four component colors to make up the general effect.

> If you need to study the PSD itself, it's on the CD-ROM called VanGogh.psd.

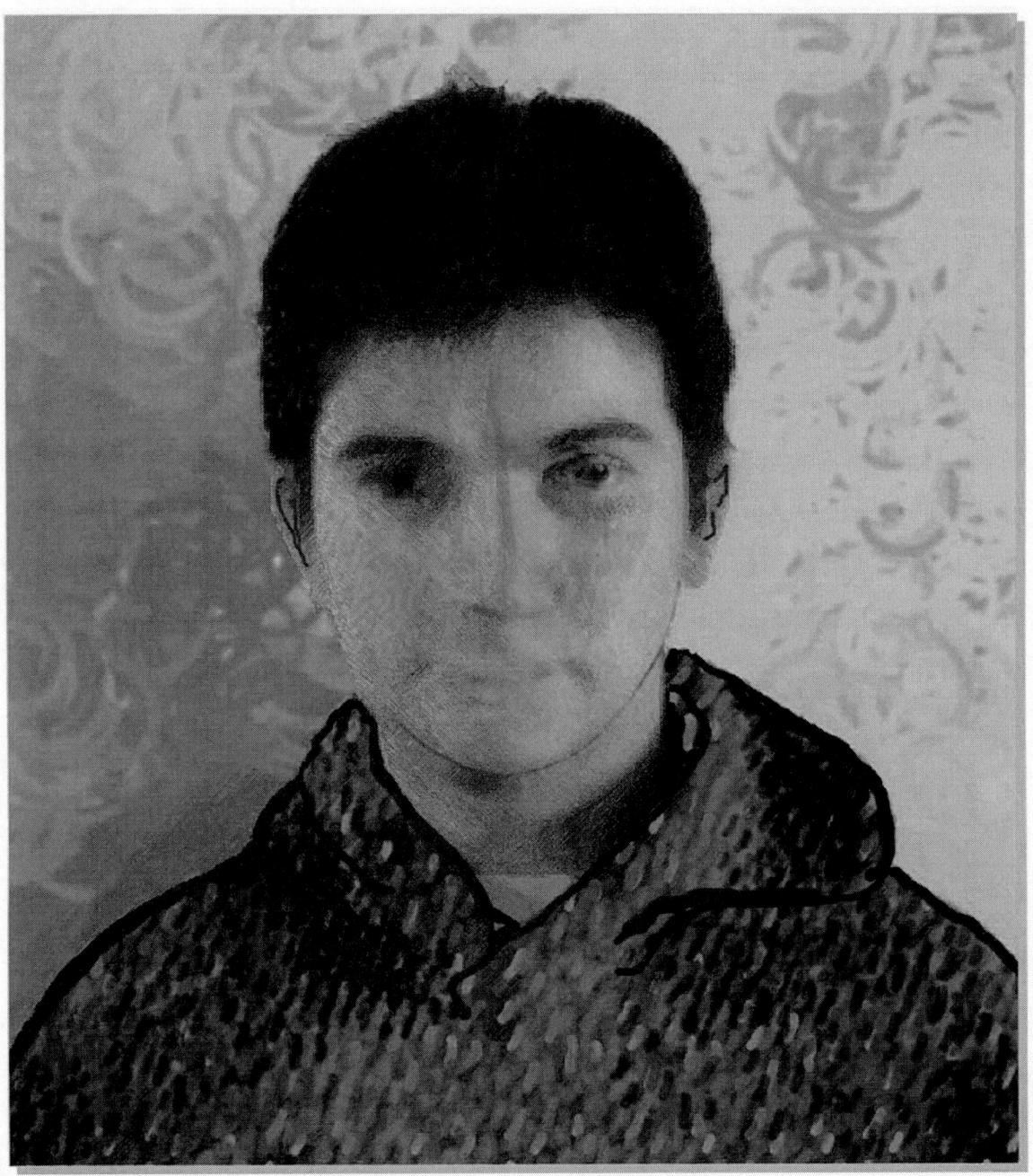

Klimt

What an excellent idea it would be to give your mother or grandmother a print of herself as a Gustav Klimt iconic lady! I'm telling you, it's a real winner! Don't you dare give me that vacant look next time her birthday comes around!

Gustav Klimt was an Austrian artist who worked at the turn of the century, in Vienna. You're most likely to know his work from *The Kiss*, which adorns card and poster stores around the Western World.

In that picture, Klimt uses patterns to represent different things. On the woman's dress you have feminine circular shapes – they remind me of cells – which contrast with the man's tunic of angular masculine shapes in black and gold.

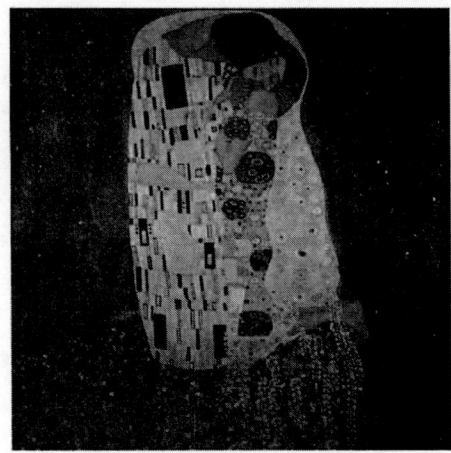

The Kiss by Gustav Klimt
© *Austrian Archives; Österreichische Galerie, Vienna/CORBIS*

Preparation

For this design we're going to prepare a small canvas to help us on our way.

1. Open a new canvas, about 600x600 pixels.

2. First of all put down a green background, with a large brush, with the opacity relatively low, just to gain a bit of texture. Add a few more leafy textural strokes with different shades of green.

3. On a new layer draw a rough sketch using a small paintbrush with a pale color of where the shapes should go. Notice how the shapes interact with each other, they kind of swim around the canvas. They are not all perfectly round, and they don't really overlap each other much. I think these particular shapes are based on anemones – they have the same colors as these flowers and the same voluptuous roundness.

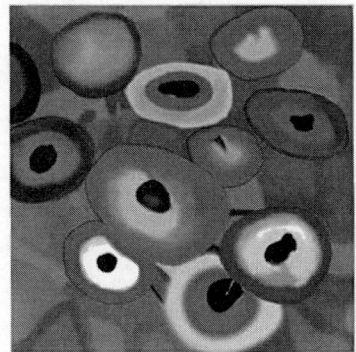

It's then a matter of filling them in. Klimt's palette for these flowers was deep reds and pinks with a hint of blue. The middles have white in them, but note that the whites are tinted with pink and orange, and even a bit of blue. This can make all the difference in whether an image looks right.

4. The technique is up to you but, to follow me, fill them in using brushes and layering colors of different opacities and smudging it all together. Put a couple over the top of each other at different opacities to gain a bit of depth.

Becky the pea - Klimting a photograph

Now on to the real thing!

1. Open pea.jpg from the CD-ROM.

2. First off, let's exercise the good practice of duplicating the background layer. Call it Klimt.

3. Select everything behind the head with the Lasso tool and cut it away so we are left with just the face and hair. Don't worry if you don't create a perfect selection for the hair – we'll be painting over it later.

4. Next, twang on a Smart Blur filter, so all the colors are smoothed out and the face is paler. I used a radius of 3.

Now on to the background. We want to create a kind of gold background. Klimt's backgrounds look like they have a million stars in them.

5. Fill a new layer (goldBack) with a goldish color. Gold is difficult to come by, and I find a lot of people go for yellow too much, but I think it's a lot greener and browner than people give it credit for.

Now we need a star-like effect.

6. Create a pattern, by opening up a new canvas, 300x300 pixels square. Create a new layer immediately and, using a small round brush with slightly softened edges, put lots of dots on it. Use both small and large dots to get a nice starry feel, and then give the whole thing a Gaussian Blur of about 2.8. Then, select everything and click through Edit > Define Pattern.

7. Back on the main canvas, on a new layer, use the Paint Bucket to fill it in with the new pattern. For a deeper effect, you might like to do this a couple of times on new layers, moving them slightly each time and altering the color.

Face style

Moving on to the face, the model is looking a little too smiley at the moment so choose a pink and close her eyes like we did with the Modigliani.

8. With a flat pink there, choose a slightly darker pink to paint in the shadows and tone. Use a soft-edged brush with a reduced opacity to keep the subtlety going!

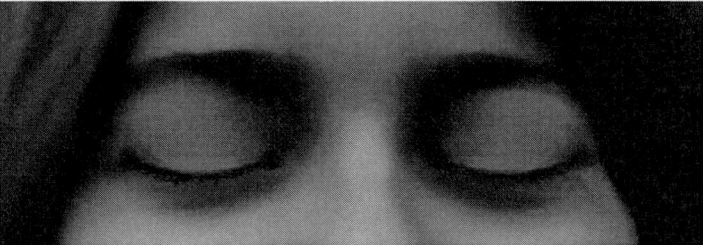

9. In order to make her slightly paler and more interesting, set the face Opacity to 90%.

10. To get the kind of blue tinge that you can see in Klimt's painting, make a new layer (facebase) and put a pale blue wash behind. You'll see a marvelous glow emanate from the serene face!

11. Create another layer, called foundation. Paint on layers of pale blue and peach, with a round paintbrush at 100% opacity, putting more blue around her nose and areas where there needs to be more definition, until you end up with something like this:

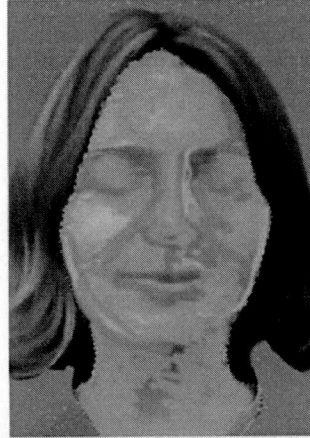

12. Then apply a Gaussian Blur of around 50.

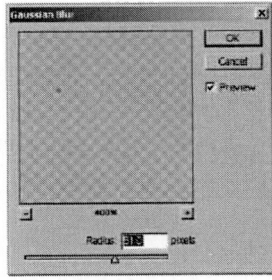

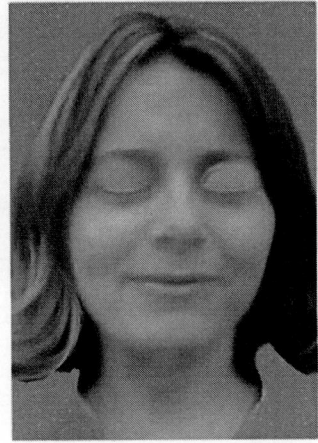

13. You end up with a blotchy face, which is quite like Klimt's faces if you look closely. You can see that they are not one smooth color but yellows, blues and peaches. Set this layer to 50% opacity in order to make it more subtle.

14. If we look at the hair now, we can see it isn't the classic burnt umber Klimt favored. So let's make it like that – all we need to do is go onto a new layer, paint over the top of the original hair with a delicious orange color, with a low opacity (about 40%). Once again we're going for depth. Set the whole layer to Multiply so it blends in with the original hair.

15. Create one more new layer called definition and, using a single pencil with a 20% opacity, sketch a thin line across the nose. Choose some colors for the hair to make up the eyebrows with the same technique, and used a dull bluish-gray to shade under the chin.

The last thing for the face is to add some color to the cheeks and lips. If you look at the cheeks and lips in *The Kiss*, you'll see how rosy and flushed they are. This typifies Klimt's paintings.

16. On a new layer called cheeks, draw in some pale peach colors and then paint on a darker pink. Smudge this all together using the Smudge tool.

17. Set the layer to Overlay at 64% opacity, and there we have it – some rosy cheeks for our lady.

18. The lips are created in a similar way. I figured I should emphasize the Cupid's Bow, brushing it all in scarlet with quite a hard small brush. Change the layer blending mode to Overlay and set the layer Opacity to 68%

Patterns

Finally, we should add the glorious patterns that typify Klimt's work.

First off, we have to add some backgrounds for the patterns to lie on. Firstly a blue dress, that comes from her shoulders.

19. Select the area you want it to clothe, and fill that area with a dark blue. For a bit of depth, add another layer and still in the same selection draw some roughly straight darker blue lines down it.

What we're going to do is make brushes of different flowers and circles just like in Klimt's paintings.

Here's a picture of the ones I made:

20. Using these, build up patterns in rich pinks, reds, blues and oranges throughout her hair and along her dress.

As you can see, it's just a question of building up as Klimt does, and thereby developing your own manner of symbolism and iconography!

> *You can look more closely at my version by checking out* `Klimt.psd` *on the CD-ROM.*

Summary

There we have it: 40 pages and 6 different artistic styles, spanning centuries. Now isn't that value for money.

We've seen that the key to mimicking art is a little bit of research beforehand and a dash of Elements creativity. And by now you'll know you're not just limited to these artists and styles. You can take the principles you've learned here and use them to reproduce the look and feel of any artist you desire.

Index

The index is arranged hierarchically, in alphabetical order, with symbols preceding the letter A. Many second-level entries also occur as first-level entries. This is to ensure that you will find the information you require however you choose to search for it.

friends of ED particularly welcomes feedback on the layout and structure of this index. If you have any comments or criticisms, please contact: feedback@friendsofED.com